A

HISTORY AND ANALYSIS

OF THE

CONSTITUTION OF THE UNITED STATES,

WITH

A FULL ACCOUNT OF THE CONFEDERATIONS WHICH PRECEDED IT; OF THE DEBATES AND ACTS OF THE CONVENTION WHICH FORMED IT; OF THE JUDICIAL DECISIONS WHICH HAVE CONSTRUED IT; WITH PAPERS AND TABLES ILLUSTRATIVE OF THE ACTION OF THE GOVERNMENT AND THE PEOPLE UNDER IT.

BY

NATHANIEL C. TOWLE,
COUNSELLOR AT LAW, WASHINGTON, D. C.

SECOND EDITION.

BOSTON:
LITTLE, BROWN AND COMPANY.
1861.

CAMBRIDGE:
Allen and Farnham, Stereotypers and Printers.

PREFACE.

I PRESENT to the citizens of the United States an account of the proceedings which established the political institutions, from which have originated, and by which are maintained, their freedom and their prosperity. I purpose to show how, by a movement at first almost imperceptible, but increasing in the progress of time, until it assumed the attitude of independence, the Colonies of America became a Confederation, and finally a republic of States. I intend to exhibit the results of the deliberations of every convention or congress of the colonies and States, from that which assembled at Boston within the first half century of their settlement, to that which, in 1787, finally established the basis of our government. My object is not so much to give a detailed history of each particular step of our national progress, as to familiarize the people with the original principles of the government under which they now live. I endeavor to do this by offering to the public such a statement of the origin of our Constitution, and of the confederations, conventions, judicial decisions, and other papers which relate to its adoption and practical operation, as will convey a clear idea of the elements of which our national polity is composed. And it need not be said, that the more widely and accurately the essential principles and the proper functions of the political institutions of a State become known to its members, the more enlightened will be the legislation emanating from those who make their laws, and the more just will be the administration of their laws, and consequently the more will their general welfare and prosperity be promoted.

In the hope that this volume will, in some degree, assist in the attainment of such results, and that its operation upon the minds of those who peruse it, may be productive of some benefit to the interests of our country, I venture to submit this work to the American people.

N. C. TOWLE.

WASHINGTON, D. C., Dec. 1, 1860.

CONTENTS.

HISTORY AND ANALYSIS

OF THE

CONSTITUTION OF THE UNITED STATES.

CONSTITUTION

OF

THE UNITED STATES OF AMERICA.

WE the People of the United States, in order to form a more perfect Union, establish Justice, insure domestic Tranquillity, provide for the common defence, promote the general Welfare, and secure the Blessings of Liberty to ourselves and our Posterity, do ordain and establish this CONSTITUTION for the United States of America.[38]

ARTICLE. I.

SECTION. 1. All legislative Powers herein granted shall be vested in a Congress of the United States, which shall consist of a Senate and House of Representatives.[41]

SECTION. 2. The House of Representatives shall be composed of Members chosen every second

Year by the People of the several States, and the Electors in each State shall have the Qualifications requisite for Electors of the most numerous Branch of the State Legislature.[illegible]

No Person shall be a Representative who shall not have attained to the Age of twenty five Years, and been seven Years a Citizen of the United States, and who shall not, when elected, be an Inhabitant of that State in which he shall be chosen.[45]

Representatives and direct Taxes shall be apportioned among the several States which may be included within this Union, according to their respective Numbers, which shall be determined by adding to the whole Number of free Persons, including those bound to Service for a Term of Years, and excluding Indians not taxed, three fifths of all other Persons.[48]

The actual Enumeration shall be made within three Years after the first Meeting of the Congress of the United States, and within every subsequent Term of ten Years, in such Manner as they shall by Law direct.[55]

The Number of Representatives shall not exceed one for every thirty Thousand, but each State shall have at Least one Representative; and until such enumeration shall be made, the State of New Hampshire shall be entitled to chuse three, Massachusetts eight, Rhode-Island and Providence Plantations one, Connecticut five, New-York six, New Jersey four, Pennsylvania eight, Delaware one, Maryland six, Virginia ten, North Carolina five, South Carolina five, and Georgia three.

When vacancies happen in the Representation from any State, the Executive Authority thereof shall issue Writs of Election to fill such Vacancies.

The House of Representatives shall chuse their Speaker and other Officers; and shall have the sole Power of Impeachment.[58]

SECTION. 3. The Senate of the United States shall be composed of two Senators from each State, chosen by the Legislature thereof, for six Years; and each Senator shall have one Vote.[61]

Immediately after they shall be assembled in Consequence of the first Election, they shall be divided as equally as may be into three Classes. The Seats of the Senators of the first Class shall be vacated at the Expiration of the second Year, of the second Class at the Expiration of the fourth Year, and of the third Class at the Expiration of the sixth Year, so that one-third may be chosen every second Year; and if Vacancies happen by Resignation, or otherwise, during the Recess of the

Legislature of any State, the Executive thereof may make temporary Appointments until the next Meeting of the Legislature, which shall then fill such Vacancies.[71]

No Person shall be a Senator who shall not have attained to the Age of thirty Years, and been nine Years a Citizen of the United States, and who shall not, when elected, be an Inhabitant of that State for which he shall be chosen.[73]

The Vice President of the United States shall be President of the Senate, but shall have no Vote, unless they be equally divided.[76]

The Senate shall chuse their other Officers, and also a President pro tempore, in the Absence of the Vice President, or when he shall exercise the Office of President of the United States.[76]

The Senate shall have the sole Power to try all Impeachments. When sitting for that Purpose, they shall be on Oath or Affirmation. When the President of the United States is tried, the Chief Justice shall preside: And no Person shall be convicted without the Concurrence of two thirds of the Members present.[78]

Judgment in Cases of Impeachment shall not extend further than to removal from Office, and Disqualification to hold and enjoy any Office of honour, Trust or Profit under the United States: but the Party convicted shall nevertheless be liable and subject to Indictment, Trial, Judgment and Punishment, according to Law.[78]

SECTION. 4. The Times, Places and Manner of holding Elections for Senators and Representatives, shall be prescribed in each State by the Legislature thereof; but the Congress may at any time by Law make or alter such Regulations, except as to the places of chusing Senators.[81]

The Congress shall assemble at least once in every Year, and such Meeting shall be on the first Monday in December, unless they shall by Law appoint a different Day.[82]

SECTION. 5. Each House shall be the Judge of the Elections, Returns and Qualifications of its own Members, and a Majority of each shall constitute a Quorum to do Business; but a smaller Number may adjourn from day to day, and may be authorized to compel the Attendance of absent Members, in such Manner, and under such Penalties as each House may provide.[84]

Each House may determine the Rules of its Proceedings, punish its Members for disorderly Behaviour, and, with the Concurrence of two thirds, expel a Member.[84]

Each House shall keep a Journal of its Proceedings, and from time to time publish the same, excepting such Parts as may in their Judgment require Secrecy; and the Yeas and Nays of the Members of either House on any question shall, at the Desire of one fifth of those Present, be entered on the Journal.[87]

Neither House, during the Session of Congress, shall, without the Consent of the other, adjourn for more than three days, nor to any other Place than that in which the two Houses shall be sitting.[89]

Section. 6. The Senators and Representatives shall receive a Compensation for their Services, to be ascertained by Law, and paid out of the Treasury of the United States. They shall in all Cases, except Treason, Felony and Breach of the Peace, be privileged from Arrest during their Attendance at the Session of their respective Houses, and in going to and returning from the same; and for any Speech or Debate in either House, they shall not be questioned in any other Place.[91]

No Senator or Representative shall, during the Time for which he was elected, be appointed to any civil Office under the Authority of the United States, which shall have been created, or the Emoluments whereof shall have been encreased during such time; and no Person holding any Office under the United States, shall be a Member of either House during his Continuance in Office.[95]

SECTION. 7. All Bills for raising Revenue shall originate in the House of Representatives; but the Senate may propose or concur with Amendments as on other Bills.[98]

Every Bill which shall have passed the House of Representatives and the Senate, shall, before it become a Law, be presented to the President of the United States; If he approve he shall sign it, but if not he shall return it, with his Objections to that House in which it shall have originated, who shall enter the Objections at large on their Journal, and proceed to reconsider it. If after such Reconsideration two thirds of that House shall agree to pass the Bill, it shall be sent, together with the Objections, to the other House, by which it shall likewise be reconsidered, and if approved by two thirds of that House, it shall become a Law. But in all such Cases the Votes of both Houses shall be determined by yeas and Nays, and the Names of the Persons voting for and against the Bill shall be entered on the Journal of each House respectively. If any Bill shall not be returned by the President within ten Days (Sundays excepted) after it shall have been presentea to him, the Same shall be a law, in like Manner as if he had signed it, unless the Congress by their Adjournment prevent its Return, in which Case it shall not be a Law.[100]

Every Order, Resolution, or Vote to which the Concurrence of the Senate and House of Representatives may be necessary (except on a question of Adjournment) shall be presented to the President of the United States; and before the Same shall take Effect, shall be approved by him, or being disapproved by him, shall be repassed by two thirds of the Senate and House of Representatives, according to the Rules and Limitations prescribed in the Case of a Bill.[101]

SECTION. 8. The Congress shall have Power

To lay and collect Taxes, Duties, Imposts and Excises, to pay the Debts and provide for the common Defence and general Welfare of the United States; but all Duties, Imposts and Excises shall be uniform throughout the United States;[103]

To borrow Money on the credit of the United States;[106]

To regulate Commerce with foreign Nations, and among the several States, and with the Indian Tribes;[108]

To establish an uniform Rule of Naturalization,

and uniform Laws on the subject of Bankruptcies throughout the United States;[117]

To coin Money, regulate the Value thereof, and of foreign Coin, and fix the Standard of Weights and Measures;[119]

To provide for the Punishment of counterfeiting the Securities and current Coin of the United States;[119]

To establish Post Offices and post Roads;[119]

To promote the progress of Science and useful Arts, by securing for limited Times to Authors and Inventors the exclusive Right to their respective Writings and Discoveries;[119]

To constitute Tribunals inferior to the supreme Court;[122]

To define and punish Piracies and Felonies committed on the high Seas, and Offences against the Law of Nations;[122]

To declare War, grant Letters of Marque and Reprisal, and make Rules concerning Captures on Land and Water;[124]

To raise and support Armies, but no Appropriation of Money to that Use shall be for a longer Term than two Years;[126]

To provide and maintain a Navy;[126]

To make Rules for the Government and Regulation of the land and naval Forces;[126]

To provide for calling forth the Militia to execute the Laws of the Union, suppress Insurrections and repel Invasions;[128]

To provide for organizing, arming, and disciplining, the Militia, and for governing such Part of them as may be employed in the Service of the United States, reserving to the States respectively, the Appointment of the Officers, and the Authority of training the Militia according to the Discipline prescribed by Congress.[128]

To exercise exclusive Legislation in all Cases whatsoever, over such District (not exceeding ten Miles square) as may, by Cession of particular States, and the Acceptance of Congress, become the Seat of the Government of the United States, and to exercise like Authority over all Places purchased by the Consent of the Legislature of the State in which the Same shall be, for the Erection of Forts, Magazines, Arsenals, Dock-Yards, and other needful Buildings;[130] — And

To make all Laws which shall be necessary and proper for carrying into Execution the foregoing Powers, and all other Powers vested by this Constitution in the Government of the United States, or in any Department or Officer thereof.[133]

SECTION. 9. The Migration or Importation of such

Persons as any of the States now existing shall think proper to admit, shall not be prohibited by the Congress prior to the Year one thousand eight hundred and eight, but a Tax or Duty may be imposed on such Importation, not exceeding ten dollars for each Person.[142]

The Privilege of the Writ of Habeas Corpus shall not be suspended, unless when in Cases of Rebellion or Invasion the public Safety may require it.[147]

No Bill of Attainder or ex post facto Law shall be passed.[148]

No Capitation, or other direct, Tax shall be laid, unless in Proportion to the Census or Enumeration herein before directed to be taken.[148]

No Tax or Duty shall be laid on Articles exported from any State.[149]

No Preference shall be given by any Regulation of Commerce or Revenue to the Ports of one State over those of another: nor shall Vessels bound to, or from, one State, be obliged to enter, clear, or pay Duties in another.[151]

No Money shall be drawn from the Treasury, but in Consequence of Appropriations made by Law; and a regular Statement and Account of the Receipts and Expenditures of all public Money shall be published from time to time.[151]

No Title of Nobility shall be granted by the United States: And no Person holding any Office of Profit or Trust under them, shall, without the Consent of the Congress, accept of any present, Emolument, Office, or Title, of any kind whatever, from any King, Prince, or foreign State.[153]

SECTION. 10. No State shall enter into any Treaty, Alliance, or Confederation; grant Letters of Marque and Reprisal; coin Money; emit Bills of Credit; make any Thing but gold and silver Coin a Tender in Payment of Debts; pass any Bill of Attainder, ex post facto Law, or Law impairing the Obligation of Contracts, or grant any Title of Nobility.[154]

No State shall, without the consent of the Congress, lay any Imposts or Duties on Imports or Exports, except what may be absolutely necessary for executing it's inspection Laws: and the net Produce of all Duties and Imposts, laid by any State on Imports or Exports, shall be for the Use of the Treasury of the United States; and all such Laws shall be subject to the Revision and Controul of the Congress.[157]

No State shall, without the Consent of Congress, lay any Duty of Tonnage, keep Troops, or Ships of War in time of Peace, enter into any Agreement or Compact with another State, or with a foreign

Power, or engage in War, unless actually invaded, or in such imminent Danger as will not admit of Delay.[159]

ARTICLE. II.

SECTION. 1. The executive Power shall be vested in a President of the United States of America. He shall hold his Office during the Term of four Years, and, together with the Vice President, chosen for the same Term, be elected, as follows[161]

Each State shall appoint, in such Manner as the Legislature thereof may direct, a Number of Electors, equal to the whole Number of Senators and Representatives to which the State may be entitled in the Congress: but no Senator or Representative, or Person holding an Office of Trust or Profit under the United States, shall be appointed an Elector.[161]

[AMENDMENT XII. — The Electors shall meet in their respective states, and vote by ballot for President and Vice President, one of whom, at least, shall not be an inhabitant of the same state with themselves; they shall name in their ballots the person voted for as President, and in distinct ballots the person voted for as Vice-President, and they shall make distinct lists of all persons voted for as President, and of all persons voted for as Vice-President, and of the number of votes for each, which lists they shall sign and certify, and transmit sealed to the seat of the government of the United States, directed to the President of the Senate; — The President of the Senate shall, in presence of the Senate and House of Representatives, open all the certificates and the votes shall then be counted; — The person having the greatest number of votes for President, shall be the President, if such number be a majority of the whole number of Electors appointed; and if no person have such majority, then from the persons having the highest numbers not exceeding three on the list of those voted for as President, the House of Representatives shall choose immediately, by ballot, the President. But in choosing the President, the votes shall be taken by states, the representation from each state having one vote; a quorum for this purpose shall consist of a member or members from two-thirds of the states, and a majority of all the states shall be necessary to a choice. And if the House of Representatives shall not choose a President whenever the right of choice shall devolve upon them, before the fourth day of March next following, then the Vice-President shall act as President, as in the case of the death or other constitutional disability of the

President. The person having the greatest number of votes as Vice-President, shall be the Vice-President, if such number be a majority of the whole number of Electors appointed, and if no person have a majority, then from the two highest numbers on the list, the Senate shall choose the Vice-President; a quorum for the purpose shall consist of two-thirds of the whole number of Senators, and a majority of the whole number shall be necessary to a choice. But no person constitutionally ineligible to the office of President shall be eligible to that of Vice-President of the United States.] [242]

NOTE. — The clause within brackets is the twelfth amendment, changing the mode of electing the President and Vice-President.

The Congress may determine the Time of chusing the Electors, and the Day on which they shall give their Votes; which Day shall be the same throughout the United States.[161]

No Person except a natural born Citizen, or a Citizen of the United States, at the time of the Adoption of this Constitution, shall be eligible to the Office of President; neither shall any Person be eligible to that Office who shall not have attained to the Age of thirty five Years, and been fourteen Years a Resident within the United States.[170]

In Case of the Removal of the President from Office, or of his Death, Resignation, or Inability to discharge the Powers and Duties of the said Office, the same shall devolve on the Vice President, and the Congress may by Law provide for the Case of Removal, Death, Resignation, or Inability, both of the President and Vice President, declaring what Officer shall then act as President, and such Officer shall act accordingly, until the Disability be removed, or a President shall be elected.[171]

The President shall, at stated Times, receive for his Services, a Compensation, which shall neither be encreased nor diminished during the Period for which he shall have been elected, and he shall not receive within that Period any other Emolument from the United States, or any of them.[172]

Before he enter on the Execution of his Office, he shall take the following Oath or Affirmation:—

"I do solemnly swear (or affirm) that I will faith-
"fully execute the Office of President of the United
"States, and will to the best of my Ability, preserve,
"protect and defend the Constitution of the United
"States.[173]

SECTION. 2. The President shall be Commander in Chief of the Army and Navy of the United States, and of the Militia of the several States, when called into the actual Service of the United States; he may require the Opinion, in writing, of the principal Officer in each of the executive Departments, upon any Subject relating to the Duties of their respective Offices, and he shall have Power to grant Reprieves and Pardons for Offences against the United States, except in Cases of Impeachment.[175]

He shall have Power, by and with the Advice and Consent of the Senate, to make Treaties, provided two thirds of the Senators present concur; and he shall nominate, and by and with the Advice and Consent of the Senate, shall appoint Ambassadors, other public Ministers and Consuls, Judges of the supreme Court, and all other Officers of the United States, whose Appointments are not herein otherwise provided for, and which shall be established by Law: but the Congress may by Law vest the Appointment of such inferior Officers, as they think proper, in the President alone, in the Courts of Law, or in the Heads of Departments.[180]

The President shall have Power to fill up all Vacancies that may happen during the Recess of the Senate, by granting Commissions which shall expire at the End of their next Session.[180]

SECTION. 3. He shall from time to time give to

the Congress Information of the State of the Union, and recommend to their Consideration such Measures as he shall judge necessary and expedient; he may, on extraordinary Occasions, convene both Houses, or either of them, and in Case of Disagreement between them, with Respect to the Time of Adjournment, he may adjourn them to such Time as he shall think proper; he shall receive Ambassadors and other public Ministers; he shall take Care that the Laws be faithfully executed, and shall Commission all the officers of the United States.[184]

SECTION. 4. The President, Vice President and all civil Officers of the United States, shall be removed from Office on Impeachment for, and Conviction of, Treason, Bribery, or other high Crimes and Misdemeanors.[186]

ARTICLE III.

SECTION. 1. The judicial Power of the United States, shall be vested in one supreme Court, and in such inferior Courts as the Congress may from time to time ordain and establish. The Judges, both of the supreme and inferior Courts, shall hold their Offices during good Behavior, and shall, at stated Times, receive for their Services, a Compensation, which shall not be diminished during their Continuance in Office.[187]

SECTION. 2. The judicial Power shall extend to all Cases, in Law and Equity, arising under this Constitution, the Laws of the United States, and Treaties made, or which shall be made, under their Authority; — to all Cases affecting Ambassadors, other public Ministers, and Consuls; — to all Cases of admiralty and maritime Jurisdiction; — to Controversies to which the United States shall be a Party; — to Controversies between two or more States; — between a State and Citizens of another State; — between Citizens of different States, — between Citizens of the same State claiming Lands under Grants of different States, and between a State, or the Citizens thereof, and foreign States, Citizens or Subjects.[190]

In all Cases affecting Ambassadors, other public Ministers and Consuls, and those in which a State shall be Party, the supreme Court shall have original Jurisdiction. In all the other Cases before mentioned, the supreme Court shall have appellate jurisdiction, both as to Law and Fact, with such Exceptions, and under such Regulations as the Congress shall make.[190]

The Trial of all Crimes, except in Cases of Impeachment, shall be by Jury; and such Trial shall be held in the State where the said Crimes shall have been committed; but when not committed within any State, the Trial shall be at such Place or Places as the Congress may by Law have directed.[195]

SECTION. 3. Treason against the United States, shall consist only in levying War against them, or in adhering to their Enemies, giving them Aid and Comfort. No Person shall be convicted of Treason unless on the Testimony of two Witnesses to the same overt Act, or on Confession in open Court.[196]

The Congress shall have Power to declare the Punishment of Treason, but no Attainder of Treason shall work Corruption of Blood, or Forfeiture except during the Life of the Person attainted.[196]

ARTICLE. IV.

SECTION. 1. Full Faith and Credit shall be given in each State to the public Acts, Records, and judicial Proceedings of every other State. And the Congress may by general Laws prescribe the Manner in which such Acts, Records and Proceedings shall be proved, and the Effect thereof.[199]

SECTION. 2. The Citizens of each State shall be entitled to all Privileges and Immunities of Citizens in the several States.[202]

A Person charged in any State with Treason, Felony, or other Crime, who shall flee from Justice, and be found in another State, shall on Demand of the executive Authority of the State from which he fled, be delivered up, to be removed to the State having Jurisdiction of the Crime.[204]

No Person held to Service or Labour in one State, under the Laws thereof, escaping into another, shall, in Consequence of any Law or Regulation therein, be discharged from such Service or Labour, but shall be delivered up on Claim of the Party to whom such Service or Labour may be due.[206]

SECTION. 3. New States may be admitted by the Congress into this Union; but no new State shall be formed or erected within the Jurisdiction of any other State; nor any State be formed by the Junction of two or more States, or Parts of States, without the Consent of the Legislatures of the States concerned as well as of the Congress.[209]

The Congress shall have Power to dispose of and make all needful Rules and Regulations respecting the Territory or other Property belonging to the United States; and nothing in this Constitution shall be so construed as to Prejudice any Claims of the United States, or of any particular State.[212]

SECTION. 4. The United States shall guarantee to every State in this Union a Republican Form of Government, and shall protect each of them against

Invasion, and on Application of the Legislature, or of the Executive (when the Legislature cannot be convened) against domestic Violence.[216]

ARTICLE. V.

The Congress, whenever two thirds of both Houses shall deem it necessary, shall propose Amendments to this Constitution, or, on the Application of the Legislatures of two thirds of the several States, shall call a Convention for proposing Amendments, which, in either Case, shall be valid to all Intents and Purposes, as Part of this Constitution, when ratified by the Legislatures of three fourths of the several States, or by Conventions in three fourths thereof, as the one or the other Mode of Ratification may be proposed by the Congress; Provided that no Amendment which may be made prior to the Year one thousand eight hundred and eight shall in any Manner affect the first and fourth Clauses in the Ninth Section of the first Article; and that no State, without its Consent, shall be deprived of its equal Suffrage in the Senate.[218]

ARTICLE. VI.

All Debts contracted and Engagements entered

into, before the Adoption of this Constitution, shall be as valid against the United States under this Constitution, as under the Confederation.[221]

This Constitution, and the Laws of the United States which shall be made in Pursuance thereof; and all Treaties made, or which shall be made, under the authority of the United States, shall be the supreme Law of the Land; and the Judges in every State shall be bound thereby, any Thing in the Constitution or Laws of any State to the Contrary notwithstanding.[223]

The Senators and Representatives before mentioned, and the Members of the several State Legislatures, and all executive and judicial Officers, both of the United States and of the several States, shall be bound by Oath or Affirmation, to support this Constitution; but no religious Test shall ever be required as a Qualification to any Office or public Trust under the United States.[225]

ARTICLE. VII.

The Ratification of the Convention of nine States, shall be sufficient for the Establishment of this Constitution between the States so ratifying the Same.[227]

DONE in Convention by the Unanimous Consent of the States present the Seventeenth Day of September in the Year of our Lord one thousand seven hundred and Eighty seven and of the Independance of the United States of America the Twelfth **In Witness** whereof We have hereunto subscribed our Names,

GEO WASHINGTON —
Presidt and deputy from Virginia

NEW HAMPSHIRE.

JOHN LANGDON, NICHOLAS GILMAN.

MASSACHUSETTS.

NATHANIEL GORHAM, RUFUS KING.

CONNECTICUT.

WM. SAML. JOHNSON, ROGER SHERMAN.

NEW YORK.

ALEXANDER HAMILTON.

NEW JERSEY.

WIL: LIVINGSTON, DAVID BREARLEY,
WM. PATERSON, JONA. DAYTON.

PENNSYLVANIA.

B. FRANKLIN, THOMAS MIFFLIN,
ROBT. MORRIS, GEO: CLYMER,
THO: FITZSIMONS, JARED INGERSOLL,
JAMES WILSON, GOUV: MORRIS.

DELAWARE.

Geo: Read, Gunning Bedford, Jun'r,
John Dickinson, Richard Bassett,
Jaco: Broom.

MARYLAND.

James M'Henry, Dan: of St. Thos. Jenifer,
Danl. Carroll.

VIRGINIA.

John Blair, James Madison, Jr.,

NORTH CAROLINA.

Wm. Blount, Rich'd Dobbs Spaight,
Hu. Williamson.

SOUTH CAROLINA.

J. Rutledge, Charles Cotesworth Pinckney,
Charles Pinckney, Pierce Butler.

GEORGIA.

William Few, Abr. Baldwin.

Attest, WILLIAM JACKSON, *Secretary*.

The Constitution was adopted on the 17th September, 1787, by the Convention appointed in pursuance of the resolution of the Congress of the Confederation, of the 21st February, 1787, and was ratified by the Conventions of the several States, as follows, viz.:

By Convention of		Delaware,	on the	7th December,	1787.
"	"	Pennsylvania,	"	12th December,	1787.
"	"	New Jersey,	"	18th December,	1787.
"	"	Georgia,	"	2d January,	1788.
"	"	Connecticut,	"	9th January,	1788.
"	"	Massachusetts,	"	6th February,	1788.
"	"	Maryland,	"	28th April,	1788.
"	"	South Carolina,	"	23d May,	1788.
"	"	New Hampshire,	"	21st June,	1788.
"	"	Virginia,	"	26th June,	1788.
"	"	New York,	"	26th July,	1788.
"	"	North Carolina,	"	21st November,	1789.
"	"	Rhode Island,	"	29th May,	1790.

ARTICLES

IN ADDITION TO, AND AMENDMENT OF,

THE CONSTITUTION OF THE UNITED STATES OF AMERICA,

Proposed by Congress, and ratified by the Legislatures of the several States, pursuant to the fifth article of the original Constitution.

(ARTICLE 1.)

Congress shall make no law respecting an establishment of religion, or prohibiting the free exercise thereof; or abridging the freedom of speech, or of the press; or the right of the people peaceably to assemble, and to petition the Government for a redress of grievances.[230]

(ARTICLE 2.)

A well regulated Militia, being necessary to the security of a free State, the right of the people to keep and bear Arms, shall not be infringed.[232]

(ARTICLE III.)

No Soldier shall, in time of peace be quartered in any house, without the consent of the Owner, nor in time of war, but in a manner to be prescribed by law.[233]

(ARTICLE IV.)

The right of the people to be secure in their persons, houses, papers, and effects, against unreasonable searches and seizures, shall not be violated, and no Warrants shall issue, but upon probable cause, supported by Oath or affirmation, and particularly describing the place to be searched, and the persons or things to be seized.[234]

(ARTICLE V.)

No person shall be held to answer for a capital, or otherwise infamous crime, unless on a presentment or indictment of a Grand Jury, except in cases arising in the land or naval forces, or in the Militia, when in actual service in time of War or public danger; nor shall any person be subject for the same offence to be twice put in jeopardy of life or limb; nor shall be compelled in any Criminal Case to be a witness against himself, nor be deprived of life, liberty, or property, without due process of law; nor shall private property be taken for public use, without just compensation.[235]

(ARTICLE VI.)

In all criminal prosecutions, the accused shall enjoy the right to a speedy and public trial, by an impartial jury of the State and district wherein the crime shall have been committed, which district shall have been previously ascertained by law, and to be informed of the nature and cause of the accusation; to be confronted with the witnesses against him; to have Compulsory process for obtaining Witnesses in his favour, and to have the Assistance of Counsel for his defence.[237]

(ARTICLE VII.)

In Suits at common law, where the value in controversy shall exceed twenty dollars, the right of trial by jury shall be preserved, and no fact tried by a jury shall be otherwise re-examined in any Court of the United States, than according to the rules of the common law.[238]

(ARTICLE VIII.)

Excessive bail shall not be required, nor excessive fines imposed, nor cruel and unusual punishments inflicted.[238]

(ARTICLE IX.)

The enumeration in the Constitution, of certain rights, shall not be construed to deny or disparage others retained by the people.[238]

(ARTICLE X.)

The powers not delegated to the United States by the Constitution, nor prohibited by it to the States, are reserved to the States respectively, or to the people.[240]

ARTICLE XI.

The Judicial power of the United States shall not be construed to extend to any suit in law or equity, commenced or prosecuted against one of the United States by Citizens of another State, or by Citizens or Subjects of any Foreign State.[241]

INTRODUCTION TO THE ANALYSIS.

When the members of the Constitutional Convention assembled in Philadelphia, to enter upon the discharge of the duties which had been assigned to them, they had very vague, undefined, and incongruous views of the work upon which they were entering. Some of them supposed that their powers and duties were limited to devising such amendments to the existing articles of confederation, as would enable Congress to provide a revenue by a tariff of duties on imports, for the purpose of raising a fund for the payment of the public debt, and to secure uniformity in the commercial regulations of the several States. This idea was sustained by the general course of the proceedings, both in Congress and in the State legislatures, which had immediately led to the assembling of a general convention. The delegates to the Annapolis convention, which was the immediate precursor to that at Philadelphia, were limited in their commissions to those objects; and the instructions given by the State legislatures to most of the members of the constitutional convention, seemed to contemplate little more than a revision and amendment of the existing Articles of Confederation.

Others of the members, particularly those from Virginia and South Carolina, were prepared to enter at once upon the construction of the organic law for a supreme general government, without regard, either in form or substance, to the existing articles of confederation. Mr. Madison, in a letter addressed to his colleague, Mr. Randolph, dated some time prior to the meeting, and prior to the election of delegates in several of the States, had suggested this view of the purpose and duty of the Convention.

On the opening of the session, Mr. Randolph submitted a series of resolutions, embodying his views (which were substantially those suggested to him by Mr. Madison), of the character of government he proposed to have established.

Mr. Charles Pinckney, of South Carolina, at the same time, submitted his plan, embodying a similar purpose, but in a more detailed form. Both of these are inserted in another part of this volume.

These two propositions were immediately referred to the committee of the whole, and became the basis of an earnest and protracted debate. In order to bring the question of the powers and purposes of the convention to a direct issue, Mr. Randolph, on the suggestion of Mr. Gouverneur Morris, modified his first resolution so as to declare, that a *national government* ought to be established, with *supreme executive, legislative,* and *judiciary departments.* Mr. Patterson, from New Jersey, in behalf of the delegates from that State, and of a majority of those from New York and some others, submitted a counter proposition, providing for such an amendment of the existing Articles of Confederation as would tend to obviate the difficulties which had been the principal subjects of complaint. After a protracted discussion of these several propositions, that of Mr. Randolph prevailed by a decisive majority. After the passage of the resolution, its phraseology was changed by substituting the words "United States" in place of the word "National." This may, perhaps, be regarded as a concession to some extent, on the part of the advocates of a strictly national government, to those who favored the maintenance of the confederacy.

This question being settled, the Convention proceeded to the formation of the new CONSTITUTION. It having been agreed that the legislature should consist of two branches, the next important question upon which the members were divided, was in regard to the manner in which the respective States were to be represented in the legislative bodies.

The States of Massachusetts, Pennsylvania, Virginia, North Carolina, and South Carolina, contended that the several States should be represented in both houses of Congress, in proportion to the population and wealth of each State. New York, Connecticut, New Jersey, and Delaware insisted that the equality which the States had enjoyed in the confederation, as sovereign political communities, should be maintained in all of the branches of the new general government. The tenacity with which the two parties adhered to their respective positions on this question, seriously threatened the disruption of the Convention.

The smaller States, together with New York, finally yielded to a proportional representation in the popular branch of Congress, but firmly adhered to their resolution to maintain their equality in the Senate, and intimated the alternative of secession, if this should be refused. The opposite party indicated its determination to accept the alternative. At this crisis, a committee of one from each State, was raised to make a further effort to effect a compromise. In this committee, the two parties were equally represented; but Dr. Franklin, the member of the committee for Pennsylvania, finding the other party resolved to adhere to their position at all hazards, yielded the point of equal State representation in the Senate, on condition that all bills for raising or appropriating money should originate in the other house. This compromise was sustained by the Convention, but by a vote less than a majority of the States represented, there being, on the final vote, but five States in the affirmative, namely — Connecticut, New Jersey, Delaware, Maryland, North Carolina; and four in the negative — Pennsylvania, Virginia, South Carolina, Georgia; New York absent, Massachusetts divided.

The basis of representation in the House of Representatives, presented the next subject of serious controversy. The northern delegates generally contended that the free population should constitute the sole basis — while those from the South insisted that the entire population should be taken into the account. A ground of compromise for this difficulty, was found in the mode of counting the population when it was to be made the basis of taxation instead of the measure of power, and when the interests of the parties were in a reversed position.

These fundamental questions having been adjusted, the Convention proceeded to the arrangement of the details of the Constitution without serious difficulty.

The usual mode of proceeding was, to consider the several propositions, as they were submitted, first in committee of the whole and then in Convention, and if approved, they were referred to a committee of detail, who embodied them in proper form and reported them back to the Convention. They were then reconsidered by the Convention and further modified, when deemed expedient, and finally referred to a committee of style and arrangement. This last committee did not report until the closing days of the session, and their report, although it varies, in some respects, from what seems to have been the action of the Convention, was adopted without being questioned. This may account for some of the paragraphs, and particularly the preamble, appearing in a somewhat different form in the Constitution from that which the journal gives them.

It is well known that the proceedings of the Convention were secret, and that, for what has transpired beyond the contents of the official journal, we are mainly indebted to Mr. Madison and Judge Lansing of New York, who kept daily notes of the proceedings and debates of the Convention, from which this part of the work is principally compiled.

It is the main purpose of this Analysis, to give such a history of the several clauses of the Constitution, as will make the objects and intentions of its framers clear and intelligible. This, it has occurred to me, could be most conveniently accomplished, by giving, in connection with each clause, its origin and the modifications it underwent or which were proposed to be given to it, and a brief statement of the debate upon it, during its progress in the Convention, until it assumed the form in which it appears in the Constitution. To this is added the judicial construction, if any, that it has received. The convenience of this arrangement will be obvious. The framers of the Constitution were certainly the most competent to explain its intended import. If the original form of a proposition was changed, the change itself or the reason assigned for it, would indicate the object aimed at. If the clause had been contained in the Articles of Confederation, its retention in the Constitution was an evidence that it had already received a satisfactory, practical construction.

EXPLANATION.

In the following *Analysis*, each clause of the Constitution is placed at the head of a page, and is immediately followed by a notice of its origin.

If the same or a similar power or provision had been contained in any of the Articles of Confederation, the article, or the portion of it containing the power, is inserted.

This is followed by the proceedings upon it, in the Convention, showing the form in which it was introduced, the modifications to which it was subjected, and a synopsis of the debate to which it gave rise, until it assumed its final shape and place in the Constitution.

To this is appended an abstract of the judicial constructions which have been given to it.

ANALYSIS OF THE CONSTITUTION.

PREAMBLE.

WE, the people of the United States, in order to form a more perfect union, establish justice, insure domestic tranquillity, provide for the common defence, promote the general welfare, and secure the blessings of liberty to ourselves and our posterity, do ordain and establish this Constitution for the United States of America.

Confederation. — Articles of confederation and perpetual union between the States of New Hampshire, Massachusetts, &c.

Mr. RANDOLPH'S PLAN. — "That the Articles of Confederation ought to be so corrected and enlarged as to accomplish the objects proposed by their institution, namely, 'common defence, security of liberty, and general welfare.'"

Mr. PINCKNEY'S PLAN. — "We, the people of the States of New Hampshire, Massachusetts, &c., do ordain, declare, and establish the following CONSTITUTION, for the government of ourselves and posterity."

In Committee of the Whole. — On motion of Mr. RANDOLPH, on the suggestion of Mr. G. MORRIS, it was,

Resolved, "That a *national government* ought to be established, consisting of a supreme legislative, executive, and judiciary." Yeas — Massachusetts, Pennsylvania, Delaware, Virginia, North Carolina, South Carolina, 6. Nay — Connecticut.

In this form it was reported to the Convention, when Mr. PATTERSON, on behalf of those members who desired to enlarge and improve the Articles of Confederation but not to establish a *national government*, proposed the following substitute: —

Resolved, "That the Articles of Confederation ought to be so revised, corrected, and enlarged as to render the Federal Constitution adequate to the exigencies of government and the preservation of the Union."

The two propositions being under discussion, Mr. LANSING stated the distinction to be, that the plan of Mr. Randolph "absorbed all power except what may be exercised in the little local matters," — while that of Mr. Patterson sustained "the sovereignty of the respective States."

Mr. RANDOLPH said, "The question is, whether we will adhere to the *federal* plan, or introduce the *national* one."

On the question whether Mr. Randolph's plan should be adhered to, or that of Mr. Patterson substituted, — Massachusetts, Connecticut, Pennsylvania, Virginia, North Carolina, South Carolina, and Georgia, 7, voted for the former; and New York, New Jersey, and Delaware, 3, for the latter; Maryland, divided.

On motion of Mr. ELLSWORTH, the words "*a government of the United States*" were substituted for "*a national government.*"

It went in this form to the committee of detail, who

reported, — "We, the people of the States of New Hampshire, Massachusetts, Rhode Island, Connecticut, New York, New Jersey, Pennsylvania, Maryland, Virginia, North Carolina, South Carolina, and Georgia, do ordain, declare, and establish the following Constitution for the government of ourselves and our posterity."

The committee of style and arrangement gave it the present form. No reason seems to have been assigned for the change.

Judicial Constructions. — The Constitution of the United States was ordained and established, not by the United States in their sovereign capacities, but, as the preamble declares, by the people of the United States.

It was competent for the people to invest the national government with all the powers they might deem proper and necessary, and to give them paramount and supreme authority. The people had a right to prohibit to the States the exercise of any powers, &c., and to reserve to themselves those sovereign powers which they might not choose to delegate to either.

The Constitution was not, therefore, carved out of existing State sovereignties, nor a surrender of powers already existing in the State governments. On the other hand, the sovereign powers vested in the State governments by their respective constitutions, remain unaltered and unimpaired, except so far as they are granted to the government of the United States.

The government of the United States can claim no powers which are not granted to it by the Constitution, either expressly or by necessary implication.

The Constitution, like every other grant, is to have a reasonable construction, according to the import of its terms. Martin *v.* Hunter's Lessee, 1 Wheat. 304, 324, 380.

The United States is a *government*, and, consequently, a body politic and corporate, capable of attaining the objects for which it was created, by means which are necessary for their attainment. United States *v.* Maurice, 2 Brock. 109.

ARTICLE I.

SECTION I.

All legislative powers herein granted shall be vested in a Congress of the United States, which shall consist of a Senate and House of Representatives.

The Continental Congress of 1774 — the first "general Congress" of the colonies — seems to have been originally proposed by the committee of correspondence of the SONS of LIBERTY of the city of New York, in May of that year. It assembled at Philadelphia, September 6th, and continued to meet annually until the adoption of the present Constitution.

On the 21st July, 1775, Dr. FRANKLIN submitted to Congress the sketch of "Articles of Confederation," the fourth article of which provides: —

"That delegates shall be annually elected in each colony, to meet in general Congress, at such times and places as shall be agreed on in the next preceding Congress."

This provision is substantially retained in the "Article of Confederation" (5th), adopted by Congress in 1777, and subsequently ratified by the several States.

In Federal Convention. Mr. RANDOLPH'S PLAN. — "That the national legislature ought to consist of two branches."

4 *

Mr. Pinckney's Plan.—"The legislative power shall be vested in a Congress, to consist of two separate Houses, one to be called the House of Delegates, and the other the Senate."

Mr. Lansing moved, "That the powers of legislation be vested in the United States in Congress."

The debate on this motion turned upon the question whether the principle of *confederation* was to be retained, or a *national* government established.

The following extracts are taken from the "Madison Papers," Elliot's edition, vol. 5, p. 214 et seq.

Mr. Lansing "observed, that the true question here was, whether the Convention would adhere to, or depart from, the foundation of the present confederacy."

Col. Mason supported Mr. Randolph's plan, but observed that, "notwithstanding his solicitude to establish a national government, he would never agree to abolish the State governments, or render them absolutely insignificant."

Mr. Luther Martin "agreed with Col. Mason as to the importance of the State governments: he would support them at the expense of the general government, which was instituted for the purpose of that support. He saw no necessity for two branches. . . . . At the separation from the British empire, the people of America preferred the establishment of themselves into thirteen separate sovereignties, instead of incorporating themselves into one. To these they look for the security of their lives, liberties, and properties—to these they must look up. The federal government they formed to defend the whole against foreign nations in time of war, and to defend the lesser States against the ambition of the larger."

Mr. Sherman, of Connecticut, "seconded and supported Mr. Lansing's motion. He admitted two branches to be necessary in the State legislatures, but saw no necessity in a *confederacy of States.* Congress carried us through the war, and perhaps as well as any government could have done. . . . If another branch were to be added to Congress, it would serve to embarrass them. The disparity of States, in point of size, he perceived, was the main difficulty. But the large States had not yet suffered from the equality of votes enjoyed by the smaller ones."

"If the difficulty on the subject of representation cannot be otherwise got over, he would agree to have two branches, *and a proportional representation in one of them, provided each State had an equal voice in the other.* This was necessary to secure the rights of the lesser States. Each State had its peculiar habits, usages, and manners, which constituted its happiness." [This appears to have been the first suggestion of the idea upon which the two Houses of Congress were ultimately organized.]

Mr. WILSON, of Pennsylvania, urged the necessity of two branches. He admitted that the large States did accede to the confederation in its present form; but it was the effect of necessity, not of choice.

Dr. JOHNSON.—"On comparison of the two plans which had been proposed from Virginia and New Jersey, it appeared that the peculiarity which characterized the latter, was its being calculated to preserve the individuality of the States. Mr. Wilson and the gentleman from Virginia (Col. Mason) . . . wished to leave the States in possession of a considerable, though subordinate jurisdiction."

Mr. MADISON "was of opinion, in the first place, that there was less danger of encroachment from the general government than from the State governments; and in the second place, that the mischiefs from encroachments would be less fatal if made by the former, than if made by the latter."

Mr. Randolph's resolution was agreed to. Yeas — Massachusetts, Connecticut, Pennsylvania, Virginia, N. Carolina, South Carolina, Georgia, 7. Nays — New York, New Jersey, Delaware, 3.

The committee of the whole reported the clause in the following form: —

"That the national legislature ought to consist of two branches. That each branch ought to possess the right to originate acts."

On motion of Mr. Ellsworth, the words "the United States" were substituted for the word "national."

As reported by the committee of detail: —

"The legislative power shall be vested in a Congress, to consist of two separate and distinct bodies of men, a House of Representatives and a Senate; each of which shall in all cases have a negative on the other."

On motion of Mr. Madison, the last clause of the sentence was stricken out.

It was then referred to the committee of style, who reported it in its present form.

ARTICLE I.

SECTION II.

Clause 1.—The House of Representatives shall be composed of members chosen every second year by the people of the several States, and the electors in each State shall have the qualifications requisite for electors of the most numerous branch of the State legislature.

Clause 2.—No person shall be a representative who shall not have attained the age of twenty-five years, and have been seven years a citizen of the United States, and who shall not, when elected, be an inhabitant of that State in which he shall be chosen.

Articles of Confederation.—Delegates shall be annually appointed, in such manner as the legislature of each State shall direct, . . . with a power reserved to each State to recall its delegates or any of them, at any time within the year, and to send others in their stead for the remainder of the year.

In Federal Convention. Mr. Randolph's Plan.—"*That the members of the first branch of the national legislature ought to be elected by the people of the several States,* every —— for the term of ——, to be of the age of —— years at least; to be incapable of reëlection for the space of —— years after the expiration of their term of service, and to be subject to recall."

Mr. CHARLES PINCKNEY'S PLAN.—"The members of the House of Delegates shall be chosen every —— year, and the qualification of the electors shall be the same as those of the electors in the several States for their legislatures. Each member shall have been a citizen of the United States for —— years, and shall be —— of age, and a resident in the State he is chosen for."

On the question for an election of the first branch of the national legislature by the people. Yeas — Massachusetts, New York, Pennsylvania, Virginia, North Carolina, and Georgia, 6. Nays — New Jersey, South Caroina, 2. Connecticut and Delaware, divided.

Mr. CHARLES PINCKNEY proposed,—"That the first branch of the national legislature be elected by the State legislatures and not by the people," which was disagreed to.

General C. C. PINCKNEY proposed,—That the election should be "in such manner as the legislature of each State should direct."

This proposition having been rejected, the question was taken on the election "by the people" and it was agreed to. Yeas — Massachusetts, New York, Pennsylvania, Virginia, North Carolina, and Georgia, 6. Nays — New Jersey, South Carolina, 2.

On motion of Mr. Randolph, the term of service was fixed at *two years*, and the clause adopted.

Judicial Constructions.—An inhabitant of a State, is one who is, *bona fide*, a member of the State, subject to all the requisitions of its laws, and entitled to all the privileges and advantages which they confer. Bailey's case, Cl. & Hall, 411.

A person residing in the District of Columbia, though in the employment of the general government, is not an inhabitant of a State, so as to be eligible to a seat in Congress. Ibid.

A public minister residing at a foreign court, does not lose his character as an inhabitant of his State. Ibid. 497.

It has been repeatedly settled by both houses of Congress, that, the constitution having fixed the qualifications of members, no additional qualifications can rightfully be required by the States. Ibid. 167.

The House of Representatives has jurisdiction to punish for contempt. Anderson *v.* Dunn, 6 Wheaton, 204.

A warrant of arrest, under the hand and seal of the speaker, attested by the clerk and directed to the sergeant-at-arms, is legal, although it does not show on its face, on what evidence it was founded, nor set forth specially in what the alleged contempt consists. Ibid.

ARTICLE I.

SECTION II.

Clause 3. — Representatives and direct taxes shall be apportioned among the several States which may be included within this Union, according to their respective numbers, which shall be determined by adding to the whole number of free persons, including those bound to service for a term of years, and excluding Indians not taxed, three-fifths of all other persons.

The first American Congress assembled at Philadelphia on the 5th day of September, 1774. The next day (September 6th), they passed the following resolution, being their first legislative act: —

"*Resolved, That in determining questions in Congress, each colony or province shall have one vote.* The Congress not being possessed of, or at present able to procure, proper materials for ascertaining the importance of each colony."

This great principle of State equality was firmly maintained through all the vicissitudes of the Revolution and until its partial surrender in the above article of the Constitution, notwithstanding often repeated efforts and struggles by the larger States, to subvert it.

On the 21st July, 1775, Dr. FRANKLIN introduced a plan for a confederation, embracing the following: —

"The number of delegates to be elected and sent to

Congress by each colony shall be regulated by the number of male polls [between 16 and 60 years]."

In providing for the redemption of the paper-money issued by Congress, it was provided —

"That the proportion or quota of each colony be determined according to the number of inhabitants of all ages, including negroes and mulattoes in each colony."

The subject was again agitated for a considerable time, and with great earnestness in the session of 1777. It was proposed that the small States of Rhode Island, Delaware, and Georgia, should each have one vote; and the other States, one vote for every 50,000 white inhabitants. Virginia and Pennsylvania alone supported this motion. It was then moved that each State should have one vote for every 30,000, which was supported by Virginia alone. It was then proposed that the representation should be in proportion to the taxes paid by each colony, which was negatived by the same vote.

Finally, after a protracted struggle of some six or eight weeks, all the States except Virginia, yielded to the principle of *State equality*, and the following article divested of the apparent qualification appended to the original resolution, was adopted in the Articles of Confederation: —

"In determining questions in the United States, in Congress assembled, each State shall have one vote."

The general treasury was to be "supplied by the several States in proportion to the value of all lands, within each State, granted to or surveyed for any person . . . together with the buildings and improvements."

On the 6th of March, 1783, the Committee on Revenue reported to Congress a series of resolutions on the means of supplying the treasury, one of which proposed to substitute for the above — that the common treasury should be supplied by the several States "*in proportion to the number of inhabitants, of every age, sex, and condition, except Indians not paying taxes, in each State*," and *excluding also* "*persons who are bound to servitude for life according to the laws of the State to which they belong*," — except those between certain ages.

It was proposed to accomplish the object of the latter part of the clause by substituting, "that two blacks be counted as one freeman."

Mr. Wilson and Mr. Clark said they were members of Congress when the article was adopted, and that the Southern States were then willing to agree to the mode now proposed, but that the Eastern States would not consent that *only half* the slaves should be counted.

Mr. Wolcott proposed, "that four slaves be rated as three freemen."

Mr. Carroll proposed, "that four slaves be rated as one freeman."

Mr. Williamson, of North Carolina, thought they should be excluded altogether, as being an incumbrance, instead of increasing the ability to pay taxes.

Mr. Rutledge, of South Carolina, would consent to the proportion of two to one, but he thought three to one a "juster proportion."

Mr. Madison proposed, as a compromise, "*that slaves should be rated as five to three*." This was seconded by Mr. Rutledge and agreed to. Yeas — New Hampshire, New Jersey, Pennsylvania, Maryland, Virginia, North Carolina, and South Carolina, 7. Nays — Rhode Island and Connecticut, 2. Massachusetts divided. It was finally agreed to by eleven States.

In Federal Convention. Mr. Randolph's Plan. — "That the rights of suffrage in the national legislature ought to be proportioned to the quotas of contribution, or to the number of free inhabitants."

Mr. PINCKNEY'S PLAN, proposed to regulate the number of delegates by "the number of inhabitants of every description."

Mr. READ stated, that the instructions of the members from Delaware restrained them from assenting to any change of the rule of suffrage.

Mr. MADISON observed, "that, whatever reason might have existed for the equality of suffrage when the Union was a federal one, among sovereign States, it must cease when a national government should be put in its place."

After it had been determined that the legislature should consist of two branches,

Mr. SHERMAN suggested, "that the proportion of suffrage in the first branch should be according to the respective numbers of free inhabitants."

Mr. RUTLEDGE proposed to substitute, "according to the quotas of contribution."

These propositions were postponed for a motion by Mr. WILSON, seconded by Mr. C. PINCKNEY, that the right of suffrage in this branch of the legislature, should be "*in proportion* to the whole number of white and other free citizens and inhabitants, of every age, sex, and condition, including those bound to service for a term of years, and three fifths of all other persons, not comprehended in the foregoing descriptions, except Indians, not paying taxes in each State." Which was agreed to — New Jersey and Delaware only in the negative.

The committee of the whole, having reported this proposition to the House, Mr. LANSING moved to modify it so as to give each State an equal vote. After a long and somewhat exciting debate, the motion was rejected. Yeas — Connecticut, New York, New Jersey, and Delaware,

4. Nays — Massachusetts, Pennsylvania, Virginia, North Carolina, South Carolina, Georgia, 6. The clause as reported was then agreed to.

The compromise committee on the mode of constituting the Senate reported, by way of concession to the small States for being allowed an equal vote in the second branch, the following: —

"That in the first branch of the legislature, each of the States now in the Union shall be allowed one member for every forty thousand inhabitants of the description reported in the seventh resolution of the committee of the whole House: that each State not containing that number shall be allowed one member: that all bills for raising or appropriating money and for fixing salaries of officers of government shall originate in the first branch of the legislature and shall not be altered or amended by the second branch, and that no money shall be drawn from the public treasury but in pursuance of appropriation to be originated in the first branch."

Mr. G. Morris objected to the ratio of one for every 40,000, and thought property should be taken into account.

Mr. Rutledge concurred with Mr. Morris, and proposed "that the suffrages of the several States be regulated and proportioned according to the sums to be paid towards the general revenue by the inhabitants of each State respectively," &c.

South Carolina alone supported this proposition.

The clause, on motion of Mr. G. Morris, was committed to a new committee, namely, Morris, Gorham, Randolph, Rutledge, and King.

This committee reported, "that, in the first meeting of the legislature, the first branch thereof consist of fifty-six members; of which number New Hampshire shall have

2, Massachusetts 7, Rhode Island 1, Connecticut 4, New York 5, New Jersey 3, Pennsylvania 8, Delaware 1, Maryland 4, Virginia 9, North Carolina 5, South Carolina 5, Georgia 2."

"But as the present situation of the States may probably alter, as well in the point of wealth as in the number of their inhabitants, that the legislature be authorized, from time to time to augment the number of representatives. And in case any of the States shall hereafter be divided, or any two or more States united, or any new States created within the limits of the United States, the legislature shall possess authority to regulate the number of representatives in any of the foregoing cases, *upon the principles of their wealth and number of inhabitants*."

The second paragraph of the report was agreed to, yeas 9, nays 2.

The first paragraph being under consideration, Mr. SHERMAN moved to refer it to a committee of one from each State.

Mr. WILLIAMSON "thought it would be necessary to return to the rule of numbers."

Mr. PATTERSON. — "What is the true principle of representation? It is an expedient, by which an assembly of certain individuals, chosen by the people, is substituted in the place of the inconvenient meeting of the people themselves."

Mr. MADISON remarked, that Mr. Patterson's "doctrine of representation, which was, in its principle, the genuine one, must forever silence the pretensions of the small States to an equality of votes with the large ones. They ought to vote in the same proportion in which their citizens would do if the people of all the States were collectively met."

Mr. KING "had always expected that, as the Southern

States are the richest, they would not league themselves with the Northern, unless some respect was paid to their superior wealth."

The commitment was then carried.

The committee reported, adding one member each to New Hampshire, Massachusetts, New York, New Jersey, Virginia, and Georgia, and two to Maryland.

General PINCKNEY and Mr. WILLIAMSON objected that the southern interests would be endangered by this arrangement.

The report of the committee was adopted.

Judicial Constructions. — A tax on carriages is not a direct tax, within the meaning of the Constitution. 3 Dall. 171.

This does not exclude the right to impose a direct tax on the District of Columbia. Loughborough *v.* Blake, 5 Wheaton, 317.

ARTICLE I.

SECTION II.

Clause 4.—The actual enumeration shall be made within three years after the first meeting of the Congress of the United States, and within every subsequent term of ten years, in such manner as they shall by law direct.

Appropriation was made, in the Congress of the Confederation, in March, 1783, for a triennial census to be taken, of the number of inhabitants of every age, sex, and condition, except Indians not taxed in each State; *provided*, that no persons should be included who were bound to servitude for life; in proportion to which the common treasury was to be supplied.

In Federal Convention.—Mr. PINCKNEY'S PLAN of a Constitution, provides for a periodical census "of the whole number of inhabitants of every description," as the basis of direct taxation.

A committee having reported that the legislature should have power to regulate the number of representatives to which each State should be entitled, "upon the principle of their wealth and number of inhabitants,"—

Mr. RANDOLPH moved that "the legislature should be required to cause a census and estimate [of population and wealth] to be taken within one year after its first meeting; and every ——— years thereafter; and that the legislature arrange the representation accordingly."

Mr. WILLIAMSON proposed to amend, by having the census show the number "of free white inhabitants, and three fifths of those of other descriptions."

"Three fifths," &c. was stricken out, and the blank filled with "fifteen." The proposition was subsequently modified so as to require the first census to be taken within *six years*, and every *ten years* thereafter, "of all the inhabitants, in the manner and according to the ratio recommended by Congress, in their resolution of 18th April, 1783 [rating the blacks at three fifths of their number]," which prevailed. Yeas — Connecticut, Pennsylvania, Maryland, Virginia, North Carolina, Georgia, 6. Nays — New Jersey, Delaware, 2. Divided — Massachusetts, South Carolina, 2.

On motion of Mr. ELLSWORTH, "three years" was substituted for "*six years.*"

Under the seventh census (1850), the States are entitled to the following representation in the House of Representatives, namely: —

Alabama, 7.
Arkansas, 2.
California, 2.
Connecticut, 4.
Delaware, 1.
Florida, 1.
Georgia, 8.
Illinois, 9.
Indiana, 11.
Iowa, 2.
Kentucky, 10.
Louisiana, 4.
Maine, 6.
Maryland, 6.
Massachusetts, 11.
Michigan, 4.
Mississippi, 5.
Missouri, 7.
New Hampshire, 3.
New Jersey, 5.
New York, 33.
North Carolina, 8.

Ohio, 21.
Oregon, 1.
Pennsylvania, 25.
Rhode Island, 2.
South Carolina, 6.
Tennessee, 10.
Texas, 2.
Vermont, 3.
Virginia, 13.
Wisconsin, 3.

By the act of 23d May, 1850 (9 Stat. 432), the House of Representatives is hereafter to consist of two hundred and thirty-three members, to be apportioned among the several States, after the taking of each census, in accordance with the provisions of the Constitution, by the Secretary of the Interior. The representatives from new States, admitted into the Union subsequently to each apportionment, are to be in addition to the above number; but such additional number is only to continue until the next apportionment.

ARTICLE I.

SECTION II.

Clause 5. — The number of Representatives shall not exceed one for every thirty thousand, but each State shall have at least one Representative; and until such enumeration shall be made, the State of New Hampshire shall be entitled to choose three, Massachusetts eight, Rhode Island and Providence Plantations one, Connecticut five, New York six, New Jersey four, Pennsylvania eight, Delaware one, Maryland six, Virginia ten, North Carolina five, South Carolina five, and Georgia three.

When vacancies happen in the Representation from any State, the Executive authority thereof shall issue writs of election to fill such vacancies.

Clause 6. — The House of Representatives shall choose their Speaker and other officers; and shall have the sole power of impeachment.

In Federal Convention. — The subject of this clause being under consideration, —

Mr. Dickinson "supposed the sums paid in each would form a better ratio" for the House of Representatives, "than either the number of inhabitants or the quantum of property."

Mr. SHERMAN proposed, — "the respective numbers of the free inhabitants."

Mr. GERRY, from the grand committee, to whom the subject had been referred, reported: —

"That in the first branch of the legislature, each of the States now in the Union shall be allowed one representative for every forty thousand inhabitants of the description" described in the third clause of this section, as the basis of taxation; and that "vacancies shall be supplied by writs of election from the executive authority of the State."

On motion of Mr. DICKINSON, — "Provided that each State shall have one representative at least," — was added.

The clause in this form was referred to a special committee, who reported, "That the first House consist of fifty-six members, to be subsequently regulated by the legislature, upon the principles of the wealth and number of inhabitants." It was finally adopted as reported by the grand committee, with Mr. Dickinson's amendment.

After its engrossment, Mr. GORHAM said, "If it was not too late, he could wish, for the purpose of lessening the objections to the Constitution, that the clause declaring that 'the number of representatives shall not exceed one for every forty thousand,' which had produced so much discussion, might yet be reconsidered, in order to strike out 'forty thousand,' and insert 'thirty thousand.'"

Mr. KING and Mr. CARROLL supported the motion.

General WASHINGTON said, "Although his situation had hitherto restrained him from offering his sentiments on questions depending in the House, and, it might be thought, ought now to impose silence on him, yet he could not forbear expressing his wish that the alteration proposed might take place. It was much to be desired, that objections to the plan recommended might be made as few as possible. The smallness of the proportion of representatives, had been considered by many members of the convention an insufficient security for the rights and interests of the people. He acknowledged that it had always appeared to himself among the exceptional parts of the plan; and late as the present moment was for admitting amendments, he thought this of so much consequence that it would give him much satisfaction to see it adopted."

Mr. MADISON says this was the only occasion in which General Washington entered at all into the discussions of the Convention.

The reconsideration was carried and the amendment agreed to.

Judicial Construction. — The executive of a State may receive the resignation of a member and issue writs for new election, without waiting to be informed by the House that a vacancy exists. Mercer's case, Cl. & Hall, 44; Edwards's case, id. 46.

ARTICLE I.

SECTION III.

Clause 1. — The Senate of the United States shall be composed of two Senators from each State, chosen by the legislature thereof, for six years; and each Senator shall have one vote.

In Federal Convention. Mr. RANDOLPH'S PLAN. — "That the second [or senatorial] branch of the national legislature ought to be elected by those of the first, out of a proper number of persons nominated by the individual legislatures; to be of the age of —— years at least, to hold their offices for a term sufficient to insure their independency; to receive liberal stipends, by which they may be compensated for the devotion of their time to the public service, and to be ineligible to any office established by a particular State, or under the authority of the United States, except those peculiarly belonging to the functions of the second branch, during the term of service and for the space of —— years after the expiration thereof."

Mr. C. PINCKNEY'S PLAN. — "The Senate shall be elected and chosen by the House of Delegates [or Representatives]." [To be apportioned amongst the States and classified.]

In Committee of the Whole. — MR. SPAIGHT, of N. C., moved to amend, so as to give the election of Senators to the State legislatures — but subsequently withdrew it.

The propositions for electing Senators by the House of Representatives, out of nominations by the State legislatures, were negatived.

Mr. DICKINSON renewed Mr. Spaight's proposition for the election of the second branch by the State legislatures.

[Mr. READ, of Delaware, proposed that "the Senate should be appointed by the executive magistrate out of a proper number of persons, to be nominated by the State legislatures." Not seconded.]

Mr. MADISON opposed Mr. Dickinson's motion, as it involved a departure from the doctrine of proportional representation, which was inadmissible, being evidently unjust — or would make the Senate too numerous a body.

Mr. PINCKNEY, of S. C., suggested a proposition for dividing the States into three classes, according to their respective sizes, and for allowing the first class three senators, the second class two, and the third class one.

Mr. Dickinson's motion prevailed.

On Mr. SHERMAN'S motion, the direct question was taken whether each State should have an equal vote in the Senate, and it was decided in the negative. Yeas — Connecticut, New York, New Jersey, Delaware, and Maryland, 5. Nays — Massachusetts, Pennsylvania, Virginia, North Carolina, South Carolina, and Georgia, 6.

The question was then taken, on the proposition for making the ratio of representation in the Senate the same as had been fixed on for the House of Representatives, and it passed in the affirmative. Yeas — Massachusetts, Pennsylvania, Virginia, North Carolina, South Carolina, and Georgia, 6; the rest nay.

Mr. GERRY moved to restrain the Senate from originating money bills. Negatived.

Mr. HAMILTON suggested his plan, namely: "The Senate to consist of persons elected to serve during good behavior;

their election to be made by electors chosen for that purpose by the people, from election districts. To have the sole power of declaring war; the power of advising and approving all treaties; the power of approving or rejecting all appointments of officers, except the heads or chiefs of the departments of finance, war, and foreign affairs."

Mr. HAMILTON, before the close of the session of the Convention, modified his views and advocated short terms of office, both for the President and Senators.

The committee of the whole reported the clause in the following form: —

"The members of the second branch of the national legislature ought to be chosen by the individual legislatures; to be of the age of thirty years at least; to hold their offices for a term sufficient to insure their independence, namely, seven years.

"That the right of suffrage in the second branch of the national legislature ought to be according to the rule established for the first."

This report being under consideration, the following proceedings were had: —

The word *national* was stricken out and "United States" inserted. The two first clauses — as to mode of election and age were agreed to.

Mr. GORHAM moved to reduce the term of service to "four years," one fourth to be elected every year.

Mr. RANDOLPH concurred in the suggestion of "rotation," "as the body might be always sitting and aiding the Executive," and moved to add, after the words "seven years," the words, "to go out in fixed proportion," which was agreed to.

Mr. WILLIAMSON suggested "six years," as the term of service.

Mr. READ suggested "during good behavior," and

General PINCKNEY, "four years."

The words "seven years" were stricken out, in order to allow a vote on these several propositions.

The question was then taken on inserting "six years," and lost. Yeas — Connecticut, New Jersey, Pennsylvania, Delaware, Virginia, 5. Nays — Massachusetts, New York, North Carolina, South Carolina, Georgia, 5.

"Five years," was moved and lost.

Mr. GORHAM renewed the motion for "six years," "one third to go out every second year."

Mr. READ moved "nine years."

Mr. MADISON favored Mr. READ's motion. He did not conceive that the term of nine years could threaten any real danger, — but he should require that the long term allowed to the second branch should not commence till such a period of life as would render a perpetual disqualification to be reëlected, little inconvenient either in a public or private view.

On the question for "nine years," Pennsylvania, Delaware, and Virginia, yea; all the rest nay.

"Six years," was then agreed to.

The proportional representation in the first branch (House of Representatives) having been agreed to,

Mr. ELLSWORTH moved, that "the rule of suffrage in the senatorial branch be the same with that established by the Articles of Confederation," — to wit: each State to have one vote.

After a very exciting debate, of several days' duration, in which Messrs. Ellsworth, Sherman, Dayton, Bedford, and others advocated the motion; and Messrs. Baldwin, Wilson, Madison, King, and Martin opposed it; and in which Mr. Ellsworth said, "To the eastward he was sure that Massachusetts was the only State that would listen to a proposition for excluding the States as equal political societies, from an equal voice in both branches of the legislature;" "the others would risk every consequence rather than part with so dear a right."

Mr. MADISON remarked, that under the operation of the equality principle, "a majority of States might injure a majority of the people," — "they could obstruct their wishes." "But he contended that the States were divided into different interests, not by their difference of size, but by other circumstances; the most material of which resulted partly from climate, but principally from the effect of their having or not having slaves. That the division of interests did not lie between the large and small States, but between the northern and southern."

Mr. KING said, "Should this wonderful illusion (of State rights) continue to prevail, his mind was prepared for every event, rather than sit down under a government founded on a vicious principle of representation, and which must be as short-lived as it would be unjust;" "he never could listen to an equality of votes as proposed in the motion."

Mr. MARTIN, "would never confederate if it could not be done on just principles."

On the 2d of July, the question was taken. In favor of giving an equal vote to each State, in the Senate, were the States of Connecticut, New York, New Jersey, Delaware, and Maryland; and against it, were the States of Massachusetts, Pennsylvania, Virginia, North Carolina, and South Carolina; Georgia was divided. Thus showing an equal division.

Mr. ELLSWORTH'S amendment having been thus lost by an equal division, the question recurred on the proportional representation, as reported from the committee of the whole.

Mr. PINCKNEY, of South Carolina, "thought an equality of vote in the second branch inadmissible;" that "there is a real distinction between the northern and the southern interests," — and that "the larger States were entitled to some, but not a full proportion."

He renewed his proposition previously submitted, namely: "The Senate shall be elected and chosen by the House of Delegates; which house, immediately after their meeting, shall choose, by ballot, —— senators from among the citizens and residents of New Hampshire; —— from among those of Massachusetts," &c., through the States, — "to be divided into classes, and one class to go out every year."

Gen. PINCKNEY. — "Although he did not entirely approve the proposition, was willing it should be considered. Some compromise seemed to be necessary, the States being exactly divided on the question of an equality of votes in the second branch."

He proposed that a committee, consisting of a member from each State, should be appointed to devise and report a *compromise*.

Mr. LUTHER MARTIN, of Maryland, said "he had no objection to a commitment, but no modification could reconcile the smaller States to the least diminution of their equal sovereignty."

Mr. GOUVERNEUR MORRIS was for commitment for other reasons. He wished to make the Senate a permanent body. He said, "It must have great personal property; it must have the aristocratic spirit," and therefore its tenure of office "should be for life."

Mr. RANDOLPH "favored a commitment, but did not expect much good to result. He warned the small States of the danger to them of a failure to unite."

Mr. WILSON and Mr. MADISON objected to commitment to *such* a committee, "because it would decide according to that rule of voting which was opposed on one side." The commitment was carried — yeas 9, nays 2.

The committee reported the following *compromise*: —

1. "That, in the first branch of the legislature, each of the States now in the Union, shall be allowed one member for every forty thousand inhabitants, of the description reported in the seventh resolution of the committee of the whole house [see Article H. R.] — that each State not containing that number shall be allowed one member: that all bills for raising or appropriating money, and for fixing the salaries of officers of the government of the United States, shall originate in the first branch of the legislature, and shall not be altered or amended in the second branch; and that no money shall be drawn from the public treasury but in pursuance of appropriations to be originated in the first branch.

2. "That in the second branch each State shall have an equal vote."

NOTE. — Mr. MADISON says this report was founded on a motion made in the committee by Dr. Franklin.

Mr. MADISON strongly opposed the report. "He conceived that the convention was reduced to the alternative of either departing from justice in order to conciliate the smaller States and the minority of the people of the United States, or of displeasing these by justly gratifying the larger States and the majority of the people. He could not hesitate as to the option he ought to make. The convention, with justice and a majority of the people on their side, had nothing to fear."

Mr. BUTLER "urged that the second branch ought to represent the States according to their property."

Mr. WILLIAMSON, of North Carolina, "thought the proposition the most objectionable of any he had yet heard."

Mr. MASON favored the general principles of the report, and deprecated the consequences to the country, of a dissolution of the Convention without any thing being done

On the question — "shall the clause *allowing each State one vote in the second branch*, stand as a part of the report?" Yeas — Connecticut, New York, New Jersey, Delaware, Maryland, North Carolina, 6. Nays — Pennsylvania, Virginia, South Carolina, 3. Divided — Massachusetts, Georgia, 2.

Mr. WILLIAMSON said, "The State of North Carolina had agreed to an equality in the Senate, merely in consideration that money bills should be confined to the other house."

NOTE. — It is a curious fact, that on all these questions, involving the equality of States, as political communities, New York is invariably found sustaining and acting in harmony with the small States — voting to allow them an equal voice with herself in the federal government — while Virginia and South Carolina contend for the proportional representation.

At a subsequent stage of the proceedings —

Mr. PINCKNEY moved, "that instead of an equality of votes, the States should be represented in the second branch as follows: New Hampshire two members, Massachusetts four," &c., being a modified classification.

Mr. MADISON, in advocating this motion, summed up his objection to an equal representation of the States in the Senate as follows, namely: "1. The minority could negative the will of a majority of the people. 2. They could extort measures, by making them a condition of their assent to other necessary measures. 3. They could obtrude measures on a majority by virtue of the peculiar powers which would be vested in the Senate. 4. The evil, instead of being cured by time, would increase with every new State that should be admitted, as they must all be admitted on the principle of equality. 5. The perpetuity it would give to the preponderance of the northern against the southern scale."

The motion of Mr. Pinckney was rejected; Pennsylvania, Maryland, Virginia, and South Carolina, 4, voting for it; and Massachusetts, Delaware, Connecticut, New Jersey, North Carolina, and Georgia, 6, against it.

The question was then taken on agreeing to the report of the committee of the whole house, as modified, the substantial points of which were, the equal vote in the Senate and a representation in the House of Representatives, in proportion to the population, counting slaves as three to five — and it passed in the affirmative by the following vote. Yeas — Connecticut, New Jersey, Delaware, Maryland, North Carolina, 5. Nays — Pennsylvania, Virginia, South Carolina, Georgia, 4. Massachusetts divided. So that this greatest and most difficult of all the important questions which the Convention was called upon to solve, was carried by less than a majority of the States present, and by the concurrence of less than one third of the represented population.

Gouverneur Morris moved that the representation in the second branch consist of three members from each State, to vote *per capita.*

Mr. Gorham suggested "two" as the better number, which was concurred in, and as thus amended the proposition was agreed to.

Report of Committee on Detail. — Art. 5, sec. 1. The Senate of the United States shall be chosen by the legislatures of the several States.

Each legislature shall choose two members.

Each member shall have one vote.

Classification as in the Constitution. In this form it went to the committee on style.

Constructions by the Senate. — Where the election is by a joint convention of the two houses of the legislature, it is not necessary that there should be a concurrent majority of each house in favor of the candidate declared to be elected. Cameron's case, U. S. Senate, 13th March, 1857.

The election, however, must be substantially by both houses, as distinct bodies; the mere fact that a majority of the joint body, or even of each body, is present, does not constitute the aggregate body a legislature, unless the two bodies, acting separately, have voted to meet, and have actually met accordingly. Harlan's case, U. S. S., 12th Jan. 1857.

The Senate is a permanent body; its existence is continual and perpetual. Cushing's Law of Legislative Assemblies, 19.

ARTICLE I.

SECTION III.

Clause 2. — Immediately after they shall be assembled in consequence of the first election, they shall be divided as equally as may be into three classes. The seats of the Senators of the first class shall be vacated at the expiration of the second year, of the second class at the expiration of the fourth year, and of the third class at the expiration of the sixth year, so that one third may be chosen every second year; and if vacancies happen by resignation or otherwise, during the recess of the Legislature of any State, the executive thereof may make temporary appointments, until the next meeting of the Legislature, which shall then fill such vacancies.

Mr. PINCKNEY'S PLAN proposed to divide the senators into three classes — the house of delegates to "fix their time of service by lot."

Mr. GORHAM moved to make the senatorial term for "six years, one third to go out biennally," which passed in the affirmative.

The committee of detail reported this clause as follows: —

"Immediately after the first election, they shall be

divided by lot into three classes, as nearly as may be, numbered one, two, and three. The seats of the members of the first class shall be vacated at the expiration of the second year, &c."

" Vacancies may be supplied, by the executive [of the State] until the next meeting of the legislature."

Mr. Wilson objected to this clause. It was unnecessary, and wrong, " that the executive should elect into the legislative department."

Mr. Randolph. — " It will be necessary in order to prevent inconvenient chasms in the Senate."

Mr. Ellsworth. —"As there will be but two members from a State, vacancies may be of great moment." " When the legislative meeting happens to be near, the power will not be exerted."

Mr. Williamson moved to add, " unless other provision be made by the legislature." Yeas 4, nays 6.

On motion of Mr. Madison, after " vacancies " the words " happening by refusals to accept, resignations, or otherwise," were inserted.

The seat of a Senator is vacated by a resignation addressed to the executive of a State, notwithstanding he may have received no notice that his resignation has been accepted. Bledsoe's case, Cl. & Hall, 869.

It is not competent for the executive of a State, during the recess of the legislature to appoint a Senator to fill a vacancy which *shall happen*, but has not happened at the time of the appointment. Lanman's case, Cl. & Hall, 871.

The commission of a Senator by executive appointment expires at the close of the next succeeding term of his State legislature, when the power of the executive over the vacancy ceases.

ARTICLE I.

SECTION III.

Clause 3.—No person shall be a Senator who shall not have attained to the age of thirty years, and been nine years a citizen of the United States, and who shall not, when elected, be an inhabitant of that State for which he shall be chosen.

The qualification in respect to age was agreed to without dissent.

Mr. MASON moved instructions to the committee of detail, to consider clauses "requiring certain qualifications of landed property and citizenship, for the executive, the judiciary, and the members of both branches of the legislature, &c.," and "disqualifying persons having unsettled accounts with the United States."

Mr. MORRIS opposed the instructions, particularly the last clause, as the delays of the government in liquidating the just claims of citizens, frequently prevented a settlement.

On Mr. KING'S suggestion that there might be great danger in requiring a landed property qualification, the word "landed" was stricken out.

Mr. DICKINSON opposed any recital of qualifications. The best defence, in his opinion, lay in the freeholders who were to elect the legislature.

The latter portion of the instructions were refused and the first part agreed to.

The committee of detail reported as follows:—

"Every member of the Senate shall be of the age of thirty years at least; shall have been a citizen of the United States for at least four years before his election; and shall be, at the time of his election, a resident of the State for which he shall be chosen."

Mr. G. MORRIS moved to strike out "four" and insert "fourteen" years of citizenship.

Mr. C. PINCKNEY seconded the motion.

Col. MASON.—"Were it not that many, not natives of the country, had acquired great credit during the Revolution, he should be for restraining the eligibility into the Senate to natives."

Mr. MADISON "thought any restriction in the Constitution unnecessary and improper. It would give a tincture of illiberality; it would put it out of the power of the national legislature, even by special acts of naturalization, to confer the full rank of citizens on meritorious strangers," &c.

Mr. BUTLER expressed his decided disapprobation to the admission of foreigners without a long residence in the country. He acknowledged, that if he himself had been called into public life within a short time after his coming to America, his foreign habits, opinions, and attachments would have rendered him an improper agent.

Mr. RANDOLPH doubted whether the immigration of foreigners was advantageous to the country, but he was not willing to disfranchise them for fourteen years.

Mr. WILSON remarked, that, not being a native, he had experienced mortification at the discrimination proposed. Notwithstanding his participation in forming the Constitution, he might be prohibited from serving under it.

Mr. G. Morris. — "We should not be polite at the expense of prudence. He would let [foreigners] worship at the same altar, but did not choose to make priests of them. The men who can shake off their attachments to their own country can never love any other."

Mr. Randolph said he would agree to nine years, which was inserted.

Note. — See Gallatin's case, Cl. & Hall, 871, and case of Shields, United States Senate, March, 1849.

ARTICLE I.

SECTION III.

Clause 4. — The Vice-President of the United States shall be President of the Senate, but shall have no vote, unless they be equally divided.

Clause 5. — The Senate shall choose their other officers, and also a President pro tempore in the absence of the Vice-President or when he shall exercise the office of President of the United States.

The first report of the committee of detail contained the following clause in reference to the executive : —

" In case of his removal as aforesaid, death, resignation, or disability to discharge the powers and duties of his office, the president of the Senate shall exercise those powers and duties until another President of the United States be chosen, or until the disability of the President be removed."

Mr. G. Morris and Mr. Madison objected to the designation of the president of the Senate as the provisional successor to the President in the cases above indicated. The former proposed to substitute the chief justice; and the latter suggested that the council to the President should execute the executive powers during the occasional vacancy.

Mr. Williamson thought the legislature should be empowered to provide for cases of occasional vacancies.

Mr. BREARLY, from the committee of eleven (the compromise committee) reported (after providing for his election) — "The vice-president shall be *ex officio* president of the Senate, except when they sit to try the impeachment of the President, in which case the chief justice shall preside, and excepting also, when he shall exercise the powers and duties of President; in which case, and in case of his absence, the Senate shall choose a president *pro tempore*. The vice-president when acting as president of the Senate, shall not have a vote unless the house be equally divided."

Mr. GERRY, in opposing this clause, remarked that, "We might as well put the President himself at the head of the legislature. The close intimacy that must subsist between the President and the vice-president makes it absolutely improper." He was against having any vice-president.

Mr. G. MORRIS. — "The vice-president, then, will be the first heir-apparent that ever loved his father."

Mr. SHERMAN. "If the vice-president were not to be president of the Senate, he would be without employment."

Mr. WILLIAMSON. — "Such an officer as vice-president is not wanted. He was introduced merely for the sake of a valuable mode of election, which required two to be chosen at the same time."

The Convention do not appear to have contemplated making provision for any such office as vice-president, until near the close of their session. But having been unable to agree upon any mode of choosing the President, the subject was referred to a special committee, of which Mr. Williamson was a member, and he probably gives, in the above remark, the true reason why such an officer was introduced.

ARTICLE I.

SECTION III.

Clause 6.—The Senate shall have the sole power to try all impeachments: when sitting for that purpose, they shall be on oath or affirmation. When the President of the United States is tried the Chief Justice shall preside: and no person shall be convicted without the concurrence of two thirds of the members present.

Clause 7.—Judgment in cases of impeachment shall not extend farther than to removal from office, and disqualification to hold and enjoy any office of honor, trust, or profit under the United States: but the party convicted shall nevertheless be liable and subject to indictment, trial, judgment, and punishment according to law.

Mr. Randolph and Mr. Pinckney proposed to give the "national judiciary" jurisdiction in cases of "impeachments of national officers."

The plan submitted by Mr. Patterson contained a similar provision.

General Hamilton's Plan, which was only suggested in a speech, but never formally submitted to the Convention, contained the following:—

"The governor, senators, and all other officers of the United States, to be liable to impeachment for mal and corrupt conduct; and upon conviction, to be removed from office, and disqualified for holding any place of trust or profit; all impeachments to be tried by a court to consist of the chief ——, or judge of the superior court of law of each State, *provided* such judge shall hold his place during good behavior and have a permanent salary."

Mr. RUTLEDGE, from the committee of detail, reported the following: —

"The jurisdiction of the Supreme Court shall extend . . . . to the trial of impeachments of officers of the United States.

"Judgments, in cases of impeachment, shall not extend further than to removal from office and disqualification to hold and enjoy any office of honor, trust, or profit, under the United States. But the party convicted shall, nevertheless, be liable and subject to indictment, trial, judgment, and punishment according to law."

Mr. GERRY moved, that the committee of detail, be instructed to report a mode of trying the supreme judges in case of impeachment; and the committee subsequently reported the following: —

"The judges of the Supreme Court shall be triable by the Senate, on impeachment by the House of Representatives."

The committee of detail, in reference to the executive, reported: —

"He shall be removed from his office on impeachment by the House of Representatives, and conviction, in the Supreme Court, of treason, bribery, or corruption."

Mr. G. MORRIS "thought the tribunal an improper one," and the subject was postponed, and referred, under a general motion by Mr. SHERMAN, "to refer such parts of the constitution and reports as had not been finally acted on," to a committee of one from each State. The committee reported:—

"He shall be removed from his office on impeachment by the House of Representatives, and conviction by the Senate, for treason or bribery."

The same committee also reported:—

"The Senate of the United States shall have power to try all impeachments, but no person shall be convicted without the concurrence of two thirds of the members present."

Mr. MADISON "preferred the Supreme Court for the trial of impeachment, or rather a tribunal of which the Supreme Court should form a part."

The report of the committee was concurred in.

ARTICLE I.

SECTION IV.

Clause 1.—The times, places, and manner of holding elections for Senators and Representatives shall be prescribed in each State by the Legislature thereof; but the Congress may at any time, by law, make or alter such regulations, except as to the places of choosing Senators.

This clause first appears in the report of the committee on detail, in the following form:—

"The times and places and manner of holding the elections of the members of each House, shall be prescribed by the legislature of each State; but their provisions concerning them may be altered by the legislature of the United States."

At the suggestion of Mr. READ, the latter part of the clause was so modified as to read—"but regulations in each of the foregoing cases, may, at any time, be made or altered by the legislature of the United States."

It was then referred to the committee on style, who gave it the present form.

ARTICLE I.

SECTION IV.

Clause 2.—The Congress shall assemble at least once in every year, and such meeting shall be on the first Monday in December, unless they shall by law appoint a different day.

The Articles of Confederation required Congress to meet "on the first Monday in November, in every year."

Mr. PINCKNEY'S PLAN, provided for an annual meeting of Congress, and the committee of detail reported:—

"The legislature shall meet on the first Monday in December in every year."

Mr. G. MORRIS moved to strike out this clause. He did not think it necessary to fix the time of meeting, or to require that it should be annual. "The public business might not require it."

Mr. GORHAM thought an annual meeting necessary, as a check on the executive department.

Mr. KING saw no necessity for an annual meeting. "A great vice in our system was that of legislating too much."

Col. MASON thought an annual meeting necessary, for exercising the inquisitorial, if not the legislative functions of Congress.

On motion of Mr. RANDOLPH, the words "unless a different day shall be appointed by law," were added — and on motion of Mr. RUTLEDGE, the words "once at least in each year," were inserted.

NOTE. The constitutional term of a Congress, by recent practice, does not expire until 12 at noon, of the 4th of March. Formerly it was held to expire at midnight preceding.

ARTICLE I.

SECTION V.

Clause 1.—Each house shall be the judge of the elections, returns, and qualifications of its own members, and a majority of each shall constitute a quorum to do business; but a smaller number may adjourn from day to day, and may be authorized to compel the attendance of absent members, in such manner, and under such penalties, as each house may provide.

Clause 2.—Each house may determine the rules of its proceedings, punish its members for disorderly behavior, and with the concurrence of two thirds, expel a member.

The committee on detail reported the following:—

"In each house, a majority of the members shall constitute a quorum to do business; but a smaller number may adjourn from day to day."

A motion to allow less than a majority to do business having been rejected, on motion of Mr. RANDOLPH and Mr. MADISON, the words, "and may be authorized to compel absent members," &c., were added.

The clause requiring "the concurrence of two thirds" to expel a member, was inserted on motion of Mr. MADISON.

Mr. PINCKNEY submitted the following for reference to the committee of detail: —

"Each house shall be the judge of its own privileges, and shall have authority to punish by imprisonment every person violating the same, or who, in the place where the legislature may be sitting, and during the time of its session, shall threaten any of its members for any thing said or done in the house; or who shall assault any of them therefor; or who shall assault or arrest any witness or other person ordered to attend either of the houses, in his way going or returning; or who shall rescue any person arrested by their order."

Messrs. RANDOLPH and MADISON doubted the expediency or propriety of conferring upon each house the power of judging as to the *extent* of their privileges. It was suggested, that what constituted privilege, should be ascertained by law, allowing the houses to judge as to their violation.

No further action appears to have been had on Mr. Pinckney's proposition.

Judicial Constructions. — The returns from the State authorities are *prima facie* evidence only of an election, and are not conclusive upon the House. Spaulding *v.* Mead, Cl. & Hall, 157; Reed *v.* Cosden, id. 353.

The refusal of the executive of a State to grant a certificate of election, does not prejudice the right of one who may be entitled to a seat. Richard's case, id. 95.

Clause 2. This does not exclude the power to punish for contempt, others than members of the House. The Constitution says nothing of contempts. These were left to the operation of the common-law principle, that every court has the right to protect itself from insult and contempt, without which right of self-protection they could not discharge their high and important duties. Nugent's case, 1 Am. L. J. 139; Anderson *v.* Dunn, 6 Wheaton, 204; Bolton *v.* Martin, 1 Dall. 296.

It seems to be settled that a member may be expelled for any misdemeanor, though not punishable by any statute, which is inconsistent with the trust and duty of a member. 1 Story, Const. 838; Smith's case, 1 Hall, L. J. 459.

ARTICLE I.

SECTION V.

Clause 3.—Each house shall keep a journal of its proceedings, and from time to time publish the same, excepting such parts as may, in their judgment, require secrecy, and the yeas and nays of the members of either house on any question shall, at the desire of one fifth of those present, be entered on the journal.

Articles of Confederation.—"The Congress . . . shall publish the journal of their proceedings monthly, except such parts thereof relating to treaties, alliances, or military operations, as in their judgment require secrecy; and the yeas and nays of the delegates shall be entered on the journal, when it is desired by any delegate."

Report of Committee of Detail.—"The House of Representatives and the Senate, when it shall be acting in its legislative capacity, shall keep a journal of their proceedings; and shall from time to time publish them."

On motion of Mr. Gerry, the words, "when acting in its legislative capacity," were stricken out; and the words "except such parts thereof as may in their judgment require secrecy," were added.

Mr. G. Morris and Mr. Randolph proposed, that a single member be authorized to call the yeas and nays. Disagreed to.

Mr. Carroll proposed to confine the call of yeas and nays to the House of Representatives, and to allow each member of the Senate to enter his dissent. It was objected that if a minority were to have the right to enter their votes and reasons, the other side would be entitled to the same right, and the consequence would be, that the journals, like records of courts, would be filled with replications and rejoinders. The proposition was rejected.

ARTICLE I.

SECTION V.

Clause 4. — Neither house, during the session of Congress, shall, without the consent of the other, adjourn for more than three days, nor to any other place than that in which the two houses shall be sitting.

Articles of Confederation. — "The Congress of the United States shall have power to adjourn to any time within the year, and to any place within the United States, so that no period of adjournment be for a longer duration than the space of six months."

Mr. PINCKNEY'S PLAN. — "Neither house, without the consent of the other, shall adjourn for more than —— days, nor to any other place but where they are sitting."

Report of Committee of Detail. — "Neither house, without the consent of the other, shall adjourn for more than three days, nor to any other place than that at which the two houses are sitting. But this regulation shall not extend to the Senate," &c.

Mr. KING remarked, that "the section authorized the two houses to adjourn to a new place," to which he objected. The changes of the place of meeting of Congress had dishonored the government, and should be remedied.

Mr. MADISON expressed the same views. They thought

a law, at least, should be required, to authorize a change of place.

Mr. Spaight. — " This will fix the seat of government at New York. The present Congress will convene them there in the first instance, and they will never be able to remove, especially if the President should be a northern man."

The clause was then amended by prefixing to it the words " During the session of the legislature," — and striking out the last line, and then adopted.

ARTICLE I.

SECTION VI.

Clause 1. — The Senators and Representatives shall receive a compensation for their services, to be ascertained by law, and paid out of the Treasury of the United States. They shall in all cases, except treason, felony and breach of the peace, be privileged from arrest during their attendance at the session of their respective Houses, and in going to and returning from the same; and for any speech or debate in either House, they shall not be questioned in any other place.

Articles of Confederation. — "Each State shall maintain its own delegates." "Freedom of speech and debate in Congress shall not be impeached or questioned in any court or place out of Congress, and the members of Congress shall be protected in their persons, from arrests and imprisonments, during the time of their going to and returning from, and attendance on Congress, except for treason, felony, or breach of the peace."

Mr. RANDOLPH'S PLAN contained the following: —

"To receive liberal stipends, by which they may be compensated for the devotion of their time to the public service."

On motion of Mr. MADISON, the words "*and fixed*" were added. He thought, "to leave them to regulate their own wages, was an indecent thing, and might in time, prove a dangerous one."

On motion of Dr. FRANKLIN, the word "*liberal*" was stricken out. As first reported from the committee of the whole, the clause read, — "*To receive fixed stipends, to be paid out of the national treasury.*"

Mr. ELLSWORTH wished to substitute payment by the States.

Mr. WILSON, was opposed to *fixing* the amount, as circumstances might change.

Mr. MADISON argued that the amount should be fixed by the Constitution and paid from the national treasury. But he "*disliked particularly the policy suggested of leaving the members from the poor States beyond the mountains to the precarious and parsimonious support of their constituents.*" He suggested the average price of wheat as a standard.

Mr. WILSON moved, that the compensation "be ascertained by the national legislature, and be paid out of the national treasury." The first branch of the motion was lost, — yeas 2, nays 7. The second branch was carried; but on a subsequent vote, the whole sentence was negatived by an equal division.

General PINCKNEY suggested, as the senatorial branch was to represent the wealth of the country, "no salary should be allowed."

Dr. FRANKLIN seconded the motion. Disagreed to, — yeas 5, nays 6.

On motion of Mr. WILLIAMSON, "fixed stipends" was stricken out, and "a compensation for the devotion of their time to the public service," substituted.

Mr. ELLSWORTH moved to strike out the words, "to be

paid out of the national treasury," and insert, "to be paid by their respective States." Decided in the negative. Yeas — Connecticut, New York, New Jersey, South Carolina, Georgia, 5. Nays — Massachusetts, Pennsylvania, Delaware, Maryland, Virginia, North Carolina, 6.

In this form the clause was sent to the committee on detail, who reported it as follows: —

"The members of each house shall receive a compensation for their services, to be ascertained and paid by the State in which they shall be chosen."

Mr. ELLSWORTH said that reflection had changed his mind on this subject, and he moved to substitute payment "out of the treasury of the United States, an allowance not exceeding —— dollars per day, or the present value thereof."

Mr. MADISON said he "could not see any chance for that stability in the general government, the want of which was a principal evil in the State governments," if the members were left dependent on the States for their compensation.

Mr. Ellsworth's motion was carried, — yeas 9, nays 2.

Judicial Constructions. — The exception to freedom from arrest, would seem to extend to all indictable offences, as well those which are in fact attended with force and violence, as those which are only constructive breaches of the peace of the government, inasmuch as they violate good order. 1 Black. Comm. 166; 1 Story, Const. 865.

They are privileged not only from arrest both on judicial and mesne process, but also from service of a summons or other civil process, while in attendance on their public duties. Geyer's Lessee *v.* Irwin, 4 Dallas, 107; Story, Const. 860. See also, 3 Dall. 478.

A claimant to a seat in Congress, duly commissioned, is entitled to the privileges of this section, although ousted of his seat. Dunton *v.* Halstead, 4 Penn. L. J. 237.

ARTICLE I.

SECTION VI.

Clause 2.—No senator or representative shall, during the time for which he was elected, be appointed to any civil office under the authority of the United States, which shall have been created, or the emoluments whereof shall have been increased during such time: and no person holding any office under the United States shall be a member of either house during his continuance in office.

Mr. RANDOLPH'S PLAN, makes members of both branches "ineligible to any office established by a particular State, or under the authority of the United States," except those pertaining to their legislative functions, "during their terms of service and for —— years thereafter,"—and the members of the first branch incapable of immediate reelection and subject to recall.

The first blank was filled with "one," and the last clause stricken out.

Mr. GORHAM moved to strike out the ineligibility of senators to office.

Mr. KING thought such a restriction would discourage merit.

The motion was lost by a tie vote, and Mr. Randolph's proposition was agreed to.

The committee on detail reported it as follows: —

"The members of each house shall be ineligible to, and incapable of, holding any office under the authority of the United States, during the time for which they shall respectively be elected; and members of the Senate ineligible to, and incapable of, holding any such office for one year afterwards."

Mr. PINCKNEY thought this provision *degrading* and *inconvenient*, and proposed to substitute the following: —

"The members of each house shall be incapable of holding any office under the United States, for which they or any others for their benefit, receive any salary, fees, or emoluments of any kind; and the acceptance of such office shall vacate their seats respectively."

This proposition was lost by a tie vote.

Mr. G. MORRIS moved to "except officers of the army and navy."

This subject was referred to a select committee, who reported the following: —

"The members of each house shall be ineligible to any civil office under the authority of the United States, during the time for which they shall respectively be elected; and no person holding an office under the United States shall be a member of either House during his continuance in office."

Mr. KING moved to insert "created" before "during," with the view of excluding the members of the first Congress, who would create most of the offices.

Mr. SHERMAN "was for entirely incapacitating members of the legislature. He thought their eligibility to offices would give too much influence to the executive. He said the incapacity ought, at least, to be extended to cases where salaries should be *increased* as well as created during the term of a member."

Mr. G. MORRIS thought if the executive could not appoint the members, he would appoint their relatives and friends, by which he would secure the votes he desired.

Mr. KING'S motion having been rejected by a tie vote, Mr. WILLIAMSON moved to insert "created or the emoluments of which shall have been increased" before "during,"—which prevailed, and the article in that form was agreed to.

Judicial Constructions.—The acceptance by a member of any office under the United States, after he has been elected to, and taken his seat in Congress, operates as a forfeiture of his seat. Van Ness's case, Cl. & Hall, 122.

Continuing to execute the duties of an office, under the United States, after one is elected to Congress, but before he takes his seat, is not a disqualification; such office being resigned before taking his seat. Hammond *v.* Herrick, Cl. & Hall, 287; Earle's case, id. 314; Mumford's case, id. 316.

ARTICLE I.

SECTION VII.

Clause 1.—All bills for raising revenue shall originate in the House of Representatives; but the Senate may propose or concur with amendments as on other bills.

This provision first appears in the report of the compromise committee on the organization of the Senate, as an equivalent for allowing the small States an equal vote in that body, in the following form:—

"That all bills for raising or appropriating money and for fixing the salaries of the officers of the government of the United States, shall originate in the first branch of the legislature, and shall not be altered or amended by the second branch."

This part of the report was concurred in, and it was sent to the committee on detail, who added the following: "No money shall be drawn from the treasury but in pursuance of appropriation that shall originate in the House of Representatives."

This modification was rejected in Convention.

Mr. PINCKNEY moved to strike out the provisions requiring revenue bills to originate in the House of Representatives.

Mr. GORHAM did not wish to allow the Senate to *origi*

nate money bills, but would allow them to make amendments.

Mr. PINCKNEY'S motion was carried, but subsequently reconsidered, and Mr. RANDOLPH proposed the following substitute : —

" Bills for raising money *for the purpose of revenue*, or for appropriating the same, shall originate in the House of Representatives; and shall not be so amended or altered by the Senate as to increase or diminish the sum to be raised, or change the mode of levying it or the object of its appropriation." Disagreed to. Yeas 4, nays 7.

Mr. STRONG moved: —

" Each house shall possess the right of originating all bills, except bills for raising money for the purposes of revenue, or for appropriating the same, and for fixing the salaries of the officers of government, which shall originate in the House of Representatives, but the Senate may propose or concur with amendments, as in other cases."

After debate, the subject was sent to the committee of eleven, who reported: " All bills for raising revenue shall originate in the House of Representatives, and shall be subject to alterations and amendments by the Senate; no money shall be drawn from the treasury, but in consequence of appropriations made by law." This was finally concurred in.

Mr. MORRIS said this clause " had been agreed to in the committee on the ground of compromise."

NOTE. — The compromise appears to have been, that the large States, whose influence would predominate in the House of Representatives, should exclusively originate revenue bills, as a compensation for giving the eventual election of President to the Senate, where the small States would have the power.

ARTICLE I.

SECTION VII.

Clause 2.—Every bill which shall have passed the House of Representatives and the Senate, shall, before it become a law, be presented to the President of the United States; if he approve he shall sign it; but if not, he shall return it, with his objections, to that house in which it shall have originated, who shall enter the objections at large on their journal, and proceed to reconsider it. If after such reconsideration two thirds of that house shall agree to pass the bill, it shall be sent, together with the objections, to the other house, by which it shall likewise be reconsidered, and if approved by two thirds of that house, it shall become a law. But in all cases the votes of both houses shall be determined by yeas and nays, and the names of the persons voting for and against the bill shall be entered on the journal of each house respectively. If any bill shall not be returned by the President within ten days (Sundays excepted) after it shall have been presented to him, the same shall be a law, in like manner as if he had signed it, unless the Congress by their adjournment prevent its return, in which case it shall not be a law.

Clause 3. — Every order, resolution, or vote, to which the concurrence of the Senate and House of Representatives may be necessary (except on a question of adjournment), shall be presented to the President of the United States; and before the same shall take effect, shall be approved by him, or, being disapproved by him, shall be repassed by two thirds of the Senate and House of Representatives, according to the rules and limitations prescribed in the case of a bill.

Mr. RANDOLPH'S PLAN. — "That the executive and a convenient number of the national judiciary ought to compose a council of revision, with authority to examine every act of the national legislature before it shall operate, and every act of a particular legislature, before a negative thereon shall be final; and that the dissent of said council shall amount to a rejection, unless the act of the national legislature be again passed or that of a particular legislature be again rejected, by —— of the members of each branch."

Mr. PINCKNEY'S PLAN contains this revisory power of the President, nearly in the words in which they were finally embodied in the Constitution.

Mr. RANDOLPH'S resolution being under consideration, —

Mr. GERRY said he was opposed to joining the judiciary in the revisory power, — and moved "that the national executive shall have a right to negative any legislative act which shall not be afterwards passed by [two thirds] of each branch of the national legislature," which was adopted.

Mr. Hamilton's Plan gave the executive a negative on all laws about to be passed.

The several propositions having been considered in *committee of the whole*, were reported as follows: —

"The national executive shall have the right to negative any legislative act, which shall not be afterwards passed by two thirds of each branch of the legislature:" which was concurred in by the convention, without debate, and referred to the committee on detail, who gave it the form in which it stands in the Constitution.

Mr. Madison offered a substitute requiring "that every bill which shall have passed the two houses, shall, before it becomes a law, be severally presented to the President of the United States and to the judges of the Supreme Court for the revision of each."

This was supported by Delaware, Maryland, and Virginia, and opposed by the other States.

On motion of Mr. Williamson, "three fourths" was substituted for "two thirds."

Mr. Randolph moved to add the clause in reference to "every order, resolution, or vote," &c., which was agreed to.

Mr. Williamson subsequently moved to restore "two thirds."

Mr. Madison. "The object of the revisory power is twofold: first, to defend the executive rights; secondly, to defend popular or factious injustice." He was opposed to the change.

The motion prevailed. Yeas 6, nays 4.

Note. — The Senate have decided [34 to 7] that two thirds of a quorum only were requisite to pass a bill over the negative of the President, and not two thirds of the whole number of Senators. Senate Journal, 7th of July, 1856; 9 Law Rep. 196.

A joint resolution, approved by the President, or duly passed without his approval, has all the effect of law. 6 Opin. Attorney-General, 680.

ARTICLE I.

SECTION VIII.

Clause 1. — The Congress shall have power to lay and collect taxes, duties, imposts and excises, to pay the debts and provide for the common defence and general welfare of the United States; but all duties, imposts and excises, shall be uniform throughout the United States.

In the Congress of the Confederation, March 6, 1783, the committee on revenue reported that "it was indispensable to the restoration of the public credit," that Congress should be vested with the power to lay duties on imports.

Mr. Pinckney's Plan. — "The legislature of the United States shall have the power to lay and collect taxes, duties, imposts, and excises."

Mr. Patterson's Plan, — proposed by him in behalf of the delegates from New Jersey, and others who were in favor of amending the Articles of Confederation, but opposed to establishing a *Federal Government:* —

That Congress be authorized "to pass acts for raising a revenue, by levying a duty or duties on all goods or merchandises of foreign growth or manufacture, imported into any part of the United States; by stamps on paper, vellum, or parchment, and by a postage on all letters or packages, passing through the general post-office; to be applied to such federal purposes as they shall deem proper and expedient; to make rules and regulations for the collection thereof," &c.

A long and animated debate occurred in committee of the whole on these two propositions, involving the question whether it was the purpose to *establish a Federal Government*, or merely to revise and amend the Articles of Confederation. The committee sustained the idea of a Federal Government, and reported the clause as contained in Mr. Pinckney's plan.

Mr. PINCKNEY then suggested the addition of a clause "restraining the legislature from establishing a perpetual revenue;" which, with the original proposition, was referred to a special committee, and subsequently reported, with the addition of the following clause: —

"For payment of the debts and necessary expenses of the United States; *provided*, that no law for raising any branch of revenue, except what may be specially appropriated for the payment of interest on debts or loans, shall continue in force more than —— years."

On motion of Mr. MCHENRY, the following clause was added.

"All duties, imposts, and excises, prohibitions or restrictions, laid or made by the legislature of the United States, shall be uniform and equal throughout the United States." The clause was then referred to the committee of eleven, who reported it in the following form: —

"The legislature shall have power to lay and collect taxes, duties, imposts, and excises, to pay the debts, and provide for the common defence and general welfare of the United States."

NOTE. — The Convention of the State of South Carolina, which adopted and ratified the Constitution, passed the following resolution, namely, —

"*Resolved*, That the General Government of the United States ought never to impose direct taxes, *but* where the moneys arising from duties, imposts, and excise, are insufficient for the public exigencies."

The States of New Hampshire, Massachusetts, and New York, expressed a similar opinion.

Judicial Constructions. — The power to lay and collect taxes, duties, imposts, and excises, is coextensive with the territory of the United States. Loughborough *v.* Blake, 5 Wheat. 317.

Congress is not empowered to tax for those purposes which are within the exclusive provision of the States. Gibbon *v.* Ogden, 9 Wheat. 199.

The States have no power to tax the loans of the United States. Weston *v.* City of Charleston, 2 Pet. 449, 465

ARTICLE I.

SECTION VIII.

Clause 2. — To borrow money on the credit of the United States.

Mr. Pinckney's Plan. — "To borrow money and emit bills of credit."

Report of Committee of Detail. — "To borrow money and emit bills on the credit of the United States."

The clause "to emit bills on the credit of the United States" being under consideration, —

Mr. G. Morris moved to strike it out.

Mr. Butler seconded the motion.

Mr. Madison asked if it would not be sufficient to prohibit the making them a *tender?*

Mr. Mason and Mr. Randolph, notwithstanding their antipathy to paper-money, expressed their objections to striking the words out, not being able to foresee what emergencies might arise.

Mr. Mercer "was a friend to paper-money."

Mr. Ellsworth, Mr. Wilson, Mr. Butler, and Mr. Read strongly advocated the rejection of the words. They thought it a favorable moment to "shut the door against paper-money."

Mr. Langdon said he "had rather reject the whole plan, than retain the three words, '*and emit bills.*'"

The motion to strike out was carried, — New Jersey and Maryland alone voting against it.

Judicial Construction. — The States have no power to tax the loans of the United States. Weston *v.* City of Charleston, 2 Peters, 449, 465.

ARTICLE I.

SECTION VIII.

Clause 3.—To regulate commerce with foreign Nations, and among the several States, and with Indian Tribes.

This short clause of the Constitution embraces the main subject which brought the Convention into existence. The navigation laws and commercial restrictions imposed upon the colonies by the mother country, had been a constant source of irritation for a long time, and contributed largely to that state of alienation which led to the Revolution. The resolutions of July 2, 1776, converted the several colonies into "free, sovereign, and independent States." No longer subject to the navigation laws of the British Parliament, which, with all their evils, brought at least one blessing, that of uniformity among the colonial ports; each of the new-born States was left in perfect liberty to adopt such regulations as appeared conducive to its individual interests, regardless of the consequences upon its neighbors. Several of the States did not hesitate to avail themselves of this new and important prerogative. The States through whose ports the natural or artificial channels of trade principally passed, were able to exact a revenue from those which were less favorably situated for commercial purposes. So unwilling were some of the States to yield any portion of their power over this and some other subjects, that, notwithstanding the pressure of the war, upon the success of which their political existence itself was suspended, no articles of confederation were finally agreed upon and ratified until 1781. Up to this time, the authority of Congress rested upon an unwritten and undefined basis — each of the individual States commissioning its own delegates and prescribing its powers. And the Articles of Confederation, when finally adopted, afforded no remedy for the conflicting and often oppressive commercial regulations of the States towards each other. That instrument conferred upon Congress no power over this subject, and it soon became manifest that its absence was fatal to successful operation of the system. The patriotic statesmen of that day immediately set about devising a remedy.

On the 20th of July, 1782, the legislature of New York passed a series of resolutions in reference to the state of the country, concluding with a resolution, proposing that Congress should recommend, and each State adopt the measure of assembling a general convention of the States, specially authorized to revise and amend the Confederation.

On the 13th July, 1785, Mr. MONROE, from a select committee, submitted to Congress a report, in which it was recommended that the ninth article of the Confederation be so amended as to confer upon Congress the power "of regulating the trade of the States, as well with foreign nations as with each other."

On the 11th September, 1786, commissioners from the States of New York, New Jersey, Pennsylvania, Delaware and Virginia, met at Annapolis, under instructions from their respective legislatures, "to take into consideration the trade and commerce of the United States, and to consider how far an uniform system in their commercial intercourse and regulations might be necessary to their common interest and permanent harmony."

This assembly, after a session of three days, unanimously adopted a report, from which the following are extracts: —

"Deeply impressed, however, with the magnitude and importance of the object confided to them on this occasion, your commissioners cannot forbear to indulge an expression of their earnest and unanimous wish, that speedy measures may be taken to effect a general meeting of the States in a future convention, for the same and such other purposes as the situation of public affairs may be found to require."

"That the idea of extending the powers of their deputies to other objects than those of commerce, . . . will deserve to be incorporated into that of a future convention," — as "the power of regulating trade is of such comprehensive extent, and will enter so far into the general system of the federal government, that to give it efficacy . . . may require a correspondent adjustment of the other parts of the federal system."

The report concludes with the recommendation that all the States appoint commissioners, "to meet at Philadelphia on the second Monday in May next, to take into consideration the situation of the United States, &c."

In the Federal Convention. Mr. PINCKNEY'S PLAN. — The legislature of the United States shall have the power:

"To regulate commerce with all nations, and among the several States."

"No tax shall be laid on articles exported from the States."

Proposition of Mr. PATTERSON, and the delegations from New York, New Jersey, Connecticut, and Delaware —

That the existing Articles of Confederation be amended so as to vest in Congress the power "to pass acts for the regulation of trade and commerce, as well with foreign nations as with each other."

Mr. MASON moved, — "Provided that no tax, duty, or imposition shall be laid by the legislature of the United States on articles exported from any State."

Mr. RUTLEDGE expressed his willingness to support the clause giving Congress power over commerce, on condition that the subsequent clause, that "Congress shall pass no law prohibiting the immigration or importation of" negroes, should also be agreed to.

Mr. PINCKNEY moved, — "That no act of the legislature for the purpose of regulating the commerce of the United States with foreign powers or among the several States, shall be passed without the assent of two thirds of the members of each house."

This proposition gave rise to a long and exciting debate, exhibiting the antagonism between the northern and southern States, and indicating the manner in which the compromises of the Constitution were brought about.

Mr. CHARLES PINCKNEY. — "The power of regulating commerce is a pure concession on the part of the southern States. They do not need the protection of the northern States at present."

General C. C. PINCKNEY. — "It is the true interest of the southern States to have no regulation of commerce; but, considering the loss brought on the commerce of the eastern States by the revolution, their liberal conduct towards the views of South Carolina [in reference to the importation of slaves], and the interest the weak southern States had in being united with the strong eastern States, he thought it proper that no fetters should be imposed on the power of making commercial regulations, and that his constituents, though prejudiced against the eastern States, would be reconciled to this liberality. He had himself prejudices against the eastern States before he came here, but would acknowledge that he had found them as liberal and candid as any men whatever."

Mr. CLYMER. — "The northern and middle States will be ruined if not enabled to defend themselves against foreign regulations."

Mr. G. MORRIS opposed the motion of Mr. Pinckney, requiring a two thirds vote to pass navigation laws. "A navy," he said, "was essential to security, particularly of the southern States, and can only be had by a navigation act, encouraging American bottoms and seamen."

Mr. WILLIAMSON favored the motion, although he did not deem it necessary; because, if the northern States should make too stringent regulations, the southern States would build ships for themselves.

Mr. SPAIGHT opposed the motion. "The southern States could at any time save themselves from oppression by building ships for their own use."

Mr. BUTLER regarded the rejection of the motion as a concession on the part of the southern States. "He considered the interests of these and of the eastern States to be as different as the interests of Russia and Turkey." But, "being desirous of conciliating the affections of the eastern States, he should vote against requiring two thirds instead of a majority."

Col. MASON. — "The southern States are the *minority* in both houses. Is it to be expected that they will deliver themselves, bound hand and foot to the eastern States?"

Mr. WILSON thought it better "to bind the minority hand and foot" than the majority.

Mr. MADISON thought the disadvantage to the South

from a navigation act, would be chiefly, a *temporary rise of freight*, resulting in an increase of southern as well as northern shipping, and in the promotion of the general security, and particularly of the southern States.

Mr. Rutledge was against requiring two thirds to pass a navigation act. He did not think the abuse of the power, if given, to be taken for granted. "At the worst, a navigation act could bear hard a little while only on the southern States." A navigation act was now necessary, to secure the West India trade to this country. He advocated enlarged and permanent views.

Mr. Randolph. — "A rejection of the motion would complete the deformity of the system."

Mr. Gorham. — "If the government is to be so fettered as to be unable to relieve the eastern States, what motive can they have to join in it, and thereby tie their own hands from measures which they could otherwise take for themselves? The eastern States were not led to strengthen the Union by fear for their own safety."

The proposition, requiring two thirds of each house to pass a navigation act was rejected, and the clause agreed to.

Judicial Constructions. — This power, like all others vested in Congress, is complete in itself, may be exercised to its utmost extent, and acknowledges no limitations, other than are prescribed in the Constitution. Gibbons *v.* Ogden, 9 Wheat. 196.

Commerce with foreign nations and among the several States, can mean nothing more than intercourse with those nations and among those States, for the purposes of trade, be the object of the trade what it may; and this intercourse must include all the means by which it can be carried on, whether by the free navigation of the waters of the several States, or by a passage overland through the States, where such passage becomes necessary to commercial intercourse between the States. Corfiely *v.* Coryell, 4 W. C. C. 378; Penn. *v.* Wheeling Br. Co. 18 How. 421; Col. Ins. Co. *v.* Peoria Br. Co. 6 McLean, 70. See also, id. 209, 237, 518.

This clause confers the power to impose embargoes, Gib. *v.* Ogden, 9 Wheat. 191; and to punish crimes upon stranded vessels, United States *v.* Coombs, 12 Peters, 72. It does not, however, interfere with the right of the several States to enact inspection, quarantine, and health laws of every description, as well as laws for regulating their internal commerce. Gibbon *v.* Ogden, 9 Wheat. 203; New York *v.* Miln, 11 Pet. 102. Nor with the power to regulate pilots, Cooley *v.* Board of Wardens, 12 How. 299. Or to protect their fisheries, Smith *v.* Maryland, 18 How. 71.

A State law, which requires the masters of vessels engaged in foreign commerce, to pay a certain sum to a State officer, on account of every passenger brought from a foreign country into the State, conflicts with the Constitution and laws of the United States. Smith *v.* Turner, 7 How. 283.

So does a State law authorizing the seizure and imprisonment of free negroes brought into any port of the State, on board of any vessel from any other State or foreign port. Elkison *v.* Deliesseline, 2 Wh. Cr. Cas. 56. See 1 Opin. 659, and 2 Opin. 426 *contra.* And so does a State law, which requires an importer to take a license, and pay fifty dollars, before he should be permitted to sell a package of imported goods. Brown *v.* Maryland, 12 Wheat. 419.

But a State law imposing a tax on brokers, dealing in

foreign exchange, is not repugnant to this clause. Nathan *v.* Louisiana, 8 How. 73.

Nor is one imposing a tax on legacies payable to aliens. Magee *v.* Grimes, id. 490.

Nor are the license laws of certain States, forbidding the sale of spirituous liquors, under less than certain large quantities. Thurlow *v.* Massachusetts, 5 How. 504.

Congress has power to prevent the obstruction of any navigable river, which is a means of commerce between any two or more States. Work *v.* Junc. R. R. 5 McLean, 426. See also, id. 237, and 3 Am. L. R. 79. See also, Vezie *v.* Moor, 14 How. 568, for exceptions.

Under the power to regulate commerce with the Indian tribes, Congress have power to prohibit all intercourse with them, except under license. United States *v.* Cisna, 1 McLean, 254.

In the clause of the Constitution of the United States, which declares that "Congress shall have power to regulate commerce," &c., the word commerce comprehends "navigation," and a power to regulate navigation is as expressly granted, as if that term had been added to the word "commerce." 9 Wheaton, 189.

The power to regulate commerce, extends to every species of commercial intercourse between the United States and foreign nations and among the several States. Id. 191.

It does not comprehend that commerce which is completely internal, which is carried on between man and man in a State, or between different parts of the same State, and does not extend to or affect other States. But it does not stop at the jurisdictional lines of the several States; it must be exercised wherever the subject exists. Id. 194–196.

This power to regulate commerce, is the power to prescribe the rules by which commerce is to be governed. Like all other powers vested in Congress, it is complete in itself, may be exercised to its utmost extent, and has no other limitations than such as are prescribed in the Constitution. Gibbons *v.* Ogden, 9 Wheat. 196.

The power to regulate commerce extends as well to vessels employed in carrying passengers, as to those employed in transporting property. Id. 215.

ARTICLE I.

SECTION VIII.

Clause 4.—To establish a uniform rule of naturalization, and uniform laws on the subject of bankruptcies throughout the United States;

Mr. PINCKNEY'S PLAN.—"To establish uniform rules of naturalization."

Mr. PINCKNEY subsequently moved to add,—

"To establish uniform laws on the subject of bankruptcies, and respecting the damages arising on the protest of foreign bills of exchange."

Mr. SHERMAN "observed that bankruptcies were, in some cases, punishable with death by the laws of England, and he did not choose to grant a power by which that might be done here."

Mr. G. MORRIS remarked, "that it was a great and delicate subject, but he would agree to it because he saw no danger of its abuse."

It was agreed to—Connecticut alone voting in the negative.

Judicial Constructions.—The individual States have a constitutional right to pass naturalization laws, provided they do not contravene the rule established by the authority of the Union. 2 Dall. 294; but idem, 371, Quære? See 2 Wheaton, 359.

The power to pass naturalization laws would seem to be exclusively in Congress. Chirac *v.* Chirac, 2 Wheat. 269; United States *v.* Villato, 2 Dall. 372; Thurlow *v.* Massachusetts, 5 How. 585; Smith *v.* Turner, 7 How. 556.

The States have authority to pass bankrupt laws, provided they do not impair the obligation of contracts, and provided there be no act of Congress in force to establish a uniform system of bankruptcy, conflicting with such laws. Sturges *v.* Crowninshield, 4 Wheat. 122; McMillan *v.* McNiell, id. 209.

An act of a State legislature, which discharges a debtor from all liability for debts contracted previous to his discharge, on his surrendering his property for the benefit of his creditors, is a law impairing the obligation of a contract, within the meaning of the Constitution of the United States. F. & M. Bank *v.* Smith, 6 Wheat. 131.

A mere insolvent law is not within the prohibition. Ogden *v.* Saunders, 12 Wheat. 213, 370.

There is nothing in the Constitution of the United States which forbids Congress to pass laws violating the obligation of contracts, though such power is denied to the States individually. Evans *v.* Eaton, 1 Peters, C. C. R. 322.

ARTICLE I.

SECTION VIII.

Clause 5.—To coin money, regulate the value thereof, and of foreign coin, and fix the standard of weights and measures;

Clause 6.—To provide for the punishment of counterfeiting the securities and current coin of the United States;

Clause 7.—To establish post-offices and post-roads;

Clause 8.—To promote the progress of science and useful arts, by securing, for limited times, to authors and inventors the exclusive right to their respective writings and discoveries;

These powers were provided for in Mr. PINCKNEY'S PLAN,—except "and post-roads," which was added on motion of Mr. GERRY.

Mr. PINCKNEY proposed to give the power—

"To establish and provide for a national university at the seat of the government of the United States."

Mr. MADISON proposed the following:—

"To secure to literary authors their copy-rights for a limited time."

"To establish a university."

"To encourage, by premiums and provisions, the advancement of useful knowledge and discoveries."

Mr. PINCKNEY proposed: —

"To establish seminaries for the promotion of literature and the arts and sciences."

"To secure to authors exclusive rights for a certain time."

These propositions were referred to the committee of eleven — but not reported back.

Mr. MADISON and Mr. PINCKNEY, near the close of the session, renewed their proposition as follows: —

"To establish a university, in which no preferences or distinctions should be allowed on account of religion."

Mr. MORRIS remarked — "It is not necessary. The exclusive power at the seat of government will reach the object." Yeas 4, nays 6.

The committee of eleven reported the clause (8) as it stands, and it was agreed to *nem. con.*

Judicial Constructions. — The power [contained in the 5th and 6th clauses] is limited to the coining and stamping the standard of value upon what the government creates or shall adopt, and to punishing the offence of producing a false representation of what may have been so created or adopted. Fox *v.* Ohio, 5 How. 433.

Whether Congress have power to provide for the punishment of the offence of *passing* counterfeit coin, has been doubted. 2 Law Rep. 90. This power is certainly possessed by the States. Fox *v.* Ohio, 5 How. 410.

But Congress may, without doubt, provide for punishing the offence of bringing into the United States, from a foreign place, false, forged, and counterfeit coins, made in the similitude of coins of the United States; and also for punishing the offence of uttering and passing the same. United States *v.* Marigold, 9 How. 560.

Clause 7.— The power to establish post-roads is restricted to such as are regularly laid out under the laws of the several States. C. P. A. R. R. Co. *v.* F. Canal Co., Pittsburg Leg. J. 24 Dec. '53. But see Penn. *v.* Wh. Br. Co. 18 How. 421.

Clause 8.— Patents are entitled to a liberal construction, since they are not granted as restrictions upon the rights of the community, but "to promote the progress of science and the useful arts." Blanchard *v.* Sprague, 3 Sumn. 535; Grant *v.* Raymond, 6 Peters, 218; Hogg *v.* Emerson, 6 How. 486; Brooks *v.* Fiske, 15 How. 223.

The power of Congress to legislate upon the subject of patents is plenary, by the terms of the Constitution, and as there are no restraints on its exercise, there can be no limitation of their right to modify them at their pleasure, so that they do not take away the rights of property in existing patents. McClure *v.* Kingsland, 1 How. 206.

Therefore Congress has the right to grant the extension, which has been renewed under the act of 1836. Bloomer *v.* Stolley, 5 M'Lean, 158. And to reserve rights and privileges to assignees. Blanchard's Gunstock T. Fac. *v.* Warner, 1 Blatch. 258.

In the United States, an author has no exclusive property in a published work, except under some act of Congress. Wheaton *v.* Peters, 8 Pet. 591.

ARTICLE I.

SECTION VIII.

Clause 9.—To constitute tribunals inferior to the Supreme Court;

Clause 10.—To define and punish piracies and felonies committed on the high seas, and offences against the law of nations;

Clause 9.— The plans of Mr. RANDOLPH and Mr. PINCKNEY both proposed the establishment of inferior courts.

Mr. RUTLEDGE moved to strike out the provision proposing that the original jurisdiction should be, in all cases, in the State courts.

Mr. MADISON argued the necessity of inferior courts with final jurisdiction in minor cases. "An effective judiciary establishment" he regarded as essential.

Mr. SHERMAN thought the expense of two new sets of courts objectionable.

Mr. DICKINSON advocated a national judiciary to be established by Congress. It was finally determined to leave the power with Congress.

Clause 10. Mr. PINCKNEY'S PLAN.—"To declare the law and punishment of piracies and felonies at sea."

Mr. MADISON moved to strike out "and punishment." Carried.

Mr. MORRIS moved to substitute "punish" for "declare the law of." Carried.

Mr. MADISON now moved to prefix "define and ——"

Mr. WILSON "thought 'felonies' sufficiently defined by common law."

Mr. MADISON thought otherwise, and the amendment was adopted. And on motion of Mr. ELLSWORTH, "offences against the law of nations" was added.

ARTICLE I.

SECTION VIII.

Clause 11. — To declare war, grant Letters of Marque and Reprisal, and make rules concerning captures on land and water;

Confederation. — Art. 9. "The United States in Congress assembled shall have the sole and exclusive right and power of determining on peace and war, &c. Of establishing rules for deciding, in all cases, what captures on land or water shall be legal, &c. Of granting letters of marque and reprisal in times of peace," &c.

Mr. PINCKNEY'S PLAN. — "To make rules concerning captures from an enemy."

Committee of detail — "To make war — to make rules concerning captures on land or water."

Mr. PINCKNEY suggested "that the Senate would be the best depository of this power."

Mr. BUTLER was for vesting the power in the President.

Mr. GERRY and Mr. MASON were opposed to vesting the power in the President.

"*Declare*" was substituted for "*make*," as being more restricted in its meaning.

Mr. PINCKNEY moved to add, "to grant letters of marque and reprisal."

Judicial Constructions. — As a consequence of the power

of declaring war and making treaties, the government possesses power of acquiring territory, either by conquest or treaty. Am. Ins. Co. *v.* Canter, 1 Peters, 542.

When the legislative power has declared war, the executive authority, to whom its execution is confided, is bound to carry it into effect; he has a discretion vested in him, as to the manner and extent; but he cannot lawfully transcend the rules of warfare established among civilized nations. Brown *v.* United States, 8 Cranch, 153.

In expounding the Constitution of the United States, a construction ought not lightly to be admitted, which would give to a declaration of war an effect in this country it does not possess elsewhere, and which would fetter that exercise of entire discretion respecting enemy's property, which may enable the government to apply to the enemy the rule that he applies to us.

The power of making "rules concerning captures on land and water" is not confined to captures which are extra-territorial, but extends to rules respecting the enemy's property found within the territory, and is an express grant to Congress of the power of confiscating enemy's property found within the territory at the declaration of war. 8 Cranch, 110.

ARTICLE I.

SECTION VIII.

Clause 12.—To raise and support armies; but no appropriation of money to that use shall be for a longer term than two years;

Clause 13.—To provide and maintain a navy;

Clause 14.—To make rules for the government and regulation of the land and naval forces;

Mr. PINCKNEY'S PLAN.—"To raise armies."

On motion of Mr. GORHAM, "and support" was added.

Mr. GERRY moved to add, "Provided, that in time of peace, the army shall not consist of more than —— thousand men." He thought that the blank should be filled with "two" or "three." Disagreed to.

Mr. PINCKNEY.—"The military shall always be subordinate to the civil power; and no grants of money shall be made by the legislature, for supporting military land forces, for more than one year at a time."

These propositions were referred to the committee of eleven, who reported the clauses as they stand.

Judicial Constructions.—Congress have a constitutional power to enlist minors, in the navy or army, without the consent of their parents. U. S. *v.* Bainbridge, 1 Mas. 71;

E. Roberts' Case, 2 Hall, L. J. 192; U. S. *v.* Stewart, Crabbe, 265; Com. *v.* Barker, 5 Binn. 423. See also, 5 Cr. C. C. 554.

Public policy requires that a minor shall be at liberty to enter into a contract to serve the State, whenever such contract is not positively forbidden by the State itself. Commonwealth *v.* Gamble, 11 S. & R. 94.

ARTICLE I.

SECTION VIII.

Clause 15.—To provide for calling forth the militia to execute the laws of the Union, suppress insurrections, and repel invasions;

Clause 16.—To provide for organizing, arming and disciplining the militia, and for governing such part of them as may be employed in the service of the United States, reserving to the States, respectively, the appointment of the officers, and the authority of training the militia according to the discipline prescribed by Congress;

Articles of Confederation.—"Every State shall always keep up a well-regulated and disciplined militia, sufficiently armed and accoutred, and shall provide and have constantly ready for use, in public stores, a due number of field-pieces and tents, and a proper quantity of arms, ammunition, and camp equipage."

Mr. Mason moved to give Congress power,—

"To make laws for the regulation and discipline of the militia of the several States, reserving to the States the appointment of the officers."

Mr. Dickinson thought "the States would not and ought not to give up all authority over the militia," and suggested "to restrain the power to one fourth at a time." This was accepted by Mr. Mason.

Mr. GERRY expressed his decided opposition to surrendering the power over the militia, to the general government.

The propositions were sent to the grand committee.

Gov. LIVINGSTON, from the grand committee, reported the clause as it stands in the Constitution.

Judicial Constructions.— The act of 1795, which confers power on the President to call forth the militia in certain exigencies, is constitutional; and the President is the exclusive and final judge whether the exigency has arisen. Martin *v.* Mott, 12 Wh. 19.

The militia of the several States are not subject to martial law, unless they are in the actual service of the United States. Mills *v.* Martin, 19 Johns. 7.

So far as Congress has provided for organizing the militia, the legislative powers of the States are excluded. Houston *v.* Moore, 5 Wh. 51.

But a State may lawfully provide for the trial by courts-martial of drafted militia, &c. Moore *v.* Houston, 3 S. & R. 169.

ARTICLE I.

SECTION VIII.

Clause 17.—To exercise exclusive legislation in all cases whatsoever, over such district (not exceeding ten miles square) as may by cession of particular States, and the acceptance of Congress, become the seat of the government of the United States, and to exercise like authority over all places purchased by the consent of the legislature of the State in which the same shall be, for the erection of forts, magazines, arsenals, dock-yards, and other needful buildings.

Mr. MADISON moved to vest in Congress the power,—"To exercise exclusively, legislative authority at the seat of the general government, and over a district around the same, not exceeding —— square miles, the consent of the legislature of the State or States comprising the same, being first obtained."

Mr. PINCKNEY submitted the following:—

"To fix and permanently establish, the seat of government of the United States, in which they shall possess the exclusive right of soil and jurisdiction."

These propositions were referred to the committee of detail, without debate, who subsequently reported the clause, substantially as it stands.

In the discussion on the fourth clause of Art. 1, Sec. 5, Mr. KING remarked, — "that the mutability of the place of the meeting of Congress had dishonored the federal government." "He thought a law, at least, should be necessary to a removal."

Mr. SPAIGHT. — "This will fix the seat of government at New York."

Mr. MADISON. — "A central place for the seat of government is so just and would be so much insisted on by the House of Representatives, that though a law should be made requisite for the purpose, it could and would be obtained."

The propositions of Mr. MADISON and Mr. PINCKNEY to give to Congress the power to establish a University, being under consideration,

Mr. MORRIS said — "It is not necessary. The exclusive power at the seat of government will reach the object."

Judicial Constructions. — Congress has authority to impose a direct tax on the District of Columbia, in proportion to the census directed to be taken by the Constitution.

The power of Congress to exercise exclusive legislation, &c., includes the power of taxing. Lough. *v.* Blake, 5 Wheaton, 317.

Congress is not bound to extend a direct tax to the District or the territories. Ibid.

The right of exclusive legislation carries with it the right of exclusive jurisdiction. U. S. *v.* Connell, 2 Mas. 60. But the purchase of the lands by the United States, for the public purposes within the limits of a State, does not of itself, oust the jurisdiction or sovereignty of such State over the lands so purchased. Ibid.

The Constitution prescribes the only mode by which they can acquire land as a sovereign power, and therefore, they hold only as an individual, when they obtain it in any other manner. Commonwealth *v.* Young, Brightly, 302; People *v.* Godfrey, 17 Johns. 225. See also, 2 Wheat. Cr. Cas. 490, 548; 2 Wall, Jr. 72; 7 Opin. 628.

ARTICLE I.

SECTION VIII.

Clause 18.—To make all laws which shall be necessary and proper for carrying into execution the foregoing powers, and all other powers vested by this Constitution in the Government of the United States, or in any department or officer thereof.

General Powers of Congress.

Articles of Confederation.—"The United States in Congress assembled, shall have the sole and exclusive right and power of determining on peace and war . . . . . of sending and receiving ambassadors; entering into treaties and alliances, *provided* that no treaty of commerce shall be made, whereby the legislative power of the respective States shall be restrained from imposing such imposts and duties on foreigners as their own people are subjected to or from prohibiting the exportation or importation of any species of goods or commodities whatsoever; of establishing rules for deciding, in all cases, what captures on land or water shall be legal . . . . . of granting letters of marque and reprisal in times of peace; appointing courts for the trial of piracies and felonies committed on the high seas, and establishing courts for receiving and determining finally appeals in all cases of captures, *provided* that no member of Congress shall be appointed a judge of any of said courts.

"The United States in Congress shall also have the sole and exclusive right and power of regulating the alloy and value of coin struck by their own authority or that of the respective States; fixing the standard of weights and measures throughout the United States; regulating the trade and managing all affairs with the Indians, not members of any of the States, *provided* that the legislative right of any State be not infringed or violated; establishing or regulating post-offices from one State to another, throughout all the United States, and exacting such postage on the papers passing through the same as may be requisite to pay the expenses of the said office; appointing all officers," &c.

Mr. RANDOLPH'S PLAN. — "*Each branch ought to possess the right of originating acts. The national legislature ought to be empowered to enjoy the legislative rights vested in Congress by the Confederation, and moreover to legislate in all cases to which the separate States are incompetent, or in which the harmony of the United States may be interrupted by the exercise of individual legislation; to negative all laws passed by the several States, contravening, in the opinion of the national legislature, the articles of union,* or any treaty subsisting under the authority of the Union, and to call forth the force of the Union against any member of the Union failing to fulfil its duty under the articles thereof." Agreed to in committee of the whole, without division, except the last clause.

When the clause giving Congress power to negative State laws came up in the Convention, Mr. PINCKNEY of South Carolina, moved the following substitute: "That the national legislature should have authority to negative all laws [of State legislatures] which they should judge to be improper."

Mr. MADISON "could not but regard an indefinite power

to negative legislative acts of the States as absolutely necessary to a perfect system."

On the question of agreeing to the proposition,— yeas, Massachusetts, Pennsylvania, and Virginia, 3. Delaware divided. All the rest nay.

NOTE.— As the plan of government became more developed, Mr. Madison changed his opinion on this subject.

Plan proposed by the delegates from New Jersey.

"SEC. —. That, in addition to the powers vested in the United States in Congress, by the present existing Articles of Confederation, they be authorized to pass acts for raising a revenue, by levying a duty or duties on all goods or merchandises of foreign growth or manufacture, imported into any port of the United States; by stamp on paper, vellum or parchment, and by a postage on all letters or packages passing through the general post-office;— to be applied to such federal purposes as they shall deem proper and expedient; to make rules and regulations for the collection thereof; and the same from time to time to alter and amend in such manner as they shall think proper; to pass acts for the regulation of trade and commerce, as well with foreign nations as with each other; — provided that all punishments, fines, forfeitures, and penalties, to be incurred for contravening such acts, rules, and regulations, shall be adjudged by the common-law judiciaries of the State in which any offence, contrary to the true intent and meaning of such acts, rules, and regulations, shall have been committed and perpetrated, with liberty of commencing in the first instance all suits and prosecutions for that purpose in the superior common-law judiciary in such States; subject, nevertheless, for the correction of all errors, both in law and fact, in rendering judgment, to an appeal to the judiciary of the United States.

"SEC. —. That whenever requisitions shall be necessary, instead of the rule for making requisitions, mentioned in the Articles of Confederation, the United States in Congress be authorized to make such requisitions in proportion to the whole number of white and other free citizens and inhabitants of every age, sex, and condition, including those bound to service for a term of years, and three fifths of all other persons, not comprehended in the foregoing description, except Indians not paying taxes; that if such requisitions be not complied with in the time specified therein, to direct the collection thereof in the non-complying States, and for that purpose to devise and pass acts directing and authorizing the same; — provided that none of the powers hereby vested in the United States in Congress shall be exercised without the consent of at least —— States, and in that proportion, if the number of confederated States should be hereafter increased or diminished.

"SEC. —. That the United States in Congress be authorized to elect a federal executive." [This plan was sustained by New York and New Jersey only.]

Mr. RANDOLPH remarked, in comparing this plan with that submitted by him, — "The true question is, whether we will adhere to the federal plan or introduce the national one."

Mr. HAMILTON'S PLAN, — suggested in his speech on Mr. Randolph's resolutions. "The supreme legislative power of the United States of America to be vested in two different bodies of men; — the one to be called the Assembly, the other the Senate, who together shall form the legislature of the United States, with power to pass all laws whatsoever, subject to the negative hereafter mentioned.

"All laws of the particular States, contrary to the Constitution and laws of the United States to be utterly void; and the better to prevent such laws being passed, the governor or president of each State shall be appointed by the general government and shall have a negative upon the laws about to be passed in the State of which he is governor or president."

These several propositions having been considered in the committee of the whole, they reported the following: —

"That the national legislature ought to be empowered to enjoy the legislative rights vested in Congress by the Confederation; and, moreover, to legislate in all cases to which the separate States are incompetent, or in which the harmony of the United States may be interrupted by the exercise of individual legislation; to negative all laws passed by the several States, contravening, in the opinion of the national legislature, the articles of union or any treaties subsisting under the authority of the Union."

This was modified on motion of Mr. BEDFORD, by inserting "for the general interests of the Union and also in those" — after the words "all cases."

The power to negative State laws was rejected in Convention — being supported by Massachusetts, Virginia, and North Carolina only.

As thus amended, the report was agreed to, and referred to the committee on detail, in the following form: —

"The legislature of the United States shall have authority to establish such uniform qualifications of the members of each house, with regard to property, as to the said legislature shall seem expedient.

"The legislature of the United States shall have the power to lay and collect taxes, duties, imposts, and excises.

"To regulate commerce with foreign nations and among the several States;

"To establish an uniform rule of naturalization throughout the United States;

"To coin money; To regulate the value of foreign coin;

"To fix the standard of weights and measures;

"To establish post-offices; [on motion of Mr. GERRY, "and post roads" was added].

"To borrow money and emit bills on the credit of the United States;

"To appoint a treasurer by ballot;

"To constitute tribunals inferior to the Supreme Court;

"To make rules concerning captures on land and water;

"To declare the law and punishment of piracies and felonies committed on the high seas, and the punishment of counterfeiting the coin of the United States, and of offences against the law of nations;

"To subdue a rebellion in any State on the application of its legislature;

"To make war; to raise armies; to build and equip fleets;

"To call forth the aid of the militia in order to execute the laws of the Union, enforce treaties, suppress insurrections, and repel invasions;

"And to make all laws that shall be necessary and proper for carrying into execution the foregoing powers, and all other powers vested by this Constitution in the government of the United States, or in any department or office thereof."

[To declare the punishment of treason.]

Mr. MADISON moved to add the following:—

"To dispose of the unappropriated lands of the United States.

"To institute temporary governments for new States arising therein.

"To grant charters of corporation in cases where the public good may require them, and the authority of a single State may be incompetent.

"To secure to literary authors their copyrights for a limited time.

"To establish a university.

"To encourage, by premiums and provisions, the advancement of useful knowledge and discoveries.

"To authorize the executive to procure and hold, for the use of the United States, landed property for the erection of forts, magazines, and other necessary building."

Mr. PINCKNEY, at the same time, moved the following:—

"To fix and permanently establish, the seat of government, &c.

"To establish seminaries for the promotion of literature, &c.

"To grant charters of incorporation.

"To grant patents for useful inventions.

"To secure to authors exclusive rights for a certain time.

"To establish public institutions, rewards, and immunities for the promotion of agriculture, commerce, trades, and manufactures."

These propositions were sent to the committee of detail, without debate.

Mr. MASON moved to add "a power to regulate the militia"—and a power "*to enact sumptuary laws.*"

Mr. ELLSWORTH, Mr. G. MORRIS, and Mr. GERRY opposed the latter power. The vote stood—yea, Delaware, Maryland, and Georgia; all the rest nay.

Mr. Rutledge reported from the committee to whom the above propositions were referred as follows — add to the clause giving the power to lay and collect taxes, duties, imposts, and excises — "for payment of the debts and necessary expenses of the United States; *provided*, that no law for raising any branch of revenue, except what may be specially appropriated for the payment of interest on debts or loans, shall continue in force more than —— years."

Mr. Charles Pinckney renewed the proposition to give the legislature of the United States the power,

"To negative all laws passed by the several States, interfering, in the opinion of the legislature, with the general interests and harmony of the Union, *provided* that two thirds of the members of each house assent to the same."

Mr. Brown, Mr. Madison, Mr. Langdon, and Mr. Wilson, favored the proposition. Mr. Wilson regarded it as "the keystone wanted to complete the arch of government we are raising."

Mr. Sherman, Mr. Williamson, Mr. Rutledge, Mr. Ellsworth, and Mr. G. Morris, opposed it. Mr. Rutledge remarked, "This alone would damn and ought to damn the Constitution."

On the question of referring the proposition to a committee, moved by Mr. Madison, it was lost by the votes of New Hampshire, Pennsylvania, Delaware, Maryland, and Virginia, in the affirmative; and Massachusetts, Connecticut, New Jersey, North Carolina, South Carolina and Georgia, in the negative. It was then withdrawn that being regarded as a test vote.

Mr. Gerry and Mr. Pinckney moved to insert — "that the liberty of the press should be inviolably preserved." Lost — yeas 4, nays 7.

The subject was then sent to the committee on style and arrangement, who reported the form as in the Constitution.

Judicial Constructions.— The word *necessary*, in this clause, does not mean absolutely necessary, nor does it imply the use of only the most direct and simple means calculated to produce the end. Commonwealth *v.* Lewis, 6 Binn. 270; McCulloch *v.* Maryland, 4 Wheaton, 413.

And, therefore, Congress had the power to charter the Bank of the United States, as a necessary and useful instrument of the fiscal operations of the government. Ibid. 316, 422.

They have the power, under this general authority, to provide for the punishment of any offences which interfere with, obstruct, or prevent commerce and navigation with foreign States and among the several States, although such offences may be done on land. U. S. *v.* Coombs, 12 Peters, 78.

If the end be legitimate and within the scope of the Constitution, all the means which are appropriate, which are plainly adapted to that end, and which are not prohibited, may constitutionally be employed to carry it into effect. 4 Wheaton, 316.

Corporations. The power of establishing corporations is not a distinct sovereign power or end of government, but only the means of carrying into effect other powers which are sovereign. Whenever it becomes an appropriate means of exercising any of the powers given by the Constitution, to the government of the Union, it may be exercised by that government. Ibid.

ARTICLE I.

SECTION IX.

Clause 1.—The migration or importation of such persons as any of the States now existing shall think proper to admit, shall not be prohibited by the Congress prior to the year one thousand eight hundred and eight; but a tax or duty may be imposed on such importation, not exceeding ten dollars for each person.

A clause of this kind was suggested by the members from South Carolina, during the debate on the navigation clause, but no formal proposition moved.

The committee to whom the subject of the general powers of Congress was referred, reported the following:—

"No tax or duty shall be laid, &c., on the migration or importation of such persons as the several States shall think proper to admit; nor shall such migration or importation be prohibited."

Mr. L. MARTIN, of Maryland, proposed to amend the clause so as to allow a tax or prohibition on the importation of slaves,—for the reasons that their importation was encouraged by their being made an element in the basis of representation, at the same time that they weak ened the power of the State, — and because it was inconsistent with the principles of the Revolution.

Mr. RUTLEDGE did not concede that slaves were an element of weakness in a State, and "would readily exempt other States from the obligation to protect the southern against them." "The true question at present is, whether the southern States shall or shall not be parties to the Union."

Mr. PINCKNEY said — "South Carolina can never receive the plan if it prohibits the slave-trade."

Mr. ELLSWORTH. — "Let every State import what it pleases. The morality or wisdom of slavery are considerations belonging to the States themselves. What enriches a part enriches the whole, and the States are the best judges of their particular interest."

Mr. SHERMAN "was for leaving the clause as it stands." "He disapproved of the slave-trade, but did not think the public good required that the proposed scheme of government should interfere with the existing rights of the States to import slaves." "It was better to let the southern States import slaves than to part with them, if they made that a *sine qua non*."

Colonel MASON, of Virginia. — "The infernal traffic originated in the avarice of British merchants. The British government constantly checked the attempts of Virginia to put a stop to it." "He held it essential, in every point of view, that the general government should have the power to prevent the increase of slavery."

General PINCKNEY. — "South Carolina and Georgia cannot do without slaves. As to Virginia, she will gain by stopping importations. Her slaves will rise in value, and she has more than she wants." "The importation of slaves will be for the interest of the whole Union."

Mr. GERRY. — "We have nothing to do with the conduct of the States as to slaves, but ought to be careful not to give any sanction to it."

Mr. King of Massachusetts, and Mr. Langdon of New Hampshire, strongly advocated, giving the prohibitory power to the general government. Mr. Langdon said he "could not, with a good conscience, leave it with the States."

General Pinckney, of South Carolina, moved to recommit the clause, "that slaves might be made liable to an equal tax with other imports."

Mr. Rutledge, of South Carolina. — "If the Convention thinks that North Carolina, South Carolina, and Georgia will ever agree to the plan, unless their right to import slaves be untouched, the expectation is vain."

Mr. G. Morris, of Pennsylvania, proposed also to recommit the clauses relating to taxes on exports, and to a navigation act — "*with the view to a bargain between the northern and southern States.*"

Mr. Randolph favored the commitment, in the hope that a compromise might be effected; but he "could never agree to the clause as it stands; he would sooner risk the Constitution."

The motion to commit was carried by the votes of Connecticut, New Jersey, Maryland, Virginia, North Carolina, South Carolina, and Georgia.

The committee, consisting of Langdon of New Hampshire, King of Massachusetts, Johnson of Connecticut, Livingston of New York, Clymer of Pennsylvania, Dickinson of Delaware, L. Martin of Maryland, Madison of Virginia, Williamson of North Carolina, C. C. Pinckney of South Carolina, and Baldwin of Georgia, reported the following, as a substitute for the propositions referred to them: —

"The immigration or importation of such persons as the

several States, now existing, shall think proper to admit, shall not be prohibited by the legislature prior to the year 1800, but a tax or duty may be imposed on such migration or importation, at a rate not exceeding the average of the duties laid on imports."

The clause in relation to the capitation tax to be retained, and that requiring a two thirds vote to pass a navigation act, to be stricken out.

The report being taken up,

General PINCKNEY moved to strike out "1800" and insert "1808."

Mr. GORHAM seconded the motion, and it prevailed.

Affirmative — New Hampshire, Massachusetts, Connecticut, Maryland, North Carolina, South Carolina, and Georgia, 7.

Negative — New Jersey, Pennsylvania, Delaware, and Virginia, 4.

Mr. G. MORRIS proposed to avoid ambiguity by making the clause read, "The importation of slaves into North Carolina, South Carolina, and Georgia, shall not be prohibited." "He wished it to be known that this part of the Constitution was a compliance with those States. If the change of language should be objected to by members from those States, he should not urge it."

Mr. WILLIAMSON said, "that both in opinion and practice he was against slavery; but he thought it more favorable to humanity, from a view of all the circumstances, to let in South Carolina and Georgia on those terms, than to exclude them from the Union."

Mr. MORRIS withdrew his motion.

Mr. SHERMAN was opposed to authorizing a "tax or duty" on such "immigration" or "importation," as implying that "men could be property."

It was answered, that this was the price of the other

part of the clause, and that not to tax would be equivalent to a bounty on the importation of slaves.

Mr. MADISON "thought it wrong to admit, in the Constitution, that there could be property in men." It was finally arranged to read, as in the Constitution. [See debate on the navigation clause.]

ARTICLE I.

SECTION IX.

Clause 2.—The privilege of the writ of *habeas corpus* shall not be suspended, unless when in cases of rebellion or invasion the public safety may require it.

Mr. PINCKNEY submitted for reference to committee of detail, the following:—

"The privilege and benefit of the writ of *habeas corpus* shall be enjoyed in this government in the most expeditious and ample manner, and shall not be suspended by the legislature except upon the most urgent and pressing occasions, and for a limited time, not exceeding —— months."

Mr. RUTLEDGE thought the privilege of *habeas corpus* should be declared inviolate.

Mr. G. MORRIS suggested the form as it stands in the Constitution, and it was adopted.

ARTICLE I.

SECTION IX.

Clause 3.—No bill of attainder or ex post facto law shall be passed.

Clause 4.—No capitation, or other direct tax, shall be laid, unless in proportion to the census or enumeration herein before directed to be taken.

Clause 3 was moved by Mr. GERRY.

Clause 4 was part of the compromise between the northern and southern States, as to the proportion of taxation, representation, navigation, and importation of slaves.

Mr. BALDWIN, of Georgia, in the House of Representatives (2d Sess., 1st. Cong.), said: "This was intended to prevent Congress from laying any special tax upon negro slaves."

Judicial Constructions.—*Ex post facto* laws are such as create or aggravate crimes or increase the punishment, or change the rules of evidence for the purpose of conviction. Calder *v.* Bull, 3 Dall. 390. The phrase only applies to penal and criminal laws, which inflict forfeitures or punishments, and not to civil proceedings which affect private rights retrospectively. Watson *v.* Mercer, 8 Peters, 110; Carpenter *v.* Penn, 17 How. 463.

ARTICLE I.

SECTION IX.

Clause 5. — No tax or duty shall be laid on articles exported from any State.

Mr. PINCKNEY'S PLAN. — "No tax shall be laid on articles exported from the States."

Mr. MASON "urged the necessity of connecting with the powers of levying taxes, duties," &c. the above prohibition. "He hoped the northern States did not mean to deny the southern this security."

Mr. G. MORRIS regarded such a prohibition as inadmissible.

Mr. MADISON "thought the power proper in itself, and that its exercise belonged to the States collectively and not individually. He argued that the tax would be paid by the consumer and not by the producer, and that, even if the burden should fall heaviest on the southern States, they ought not to complain, because they were more in need of naval protection than the northern."

Messrs. WILLIAMSON, ELLSWORTH, GERRY, MERCER, and SHERMAN supported the prohibition, and Messrs. WILSON and G. MORRIS opposed it.

Mr. MADISON moved to amend by adding, "unless by consent of two thirds of the legislature." Lost Yeas 5, nays 6.

Mr. MORRIS proposed that the clauses relating to the importation of slaves, the navigation laws, and the tax on exports, be referred to a special committee, and suggested that they might be the subjects "of a bargain between the northern and southern States."

Mr. BUTLER "declared he never would agree to the power of taxing exports."

Mr. MORRIS'S motion prevailed. Yeas — Connecticut, New Jersey, Maryland, Virginia, North Carolina, South Carolina, Georgia, 7. Nays — New Hampshire, Pennsylvania, and Delaware, 3.

The committee subsequently reported the several clauses on the subjects referred to them, substantially as finally adopted.

ARTICLE I.

SECTION IX.

Clause 6. — No preference shall be given by any regulation of commerce or revenue to the ports of one State over those of another; nor shall vessels bound to or from one State, be obliged to enter, clear, or pay duties in another.

Clause 7. — No money shall be drawn from the Treasury, but in consequence of appropriations made by law; and a regular statement and account of the receipts and expenditures of all public money shall be published from time to time.

Mr. CARROLL and Mr. MARTIN suggested the sixth clause in order to prevent the general legislature from favoring the ports of particular States. This proposition was referred to a committee, who reported in its favor, and the report was concurred in.

The seventh clause grew out of the compromise which conceded the equality of the States in the Senate. As first agreed to, it was in the following form: —

"No money shall be drawn from the treasury but in pursuance of appropriations that shall originate in the House of Representatives."

The committee of style and arrangement gave it its

present form. The requirement of a publication of the public expenditures, was moved by Col. MASON.

Judicial Construction.— A State law requiring the payment of pilotage fees, does not infringe this clause. Cooley *v.* Board of Wardens, 12 How. 314, 315. See 18 How. 421.

ARTICLE I.

SECTION IX.

Clause 8.—No title of nobility shall be granted by the United States: and no person holding any office of profit or trust under them, shall, without the consent of the Congress, accept of any present, emolument, office, or title, of any kind whatever, from any king, prince, or foreign State.

Articles of Confederation.—"Nor shall any person holding any office of profit or trust under the United States, or any of them, accept of any present, emolument, office, or title of any kind whatever, from any king, prince, or foreign State. Nor shall the United States in Congress assembled or any of them, grant any title of nobility."

These prohibitions were transferred to the Constitution, on motion of Mr. C. PINCKNEY, without opposition.

ARTICLE I.

SECTION X.

Clause 1.— No State shall enter into any treaty, alliance, or confederation; grant letters of marque and reprisal; coin money; emit bills of credit; make any thing but gold and silver coin a tender in payment of debts; pass any bill of attainder, ex post facto law, or law impairing the obligation of contracts, or grant any title of nobility.

Articles of Confederation.— No State, without the consent of the United States in Congress assembled, shall send any embassy to, or receive any embassy from, or enter into any conference, agreement, alliance, or treaty with any king, prince, or State . . . . . or grant any title of nobility.

The committee of detail transferred the above article to the Constitution in the following form:—

" No State shall coin money; nor grant letters of marque and reprisal; nor enter into any treaty, alliance, or confederation, nor grant any title of nobility. No State, without the consent of the legislature of the United States, shall emit bills of credit, or make any thing but specie, a tender for the payment of debts . . . nor enter into any agreement or compact with another State or with any foreign power."

Mr. WILSON and Mr. SHERMAN proposed to make the prohibition on the States, "to emit bills of credit," or "make any thing but gold and silver coin a tender in payment of debts," peremptory, instead of allowing the States to exercise the power, by obtaining the consent of Congress.

Mr. SHERMAN argued with great earnestness that this was a favorable crisis "for crushing paper-money." The motion was carried — Virginia alone voting in the negative.

On motion of Mr. RUTLEDGE, — "nor pass bills of attainder nor *ex post facto* laws," was added.

Judicial Constructions. — To constitute a *bill of credit*, within the Constitution, it must be issued by a State, involve the faith of the State, and be designed to circulate as money, on the credit of the State, in the ordinary use of business. Briscoe *v.* Bk. Ky. 11 Peters, 257. See also, 4 Pet. 410; 8 Pet. 40; 10 How. 205; 13 How. 12; 15 How. 317.

The Constitution does not prohibit the States from passing retrospective laws generally, but only *ex post facto* laws. Watson *v.* Mercer, 8 Pet. 110. See also, Baltimore & Susquehanna Railroad *v.* Nesbit, 10 How. 401.

The provision relative to *impairing the obligation of contracts* has never been understood to embrace other contracts than those which respect property, or some object of value, and confer rights which may be asserted in a court of justice. A private charter is such a contract. Dart. Coll. *v.* Woodward, 4 Wheat. 518, 629.

An act incorporating a bank. Providence Bank *v.* Billings, 4 Pet. 514. An appointment to a salaried officer is not such a contract. Butler *v.* Pennsylvania, 10 How. 402. All contracts are subject to the eminent domain existing in the several States. W. R. Br. Co. *v.* Dix, 6 How. 507. See also, 12 Wheat. 370; 1 How. 316. Any postponement or acceleration of the performance of the contract impairs its obligation. Green *v.* Biddle, 8 Wheat. 175; McCracken *v.* Hayward, 2 How. 608.

ARTICLE I.

SECTION X.

Clause 2. — No State shall, without the consent of the Congress, lay any imposts or duties on imports or exports, except what may be absolutely necessary for executing its inspection laws: and the net produce of all duties and imposts, laid by any State on imports or exports, shall be for the use of the Treasury of the United States; and all such laws shall be subject to the revision and control of the Congress.

Articles of Confederation. — "No State shall lay any imposts or duties, which may interfere with any stipulations in treaties."

The committee of detail, transferred this article, in the following form: —

"No State, without the consent of the legislature of the United States, shall . . . lay imposts or duties on imports."

On motion of Mr. KING, "or exports" was added; and on motion of Mr. SHERMAN, "nor with such consent, but for the use of the United States."

On motion of Col. MASON, the following was added: —

"Provided that no State shall be restrained from imposing the usual duties on produce exported from such

State, for the sole purpose of defraying the charges of inspecting, packing, storing, and indemnifying the losses on such produce while in the custody of public officers; but all such regulations shall, in case of abuse, be subject to the revision and control of Congress."

The committee of style and revision gave it the form in which it stands.

ARTICLE I.

SECTION X.

Clause 3.—No State shall, without the consent of Congress, lay any duty of tonnage, keep troops, or ships of war in time of peace, enter into any agreement or compact with another State, or with a foreign power, or engage in war, unless actually invaded, or in such imminent danger as will not admit of delay.

Articles of Confederation.—"No two or more States shall enter into any treaty, confederation, or alliance between them, without the consent of the United States in Congress assembled, specifying accurately the purpose for which the same is to be entered into, and how long it shall continue. No State shall lay any imposts or duties which may interfere with any stipulations in treaties," &c.

"No vessels of war shall be kept up in time of peace by any State, except such number only, as shall be deemed necessary by the United States in Congress assembled, for the defence of such State or its trade—nor shall any body of forces be kept up by any State, in time of peace—except," &c.

"No State shall engage in war without the consent &c., unless such State be actually invaded by enemies," &c.

The committee of detail transferred these powers to the new Constitution, nearly as they stand.

Judicial Constructions. — The words in this clause are used in their broadest sense; they were intended to cut off all negotiation and intercourse between the State authorities and foreign nations. Holmes *v.* Jennison, 14 Peters, 572.

This prohibition is political in its character, and has no reference to mere matters of contract, or to the grant of a franchise, which in nowise conflicts with the powers delegated to the general government by the States. Un. Br. R. R. Co. *v.* Ga. R. R. Co. 14 Ga. 327.

ARTICLE II.

SECTION I.

Clause 1.—The Executive power shall be vested in a President of the United States of America. He shall hold his office during the term of four years, and together with the Vice-President, chosen for the same term, be elected as follows:

Clause 2.—Each State shall appoint, in such manner as the legislature thereof may direct, a number of electors, equal to the whole number of Senators and Representatives to which the State may be entitled in the Congress; but no Senator or Representative, or person holding an office of trust or profit under the United States, shall be appointed an elector.

Clause 3.—The Congress may determine the time of choosing the electors, and the day on which they shall give their votes; which day shall be the same throughout the United States.

MR. RANDOLPH'S PLAN.— *That a national executive be instituted*, to be chosen by the national legislature for the term of —— years,—to be ineligible thereafter—to possess the executive power of Congress, &c.

Mr. PINCKNEY'S PLAN. — "The executive power of the United States shall be vested in a President of the United States of America, which shall be his style; and his title shall be His Excellency. He shall be elected for —— years, and shall be reëligible."

Mr. Randolph's Plan being under consideration, in committee of the whole, —

Mr. WILSON moved, — "That the national executive consist of a single person."

Mr. GERRY and Mr. RANDOLPH opposed a unity in the executive magistracy. Before the question was taken,

Mr. WILSON suggested a further amendment, that the election be by the people for a term of three years, and that the President should be eligible for a second term.

Mr. PINCKNEY, of South Carolina, and Mr. MASON, of Virginia, expressed their views in favor of a term of seven years and ineligibility for reëlection. On the question of seven years, it was carried. Yeas — New York, New Jersey, Pennsylvania, Delaware, Virginia, 5. Nays — Connecticut, North Carolina, South Carolina, Georgia, 4. Massachusetts divided.

On the question of ineligibility for a second term, it was also carried.

Mr. WILSON, of Pennsylvania, moved, "that the executive magistrate should be elected by *electors*, to be chosen by the people in prescribed election districts." Lost. Yeas — Pennsylvania and Maryland, 2. Nays — 8.

For electing the executive by the national legislature, as proposed by Mr. Randolph's plan, for a term of seven years, it was agreed to. Yeas — Massachusetts, Connecticut, New York, Delaware, Virginia, North Carolina, South Carolina, and Georgia, 8. Nays — Pennsylvania and Maryland, 2.

Mr. RUTLEDGE moved that the executive consist of "one person." Agreed to.

Plan proposed by Mr. PATTERSON, in behalf of the New Jersey delegates: —

That the United States in Congress be authorized to elect a federal executive, to consist of —— persons, to continue in office for the term of —— years.

Mr. HAMILTON suggested his plan, namely, — The supreme executive authority of the United States, to be vested in a governor, to be elected to serve during good behavior; the election to be made by electors chosen by the people in election districts.

These several propositions were considered in the committee of the whole, who reported the following: —

"That a national executive be instituted, to consist of a single person; to be chosen by the national legislature for the term of seven years."

Mr. GOUVERNEUR MORRIS moved to strike out "*national legislature*," and insert "*citizens of the United States*," so as to make the choice of President by the popular vote.

PENNSYLVANIA alone supported this motion.

The words, "to be chosen by the national legislature," agreed to, *nem. con.* as also were the two following clauses.

The words, "to be ineligible a second term" were stricken out, on motion by Mr. HOUSTON. This vote was subsequently reconsidered.

Dr. McCLUNG, of Virginia, moved to strike out "seven years," and insert "during good behavior."

Mr. G. MORRIS and Mr. BROOME supported the motion.

Mr. MADISON suggested, that there was an analogy between the executive and judiciary departments, but whether the plan proposed was a proper one, was another question.

The motion was disagreed to. New Jersey, Delaware, Pennsylvania, and Virginia, having voted in the affirmative, and the other States in the negative.

NOTE. — These remarks of Mr. Madison, and the vote of that State on Dr. McClung's proposition, are understood to have been given, rather in compliment to the mover than as expressing the real sentiments of the parties.

On motion by Mr. MORRIS, the whole subject of the constitution of the executive was reconsidered.

Mr. ELLSWORTH moved to strike out "to be chosen by the national legislature," and insert "to be chosen by electors, to be appointed by the legislatures of the States," which was agreed to. Subsequently reconsidered, and appointment by the national legislature was reinstated.

"To be ineligible a second term," disagreed to.

To continue "seven years," disagreed to, and "six years" substituted.

"To be removable by impeachment," to receive fixed compensation, and "to be paid out of the national treasury," and the qualified veto, were agreed to.

On Col. MASON'S motion, the term of seven years, to be ineligible to a second term, was reinstated.

Referred to the committee of detail, who reported as follows: —

"The executive power of the United States shall be vested in a single person. His style shall be, 'The President of the United States of America,' and his title shall be, 'His Excellency.' He shall be elected by ballot by the legislature. He shall hold his office during the term of seven years; but shall not be elected a second time."

The clause, "he shall be elected by ballot, by the legislature," being up,

Mr. CARROLL moved to strike out "legislature," and insert "people." Pennsylvania and Delaware alone supported the motion.

Mr. RUTLEDGE moved to insert "joint" before "ballot."

Messrs. Sherman, Dayton, and Brearly, opposed, and

Messrs. Gorham, Wilson, Langdon, and Madison, supported the motion, which prevailed.

Mr. DAYTON then moved to add — "*each State having one vote,*" which was lost. Yeas — Connecticut, New Jersey, Delaware, Maryland, and Georgia, 5. Nays — New Hampshire, Massachusetts, Pennsylvania, Virginia, North Carolina, and South Carolina, 6.

Mr. G. MORRIS expressed strong opposition to the election of the President by the legislature, and proposed to substitute "*he shall be chosen by electors to be chosen by the people of the several States.*" Disagreed to. Yeas 5, nays 6.

In this condition, the subject was referred to the committee of one from each State, — raised on motion of Mr. SHERMAN, to consider and report on the unfinished parts of the Constitution. The committee consisted of Messrs. Gilman, King, Sherman, Brearly, Morris, Dickinson, Carroll, Madison, Williamson, Butler, and Baldwin. The committee was appointed on the 31st of August, and on the 4th of September, reported the following: —

"The executive power of the United States shall be vested in a single person. His style shall be, 'The President of the United States of America.' And his title shall be 'His Excellency.' He shall hold his office during the term of four years, and together with the vice-president, chosen for the same term, be elected in the following manner, namely: Each State shall appoint, in such manner as its legislature may direct, a number of electors equal to the whole number of senators and members of the House of Representatives, to which the State may be entitled in the legislature.

"The electors shall meet in their respective States, and vote by ballot for two persons, of whom one at least shall not be an inhabitant of the same State with themselves.

And they shall make a list of all the persons voted for, and of the number of votes for each; which list they shall sign and certify, and transmit sealed to the seat of government of the United States, directed to the president of the Senate. The president of the Senate shall, in that house, open all the certificates, and the votes shall be then and there counted. The person having the greatest number of votes shall be the President, if such number be a majority of that of the electors; and if there be more than one who have such majority, and have an equal number of votes, then the Senate shall immediately choose, by ballot, one of them for President; but if no person have a majority, then, from the five highest on the list, the Senate shall choose, by ballot, the President; and in every case, after the choice of the President, the person having the greatest number of votes, shall be vice-president, but if there should remain two or more, who have equal votes, the Senate shall choose from them the vice-president. The legislature may determine the time of choosing and assembling the electors, and the manner of certifying and transmitting the votes."

Mr. Gorham thought it objectionable that the next highest candidate after the election of President should become the vice-president without referring the decision to the Senate, as an obscure man, with few votes, might obtain the office.

Mr. Sherman.—"The object of this clause of the report was, to get rid of the ineligibility which was attached to the mode of election by the legislature, and to render the executive independent of the legislature."

Mr. Madison suggested, as objections to allowing the elections to be made from the *five highest candidates*, that "the attention of electors would be turned too much to making candidates," thereby consigning the election altogether to the Senate.

Mr. RANDOLPH and Mr. PINCKNEY called for an explanation from the committee, of their reasons for changing the mode of election which had been previously agreed to by the Convention.

Mr. G. MORRIS explained. — "The first was, the danger of intrigue and faction, if the appointment should be made by the legislature. The next was, the inconvenience of an ineligibility required by that mode, in order to lessen its evils. The third was, the difficulty of establishing a court of impeachments, other than the Senate, which would not be so proper for the trial, nor the other branch for the impeachment of the President, if appointed by the legislature. In the fourth place, nobody had appeared to be satisfied with an appointment by the legislature. In the fifth place, many were anxious even for an immediate choice by the people. And finally, the sixth reason was, the indispensable necessity of making the executive independent of the legislature."

Colonel MASON "confessed that the plan of the committee had removed some capital objections, particularly the danger of cabal and corruption. It was liable, however, to this strong objection, that nineteen times in twenty, the President would be chosen by the Senate, an improper body for the purpose."

Mr. PINCKNEY objected, that it in fact threw the appointment into the hands of the Senate.

Mr. WILSON regarded this as the most difficult question the Convention had had to decide. He thought the present plan a valuable improvement on the former. "He thought it might be better, however, to refer the eventual appointment to the *legislature* than to the Senate, and to confine it to a smaller number than five candidates."

Mr. RANDOLPH "preferred the former mode; but if the

change was to be made," he preferred that the eventual election should be made by the *legislature.*

GOUVERNEUR MORRIS. — "The Senate was preferred, because fewer could then say to the President, '*You owe your appointment to us.*'"

Mr. PINCKNEY and Mr. RUTLEDGE expressed their objections to the mode reported by the committee, and their preference for adhering to the mode of election by joint-ballot of the legislature and the ineligibility to a reëlection.

On the motion to reject this part of the report, North Carolina and South Carolina alone supported it.

Mr. WILSON moved to strike out "Senate," and insert "legislature," as the body on whom the contingent election should devolve, which was lost. Yeas — Pennsylvania, Virginia, South Carolina; the rest nay.

Mr. GERRY "suggested that the eventual election should be made by six senators and seven representatives, to be chosen by joint ballot of the two houses," but the suggestion was not favorably received.

On motion of Mr. KING and Mr. GERRY, the following words were added: —

"But no person shall be appointed an elector who is a member of the legislature of the United States, or who holds any office of trust or profit under the United States."

Motions by Mr. SPAIGHT and Mr. WILLIAMSON for extending the term to "seven" and "six" years having been rejected, "four," was agreed to.

The same members then moved "that the electors meet at the seat of the government," with the view of requiring them to make an election, without a reference to the Senate. North Carolina alone supported the motion.

Mr. WILLIAMSON moved to substitute for "Senate," "the legislature voting by States."

Mr. SHERMAN concurring in this view, moved to strike out "the Senate shall immediately choose," and substitute: —

"The House of Representatives shall immediately choose by ballot, one of them for President, the members from each State having one vote." This, after considerable debate, was agreed to, and on motion of Mr. KING, the words, — "But a quorum for this purpose shall consist of a member or members from two thirds of the States," — and on motion of Mr. GERRY, the words, — "and a concurrence of a majority of all the States shall be necessary to make a choice," were severally added.

It was then sent to the committee on style and revision, who gave it the form in which it was adopted.

NOTE. — The time of choosing the electors, is the Tuesday next after the first Monday in November. 5 Stat. 721.

The electors are to meet on the first Wednesday in December. 1 Stat. 239.

ARTICLE II.

SECTION I.

Clause 5.—No person except a natural born citizen, or a citizen of the United States, at the time of the adoption of this Constitution, shall be eligible to the office of President; neither shall any person be eligible to that office who shall not have attained to the age of thirty-five years, and been fourteen years a resident within the United States.

Mr. GERRY moved, "that the committee on detail be instructed to report proper qualifications for the President," &c.

Mr. RUTLEDGE, from the committee, reported:—

"He shall be of the age of thirty-five years, and a citizen of the United States, and shall have been an inhabitant thereof for twenty-one years."

This was subsequently referred, with such parts of reports as had not been acted on, to a committee of a member from each State, who reported this clause of the Constitution as it stands.

ARTICLE II.

SECTION I.

Clause 6.—In case of the removal of the President from office, or of his death, resignation, or inability to discharge the powers and duties of the said office, the same shall devolve on the Vice-President, and the Congress may by law provide for the case of removal, death, resignation, or inability, both of the President and Vice-President, declaring what officer shall then act as President, and such officer shall act accordingly, until the disability be removed, or a President shall be elected.

Mr. PINCKNEY'S PLAN.—"In case of his removal, death, resignation, or disability, the president of the Senate shall exercise the duties of his office until another President be chosen, and in case of the death of the President of the Senate, the speaker of the House of Delegates shall do so."

The committee on detail reported the following:—

"In case of his removal [by impeachment], death, resignation, or disability to discharge the powers and duties of his office, the president of the Senate shall exercise those powers and duties, until another President of the United States be chosen, or until the disability of the President be removed."

Mr. Morris and Mr. Madison objected to the provision making the president of the Senate provisional President of the United States, — the former suggesting the chief justice.

Mr. Williamson thought this subject should be left with Congress.

Mr. Dickinson asked, — "What is the extent of the term disability? and who is to judge of it?"

In this condition the subject was sent to the committee on the unfinished reports, &c., who reported the following: —

"In case of his removal, as aforesaid, death, absence, resignation, or inability to discharge the powers or duties of his office, the vice-president shall exercise those powers and duties, until another President be chosen, or until the inability of the President be removed."

This was amended, on motion of Mr. Randolph (and Mr. Madison), by adding —

"The legislature may declare by law what officer of the United States shall act as President, in case of the death, resignation, or disability of the President and vice-president, and such officer shall act accordingly, until such disability be removed or a President shall be elected."

In this shape the subject was sent to the committee of style, &c.

Note. — By the act of 1792, in case of vacancy in the offices of President and vice-president, the president of the Senate, and if there be none, the speaker of the House of Representatives, assumes the duties of President, until an election is had.

By the act of 1845, the electors of President and vice-president, are to be chosen on the Tuesday after the first Monday of November, in all the States.

ARTICLE II.

SECTION I.

Clause 7.—The President shall, at stated times, receive for his services, a compensation, which shall neither be increased or diminished during the period for which he shall have been elected, and he shall not receive within that period any other emolument from the United States, or any of them.

Before he enter on the execution of his office, he shall take the following oath or affirmation:—

"I do solemnly swear (or affirm) that I will faithfully execute the office of President of the United States, and will to the best of my ability, preserve, protect, and defend the Constitution of the United States."

Mr. RANDOLPH'S PLAN.—"To receive punctually, at stated times, a fixed compensation for the services rendered, in which no increase or diminution shall be made, so as to affect the magistracy existing at the time of the increase or diminution."

Mr. PINCKNEY'S Plan contained a similar provision—as did also Mr. PATTERSON'S.

Dr. FRANKLIN proposed to substitute the following:—

"Whose necessary expenses shall be defrayed, but who

shall receive no stipend, fee, or reward whatsoever for his services."

This was seconded by Col. HAMILTON, but no further action had on it.

These "plans" also provided for the oath "faithfully to execute the office," &c.; but the latter clause, "and will to the best of my judgment and power preserve, protect, and defend the Constitution of the United States," was added on motion of Col. MASON, seconded by Mr. MADISON.

ARTICLE II.

SECTION II.

Clause 1.—The President shall be commander-in-chief of the army and navy of the United States, and of the militia of the several States when called into the actual service of the United States; he may require the opinion, in writing, of the principal officer in each of the executive departments, upon any subject relating to the duties of their respective offices; and he shall have power to grant reprieves and pardons for offences against the United States, except in cases of impeachment.

Mr. PINCKNEY'S PLAN.—"He shall be commander-in-chief of the army and navy, and of the militia of the several States."

Mr. SHERMAN moved to amend the first part of this clause, by adding, in regard to the militia, "when called into the actual service of the United States," which was agreed to.

Mr. ELLSWORTH suggested that a council ought to be provided for the President, and proposed that it should consist of "the president of the Senate, the chief justice, and the ministers as they might be established for the departments of foreign and domestic affairs, war, finance, and marine; who should advise but not conclude the President."

Mr. PINCKNEY expressed the opinion that "the President should be at liberty to call for advice or not, as he might choose. He remarked, 'Give him an able council and it will thwart him; a weak one and he will shelter himself under their sanction.'"

Mr. GERRY was opposed to heads of departments or the chief justice having any thing to do with business connected with legislation.

Mr. DICKINSON was of opinion that the heads of departments and other principal officers should be appointed by the legislature, but if made by the executive they would not be suitable councillors.

Mr. GOUVERNEUR MORRIS submitted, for the consideration of the committee of detail, the following: —

"To assist the President in conducting the public affairs, there shall be a council of State composed of the following officers: —

"The chief justice of the supreme court, who shall, from time to time, recommend such alterations of, and additions to, the laws of the United States as may, in his opinion, be necessary to the due administration of justice, and such as may promote useful learning, and inculcate sound morality throughout the Union. He shall be president of the council, in the absence of the President."

He proposed that the other members of the council should consist of "the heads of the department of domestic affairs, of commerce and finance, of foreign affairs, of war, and of marine — all to be appointed during pleasure by the President.

"The President shall appoint a secretary of state, to hold his office during pleasure; who shall be secretary to the council of State, and also public secretary to the

President. It shall be his duty to prepare all public despatches from the President, which he shall countersign.

"The President may, from time to time, submit any matter to the discussion of the council of State, and he may require the written opinions of any one or more of the members. But he shall in all cases exercise his own judgment, and either conform to such opinions or not as he may think proper; and every officer above mentioned shall be responsible for his opinion on the affairs relating to his particular department."

The committee reported the following: —

"The President of the United States shall have a privy council, which shall consist of the president of the Senate, the speaker of the House of Representatives, the chief justice of the Supreme Court, and the principal officer in the respective departments of foreign affairs, domestic affairs, war, marine, and finance, as such departments of office shall, from time to time, be established; whose duty it shall be to advise him in matters respecting the execution of his office, which he shall think proper to lay before them; but their advice shall not conclude him nor affect his responsibility for the measures which he shall adopt."

This proposition having been sent to the committee of States, they reported, in lieu of it, the following, to be added to the powers of the President: —

"And may require the opinion in writing, of the principal officer in each of the executive departments, upon any subject relating to the duties of their respective offices."

Col. MASON said, "That in rejecting a council to the President, we were about to try an experiment, on which the most despotic government had never ventured. The grand seignior himself had his divan."

He moved to instruct the committee of States "to prepare a clause or clauses for establishing an executive council, as a council of State for the President of the United States; to consist of six members, two of which from the eastern, two from the middle, and two from the southern States, with a rotation of office similar to those of the Senate; such council to be appointed by the legislature, or the Senate."

Dr. FRANKLIN seconded the motion. "We seemed," he said, "too much to fear cabals in appointments by a number, and to have too much confidence in those of single persons. Experience showed that caprice, the intrigues of favorites and mistresses, were, nevertheless, the means most prevalent in monarchies. . . . He thought a council would not only check a bad President, but be a relief to a good one."

Mr. MORRIS. — "The question of a council was considered in the committee, where it was judged that the President, by persuading his council to concur in wrong measures, would acquire their protection for them."

Mr. MADISON, Mr. DICKINSON, and Mr. WILSON favored the motion for a council, but it was negatived — Maryland, South Carolina, and Georgia, yea; the rest nay, and the clause was agreed to, as reported.

Judicial Constructions. — The President may pardon as well before trial and conviction as afterward. 6 Opin. 20. He may grant a conditional pardon. Ex parte Welles, 18 How. 307. See also, 5 How. 368, 7 Pet. 161. The pardoning power includes that of remitting fines, penalties, and forfeitures under the revenue laws. 6 Opin. 329. See also, 6 Opin. 393; 4 id. 573; 3 id. 317, 362. He has no power to remit the forfeiture of a bail-bond. 4 id. 144. A pardon is a private, though official act; it must be delivered to and accepted by the criminal. United

States *v.* Wilson, 7 Peters, 150. He can order a *nolle prosequi* at any stage of a criminal proceeding in the name of the United States. 5 Opin. 729.

The President is not obliged to take, personally, the command of the militia . . . but may place them under command of officers of the army of the United States. Any officer of the army may, therefore, be required, by orders emanating from the President, to perform the appropriate duties of his station in the militia, when in the service of the United States. 2 Opin. 711; 2 Story, Const. 1490.

ARTICLE II.

SECTION II.

Clause 2. — He shall have power, by and with the advice and consent of the Senate, to make treaties, provided two thirds of the Senators present concur; and he shall nominate, and, by and with the advice and consent of the Senate, shall appoint ambassadors, other public ministers and consuls, judges of the Supreme Court, and all other officers of the United States whose appointments are not herein otherwise provided for, and which shall be established by law; but the Congress may by law vest the appointment of such inferior officers as they think proper, in the President alone, in the courts of law, or in the heads of departments.

Clause 3. — The President shall have power to fill up all vacancies that may happen during the recess of the Senate, by granting commissions which shall expire at the end of their next session.

MR. PINCKNEY'S PLAN. — " The Senate shall have the sole and exclusive power to declare war, and to make treaties, and to appoint ambassadors, and other ministers to foreign nations, and judges of the Supreme Court."

First Report of Committee of the Whole. — That the national executive have power "to appoint to offices in cases not otherwise provided for."

Report of Committee of Detail. — The President "shall commission all the officers of the United States; and shall appoint officers in all cases not otherwise provided for by this Constitution."

Mr. MADISON suggested that the President should have an agency in making treaties.

Mr. DICKINSON moved, as a substitute for "and shall appoint," &c., "and he shall appoint to all offices established by this constitution, except in cases herein otherwise provided for; and to all offices which may hereafter be created by law." Agreed to.

These propositions having been referred to the committee of eleven, Mr. BREARY, from the committee, reported as follows: —

"The President, by and with the advice and consent of the Senate, shall have power to make treaties; and he shall nominate, and by and with the advice and consent of the Senate, shall appoint ambassadors and other public ministers, judges of the Supreme Court, and all other officers of the United States, whose appointments are not otherwise herein provided for. But no treaty shall be made without the consent of two thirds of the members present."

On motion of Mr. SPAIGHT, the following was added: —

"The President shall have power to fill all vacancies that may happen during the recess of the Senate, by granting commissions, which shall expire at the end of the next session of the Senate."

On motion of Mr. MADISON, "except treaties of peace," was inserted, so as not to require two thirds to make such treaties. He then moved to authorize two thirds of the Senate to make treaties without the President, but it was not agreed to. After further debate, "except treaties of peace," was again stricken out.

On motion of Mr. G. MORRIS, this clause was inserted: —

"But the Congress may by law vest the appointment of such inferior officers as they think proper, in the President alone, in the courts of law, or in the heads of departments."

Judicial Constructions. — 1. The nomination is the sole act of the President, and is completely voluntary.

2. The appointment. This is also the act of the President, though it can only be performed by and with the advice and consent of the Senate.

3. The commission. To grant a commission to a person appointed, might perhaps be deemed a duty enjoined by the Constitution.

The act of appointing to office, and commissioning the person appointed, are distinct acts.

The Constitution contemplates cases where the law may direct the President to commission an officer, appointed by the courts or by the heads of departments. In such a case, to issue a commission would be apparently a duty distinct from the appointment, the performance of which, perhaps, could not be legally refused.

Where the officer is not removable at the will of the executive, the appointment is not revocable, and cannot be annulled; it has conferred legal rights which cannot be resumed. Marbury *v.* Madison, 1 Cranch, 137–162.

The power to appoint necessarily includes the power to remove. *Ex parte* Heman, 13 Peters, 259. See 2 Story, Const. 1538.

He may fill, during the recess of the Senate, a vacancy which occurred during the previous session (1 Opin. 631), or a vacancy which has occurred by the expiration of a former temporary appointment, the Senate having neglected to act on a nomination to fill the place. 3 Ibid. 673; 4 Ibid. 523–530.

ARTICLE II.

SECTION III.

He shall from time to time give to the Congress information of the state of the Union, and recommend to their consideration such measures as he shall judge necessary and expedient; he may, on extraordinary occasions, convene both Houses, or either of them, and in case of disagreement between them, with respect to the time of adjournment, he may adjourn them to such time as he shall think proper; he shall receive ambassadors and other public ministers; he shall take care that the laws be faithfully executed, and shall commission all the officers of the United States.

Mr. PINCKNEY'S PLAN. — He shall, from time to time, give information to the legislature, of the state of the Union, and recommend to their consideration the measures he may think necessary. He shall take care that the laws of the United States be duly executed. He shall commission all the officers of the United States. He shall receive public ministers from foreign nations.

Mr. RUTLEDGE, from the committee of detail, reported to add: —

"He may convene them [the legislature] on extraordinary occasions. In case of disagreement between the two houses, with regard to the time of adjournment, he may adjourn them to such time as he may think proper."

Mr. McHenry moved to strike out, "he may convene them," and insert, "he may convene both or either of the houses," in order to provide for convening the Senate separately.

Mr. Wilson opposed the motion, on the ground that "it implied that the Senate might be in session when the legislature was not, which he thought improper."

The motion prevailed. Yeas — New Hampshire, Connecticut, New Jersey, Delaware, Maryland, North Carolina, and Georgia, 7. Nays — Massachusetts, Virginia, Pennsylvania, and South Carolina, 4.

Note. — He has power to appoint commissioners and agents to make investigations required by acts or resolutions of Congress. 4 Opin. 248.

ARTICLE II.

SECTION IV.

The President, Vice-President, and all the civil officers of the United States, shall be removed from office on impeachment for, and conviction of, treason, bribery, and other high crimes and misdemeanors.

The Virginia, the South Carolina, and the New Jersey plans for the federal government, provided severally for the impeachment of the executive and other civil officers, before the Supreme Court.

NOTE. — A senator or representative in Congress is not such a civil officer. Blount's Trial, 22, 102; Whart. State Trials, 260, 316. 1 Story, Const. 793, 802. Nor is a territorial judge, being not a constitutional, but a legislative officer merely. 3 Opin. 409.

ARTICLE III.

SECTION I.

The judicial power of the United States shall be vested in one Supreme Court, and in such inferior courts as the Congress may from time to time ordain and establish. The judges, both of the supreme and inferior courts, shall hold their offices during good behavior, and shall, at stated times, receive for their services a compensation, which shall not be diminished during their continuance in office.

Mr. RANDOLPH'S PLAN.—"That a national judiciary be established; to consist of one or more supreme tribunals and of inferior tribunals; to be chosen by the national legislature," &c.

On motion of Mr. MADISON, "appointment by the legislature" was stricken out.

Mr. PINCKNEY'S PLAN.—"The legislature of the United States shall have the power, and it shall be their duty to establish such courts of law, equity, and admiralty as shall be necessary," &c.

Mr. Randolph's resolution being under consideration in committee of the whole, the words "inferior tribunals" were stricken out, and on motion of Mr. WILSON, the words, "that the national legislature be empowered to institute inferior tribunals," were added.

Mr. MADISON moved, "that the appointment of the judges should be made by the Senate." Agreed to, *nem. con.*

Mr. HAMILTON'S PLAN — suggested in a speech on the general subject. "The supreme judicial authority to be vested in judges to hold their offices during good behavior, with adequate and permanent salaries. The legislature of the United States to have power to institute courts in each State, for the determination of all matters of general concern."

Mr. PATTERSON'S (the New Jersey and New York) PLAN. — "That a federal judiciary be established, to consist of a supreme tribunal, the judges of which, to be appointed by the executive and to hold their offices during good behavior; to receive punctually, at stated times, a fixed compensation for their services, in which no increase nor diminution shall be made, so as to affect the persons actually in office at the time of such increase or diminution."

The committee of the whole reported the following: — "That a national judiciary be established, to consist of one supreme tribunal, the judges of which shall be appointed by the second branch of the national legislature; to hold their offices during good behavior, and to receive punctually, at stated times, a fixed compensation for their services, in which no increase or diminution shall be made, so as to affect the persons actually in office at the time of such increase or diminution.

"That the national legislature be empowered to appoint inferior tribunals."

Mr. GORHAM moved to amend, by substituting the following, for the mode of appointing the judges: —

"That the judges be nominated and appointed by the executive, by and with the advice and consent of the second branch."

This proposition was at first rejected by the Convention, but subsequently adopted.

On motion of Mr. G. MORRIS, the words "increase or" were stricken out, so as to leave it in the power of the legislature to increase, but not diminish the salaries.

The subject was then referred to the committee of detail, who reported as follows: —

"The judicial power of the United States shall be vested in one Supreme Court, and in such inferior courts as shall, when necessary, from time to time, be constituted by the legislature of the United States."

"The judges of the Supreme Court and of the inferior courts shall hold their offices during good behavior. They shall at stated times, receive for their services a compensation, which shall not be diminished during their continuance in office."

Mr. DICKINSON proposed to add, — "Provided, that they may be removed by the executive, on application by the Senate and House of Representatives."

Connecticut alone supported the motion.

A motion to reinstate the words "increased or" before "diminished," was supported by Virginia alone.

Judicial Constructions.— The jurisdiction of the courts of the United States depends entirely on the constitution and laws of the United States. Am. Ins. Co. *v.* Canter, 1 Peters, 511.

Congress has the power to define the jurisdiction of the inferior courts. 8 How. 448.

A territorial court, held by judges whose appointments are for four years, cannot be the depository of any part of the judicial power conferred by the Constitution on the general government. Am. Ins. Co. *v.* Bales of Cotton, 1 Peters, 511.

ARTICLE III.

SECTION II.

Clause 1.—The judicial power shall extend to all cases, in law and equity, arising under this Constitution, the laws of the United States, and treaties made, or which shall be made, under their authority; to all cases affecting ambassadors, other public ministers and consuls; to all cases of admiralty and maritime jurisdiction; to controversies to which the United States shall be a party; to controversies between two or more States; between a State and citizens of another State; between citizens of different States; between citizens of the same State claiming lands under grants of different States; and between a State, or the citizens thereof, and foreign States, citizens, or subjects.

Clause 2.—In all cases affecting ambassadors, other public ministers, and consuls, and those in which a State shall be a party, the Supreme Court shall have original jurisdiction. In all the other cases before mentioned, the Supreme Court shall have appellate jurisdiction, both as to law and fact, with such exceptions, and under such regulations, as the Congress shall make.

Mr. RANDOLPH'S PLAN. — "That the jurisdiction of the inferior tribunals shall be to have and determine, in the first instance, and of the supreme tribunal, in the *dernier resort*, all piracies and felonies on the high seas; captures from an enemy; cases in which foreigners, or citizens of other States, applying to such jurisdictions may be interested; or which respect the collection of the national revenue, impeachment of any national officers, and questions which may involve the national peace and harmony."

Mr. PINCKNEY'S PLAN. — "One of these courts shall be termed the Supreme Court; whose jurisdiction shall extend to all cases arising under the laws of the United States, or affecting ambassadors, other public ministers and consuls; to the trial or impeachment of officers of the United States; to all cases of admiralty and maritime jurisdiction. In cases of impeachment affecting ambassadors and other public ministers, this jurisdiction shall be original; and in all other cases, appellate."

Mr. HAMILTON'S PLAN. — "This court to have original jurisdiction in all cases of capture, and an appellate jurisdiction in all cases in which the revenues of the general government or the citizens of foreign nations are concerned."

Mr. PATTERSON'S PLAN. — "That the judiciary so established shall have authority to hear and determine, in the first instance, on all impeachments of federal officers, and by way of appeal, in the *dernier resort*, in all cases touching the rights of ambassadors; in all cases of captures from the enemy; in all cases of piracies and felonies on the high seas; in all cases in which foreigners may be interested; in the construction of any treaty or treaties, or which may arise on any of the acts for the regulation of trade, or the collection of the federal revenue."

These several propositions having been considered in

committee of the whole, the committee recommended the following: "That the jurisdiction of the national judiciary shall extend to all cases which respect the collection of the revenue, impeachments of any national officers, and questions which involve the national peace and harmony."

Mr. PINCKNEY proposed to add,—

"The jurisdiction of the Supreme Court shall be extended to all controversies between the United States and an individual State, or the United States and the citizens of an individual State."

These propositions being approved by the Convention, were referred to the committee of detail, who embodied them in the following form:—

"The jurisdiction of the Supreme Court shall extend to all cases arising under laws passed by the legislature of the United States; to all cases affecting ambassadors, other public ministers and consuls; to the trial of impeachments of all officers of the United States; to all cases of admiralty and maritime jurisdiction; to controversies between two or more States (except such as shall regard territory or jurisdiction); between a State and citizens of another State; between citizens of different States, and between a State or citizens thereof and foreign States, citizens, or subjects. In cases of impeachment, cases affecting ambassadors, other public ministers and consuls, and those in which a State shall be a party, this jurisdiction shall be original. In all other cases before mentioned, it shall be appellate, with such exceptions and under such regulations as the legislature shall make.

"The legislature may assign any part of the jurisdiction above mentioned (except the trial of the President of the United States), in the manner and under the limitations which it shall think proper, to such inferior courts as it shall constitute from time to time."

On motion of Dr. JOHNSON, the words "both in law and equity," were inserted in the first paragraph.

The words "this constitution and the," were inserted in the first clause, on motion of Dr. JOHNSON.

Mr. MADISON says, "the motion of Dr. Johnson was agreed to *nem. con.*, it being generally supposed that the jurisdiction given was constructively limited to cases of a judiciary nature."

The last clause of the committee's report was stricken out, and then the clause was sent to the committee of style and revision.

Judicial Constructions. — Congress may pass all laws which are necessary for giving the most complete effect to the exercise of the admiralty and maritime jurisdiction granted in the Constitution to the United States; but the general jurisdiction, subject to this grant, adheres to the territory, as a portion of sovereignty not yet given away. 3 Wheat. 336.

Jurisdiction is given to the courts of the United States in two classes of cases. In the first, their jurisdiction depends on the *character of the cause*, whoever may be the parties. This class comprehends all cases in law and equity arising, &c. In the second class, the jurisdiction depends entirely on the *character of the parties.* In this class are comprehended controversies between, &c. If these be the parties, it is entirely unimportant who may be the subjects of the controversy. A case in law or equity consists of the rights of the one party as well as of the other, and it is said to arise under the Constitution or a law of the United States, whenever its correct decision depends on the construction of either. Osborn *v.* United States, 9 Wheat. 819. See also, 6 Wheat. 378.

The original jurisdiction of the Supreme Court cannot be enlarged, but its appellate jurisdiction may be exercised in every case cognizable under the 3d Article of the Constitution, &c. 6 Wheat. 397.

The executive department may constitutionally execute every law which the legislature may constitutionally make, and the judicial department may receive from the legislature the power of construing every such law. 9 Wheat. 733.

Congress cannot by law assign the judicial department any duties but such as are of a judicial character; that is, appointing the judges of the circuit court, to receive and determine upon claims of persons to be placed on the pension list. 2 Dall. 409.

The words of the Constitution must be taken to refer to the admiralty and maritime jurisdiction of England. 4 Dall. 426, 429.

The authority given to the Supreme Court, by the act establishing the judicial courts of the United States, to issue writs of *mandamus* to public officers, is not warranted by the Constitution. 1 Cranch, 176.

An act of Congress cannot invest the Supreme Court with an authority not warranted by the Constitution. 1 Cranch, 175, 176.

The legislature of a State cannot annul the judgment or determine the jurisdiction of the courts of the United States. 5 Cranch, 115.

Congress cannot vest any portion of the judicial power of the United States, except in courts ordained and established by itself. 1 Wheat. 304, 380.

The grant in the Constitution, to the United States, of all cases of admiralty and maritime jurisdiction, does not extend to a cession of the waters in which those cases may arise, or of the general jurisdiction over them. 3 Wheat. 336.

ARTICLE III.

SECTION II.

Clause 3. — The trial of all crimes, except in cases of impeachment, shall be by jury; and such trial shall be held in the State where the said crimes shall have been committed; but when not committed within any State, the trial shall be at such place or places as the Congress may by law have directed.

Mr. PINCKNEY'S PLAN. — "All criminal offences, except in cases of impeachment, shall be tried in the State where they shall be committed. The trials shall be open and public, and shall be by jury."

This clause does not appear to have attracted any notice in the Convention, and was probably introduced by the committee of style and revision, upon their own motion.

ARTICLE III.

SECTION III.

Treason against the United States, shall consist only in levying war against them, or in adhering to their enemies, giving them aid and comfort. No person shall be convicted of treason unless on the testimony of two witnesses to the same overt act, or on confession in open court.

The Congress shall have power to declare the punishment of treason, but no attainder of treason shall work corruption of blood, or forfeiture except during the life of the person attainted.

Mr. Pinckney's Plan. — " The legislature of the United States shall have the power to declare the punishment of treason, which shall consist only in levying war against the United States, or any of them, or in adhering to their enemies. No person shall be convicted of treason but by the testimony of two witnesses."

Committee on detail recommended the following: —

" Treason against the United States shall consist only in levying war against the United States or any of them, and in adhering to the enemies of the United States or any of them. The legislature of the United States shall have power to declare the punishment of treason. No person shall be convicted of treason unless on the testimony of two witnesses. No attainder of treason shall work corruption of blood, nor forfeiture, except during the life of the person attainted."

On motion of Mr. WILSON, the words "or any of them" were stricken out, and the words "to the same overt act," after "witnesses" were added.

Mr. WILSON and others still thought the clause ambiguous, and it was modified by general consent, so as to read, "Treason against the United States shall consist only in levying war against them, or in adhering to their enemies."

Col. MASON moved to add the words, "*giving them aid and comfort*," and Mr. L. MARTIN the words "or on confession in open court;" both of which motions were agreed to.

Mr. DICKINSON thought the definition still vague, and suggested whether the two witnesses should concur in the same "overt act."

Mr. MADISON expressed the opinion that the definition of treason was too restricted, and that more latitude over the subject should be left to the discretion of the legislature.

Mr. MORRIS thought Congress should have the *exclusive* right to declare what should constitute treason against the United States. In case of a contest between the United States and a particular State, the people of the latter must, under the disjunctive terms of the clause, be traitor to one or other authority.

In order to remove this difficulty, the words "or any of them" were stricken out.

Mr. MADISON.—"This has not removed the embarrassment. The same act might be treason against the United States, as here defined, and against a particular State under its laws."

Dr. Johnson "was of opinion that there could be no treason against a particular State — the sovereignty being in the Union."

Mr. Morris suggested the form in which the clause was finally adopted.

Judicial Constructions. — There must be an actual levying of war; a conspiracy to subvert the government by force is not treason; nor is the mere enlistment of men, who are not assembled, a levying of war. *Ex parte* Bolman, 4 Cr. 75. No man can be convicted of treason who was not present when the war was levied. 2 Burr's Trial, 401, 439.

ARTICLE IV.

SECTION I.

Clause 1.—Full faith and credit shall be given in each State to the public acts, records, and judicial proceedings of every other State. And the Congress may by general laws prescribe the manner in which such acts, records, and proceedings shall be proved, and the effect thereof.

Articles of Confederation.—"Full faith and credit shall be given in each of these States to the records, acts, and judicial proceedings of the courts and magistrates of every other State."

The committee of detail gave the article the following form:—

"Full faith shall be given in each State to the acts of the legislatures, and to records and judicial proceedings of the courts and magistrates of every other State."

Mr. WILLIAMSON preferred the provision in the Articles of Confederation.

Mr. PINCKNEY wished the article to be recommitted, with a proposition "to establish uniform laws upon the subject of bankruptcies," &c.

Mr. RANDOLPH submitted the following:—

"Whenever the act of any State, whether legislative, executive, or judiciary, shall be attested and exemplified, under the seal thereof, such attestation and exemplification shall be deemed, in other States, as full proof of the existence of that act; and its operation shall be binding in every other State in all cases to which it may relate, and which are within the cognizance and jurisdiction of the State wherein the said act was done."

Mr. G. MORRIS moved the following:—

"Full faith ought to be given, in each State, to the public acts, records, and judicial proceedings of every other State; and the legislature shall, by general laws, determine the proof and effect of such acts, records, and proceedings."

These propositions were all referred to a select committee, who reported the following:—

"Full faith and credit ought to be given, in each State, to the public acts, records, and judicial proceedings, of every other State; and the legislature shall, by general laws, prescribe the manner in which such acts, records, and proceedings shall be proved, and the effect which judgments, obtained in one State, shall have in another."

Mr. G. MORRIS, moved to strike out all after the word "effect" in the last line, and insert "thereof."

Dr. JOHNSON, "thought the amendment as worded, would authorize the general legislature to declare the effect of legislative acts of one State in another State."

Mr. RANDOLPH "considered it as strengthening the general objection against the plan, that its definition of the powers of the government was so loose as to give it opportunities of usurping all State powers. He was for not going further than the report, which enables the legislature to provide for the effect of *judgments*."

The amendment of Mr. Morris prevailed. Yeas 6; Nays 3 (Maryland, Virginia, Georgia).

On Mr. MADISON'S motion, "shall" was substituted for "ought to," and then the article was agreed to.

Judicial Construction. — A judgment of a State court has the same credit, validity, and effect, in every court within the United States, which it had in the State in which it was rendered. Hampton *v.* McConnell, 3 Wheat. 234.

They have *only such* effect as they possessed in the State in which they were taken. Bank of Ala. *v.* Dalton, 9 How. 528. See also, 1 Stat. 129, and 9 How. 528.

ARTICLE IV.

SECTION II.

Clause 1.—The citizens of each State shall be entitled to all privileges and immunities of citizens in the several States.

Articles of Confederation.—"The better to secure and perpetuate mutual friendship and intercourse among the people of the different States in this Union, the free inhabitants of each of these States, paupers, vagabonds, and fugitives from justice excepted, shall be entitled to all privileges and immunities of free citizens in the several States; and the people of each State shall have free ingress and regress to and from any other State, and shall enjoy therein all the privileges of trade and commerce, subject to the same duties, impositions, and restrictions as the inhabitants thereof respectively, provided that such restriction shall not extend so far as to prevent the removal of property imported into any State, to any other State of which the owner is an inhabitant; provided, also, that no impositions, duties, or restriction shall be laid by any State, on the property of the United States, or either of them."

The committee on detail, reported the clause as it stands in the Constitution.

Gen. PINCKNEY expressed his dissatisfaction with it as

reported. He wished "some provision should be included in favor of slave property."

On its adoption, South Carolina voted nay, and Georgia was divided. All the other States voted in the affirmative

---

Judicial Constructions. — Since the adoption of the Constitution, no State can, by any subsequent law, make a foreigner, or any other description of persons, citizens of the United States, nor entitle them to the rights and privileges secured to citizens by that instrument. Dred Scott *v.* Sanford, 19 How. 393.

Citizenship, when spoken of in the Constitution, in reference to the jurisdiction of federal courts, means nothing more than residence. Gas. *v.* Bal., 6 Pet. 761.

A free negro, of the African race, whose ancestors were brought to this country and sold as slaves, is not a citizen within the meaning of the Constitution. Dred Scott *v.* Sanford, 19 How. 393.

It does not embrace privileges conferred by the local laws of a State. Conner *v.* Elliot, 18 How. 591.

ARTICLE IV.

SECTION II.

Clause 2.—A person charged in any State with treason, felony, or other crime, who shall flee from justice, and be found in another State, shall on demand of the executive authority of the State from which he fled, be delivered up, to be removed to the State having jurisdiction of the crime.

Articles of Confederation.—"If any person guilty of, or charged with, treason, felony, or other high misdemeanor in any State, shall flee from justice, and be found in any of the United States, he shall, upon demand of the governor or executive power of the State from which he fled, be delivered up and removed to the State having jurisdiction of the offence."

This article was reported by the committee of detail, as it stood in the Articles of Confederation.

In Convention, the words "other crime" were substituted for "high misdemeanor," as more comprehensive and less liable to technical restriction.

Mr. BUTLER moved to add a clause requiring "fugitive slaves and servants to be delivered up like criminals."

It was objected by Mr. WILSON, that "that would oblige the executive of the State to do it at the public expense."

Mr. SHERMAN saw "no more propriety in the public seizing and surrendering a slave or servant than a horse."

The proposition was withdrawn for the present, and the article adopted.

Judicial Construction. — It is not necessary that the crime alleged should constitute an offence at the common law. It is enough that it is a crime against the laws of the State from which he fled. Johnson *v.* Riley, 13 Geo. 97.

A fugitive from justice may be arrested and detained until a formal requisition can be made by the proper authority. Com. *v.* Deacon, 10 S. & R. 135; Dow's case, 6 Harris, 39; Wm. Fetter's case, 3 Zabr. 311.

The crime must have been committed in the State from which the party is claimed to have been a fugitive — and he must be actually a fugitive from that State. *Ex parte* Jos. Smith, 3 M'Lean, 133.

ARTICLE IV.

SECTION II.

Clause 3.—No person held to service or labor in one State, under the laws thereof, escaping into another, shall, in consequence of any law or regulation therein, be discharged from such service or labor, but shall be delivered up on claim of the party to whom such service or labor may be due.

Articles of Confederation of the United Colonies of New England, adopted in 1643.

"It is also agreed, that if any servant run away from his master into any other of these confederated jurisdictions, that in such case, upon the certificate of one magistrate in the jurisdiction out of which the said servant fled, or upon other due proof, the said servant shall be delivered either to his master or to any other that pursues and brings such certificate or proof."

In the Constitutional Convention— The clause requiring the rendition of fugitives from justice to be delivered up, being under consideration,—

Mr. Butler and Mr. C. Pinckney, "moved to require *fugitive slaves and servants* to be delivered up like criminals."

Mr. Wilson suggested that the effect of that proposition would be to "oblige the executive of a State to do it at the public expense."

Mr. SHERMAN "saw no more propriety in the public seizing and surrendering a slave or servant than a horse."

Mr. BUTLER then withdrew the proposition, and at a subsequent day moved it, as an independent proposition, as follows: —

"If any person bound to service or labor in any of the United States shall escape into another State, he shall not be discharged from such service or labor, in consequence of any regulations subsisting in the State to which they escape, but shall be delivered up to the person justly claiming their service or labor." This was now agreed to without a division, being regarded as a part of the compromise for the authority given to Congress to pass navigation laws by majority vote.

Mr. MADISON says, that when this article, as reported by the committee of style and arrangement, was under consideration, "on motion of Mr. RANDOLPH, the word '*servitude*' was struck out and '*service*,' unanimously inserted, the former being thought to express the condition of slaves, and the latter the obligation of free persons."

Judicial Constructions. — This includes apprentices. Bouler *v.* Cuin, 1 Am. Law Rep. 654.

This does not extend to the case of a slave voluntarily carried by his master into another State, and there leaving him under the protection of some law declaring him free. Vaughan *v.* Williams, 3 McLean, 530. Slavery is a municipal regulation; is local, and cannot exist without authority of law. Miller *v.* McQuerry, 5 McLean, 469. But the question, whether slaves are made free by going into a State in which slavery is not tolerated, with the permission of their master, is purely one of local law, and to be determined by the courts of the State in which they are found. Stroder *v.* Graham, 10 Howard, 82; Dred Scott *v.* Sanford, 19 How. 396.

The owner of a slave is clothed with full authority in every State of the Union, to seize and recapture his slave, whenever he can do it without a breach of the peace or any illegal violence. Prigg *v.* Pa. 16 Pet. 539. But it is under the Constitution and laws of the United States only, that the owner of a slave has a right to reclaim him in a State where slavery does not exist. There is no principle in the common law, in the law of nations or of nature which authorizes such recapture. Giltna *v.* Gorham, 4 McLean, 412. The Constitution recognizes slaves as property, and pledges the general government to protect it. Dred Scott *v.* San. 19 How. 395.

A statute which punishes harboring or secreting a slave is not unconstitutional. Moore *v.* Illinois, 14 How. 13.

The 2d Sec. 4th Art. of the Constitution, does not extend to a slave voluntarily carried by his master into another State and then left under the protection of a law declaring him free, but to slaves escaping from one State to another. Butler *v.* Hopper, 1 Wash. C. C. R. 499.

ARTICLE IV.

SECTION III.

Clause 1.—New States may be admitted by the Congress into this Union; but no new State shall be formed or erected within the jurisdiction of any other State; nor any State be formed by the junction of two or more States, or parts of States, without the consent of the legislatures of the States concerned, as well as of the Congress.

Articles of Confederation.—"Canada acceding to this confederation, and joining in the measures of the United States, shall be admitted into, and entitled to all the advantages of this Union, but no other colony shall be admitted into the same, unless such admission be agreed to by nine States."

Mr. RANDOLPH'S PLAN.—"That provision ought to be made for the admission of States lawfully arising within the limits of the United States, whether from a voluntary junction of government and territory or otherwise, with the consent of a number of voices in the national legislature less than the whole."

Mr. PINCKNEY'S PLAN.—"The legislature shall have power to admit new States into the Union on the same terms with the original States, provided that two thirds of the members present in both houses agree."

Mr. PATTERSON'S (N. J.) PLAN. — "That provision be made for the admission of new States into the Union."

These several propositions having been considered in the committee of the whole, they reported the following: —

"That provision ought to be made for the admission of States, lawfully arising within the limits of the United States, whether from a voluntary junction of government and territory, or otherwise, with the consent of a number of voices in the national legislature, less than the whole."

The Convention concurred in this report, and sent the clause to the committee of detail.

Report of Committee of Detail. — "New States, lawfully constituted or established within the limits of the United States, may be admitted by the legislature, into this government; but to such admission, the consent of two thirds of the members present in each house, shall be necessary. If a new State shall arise within the limits of any of the present States, the consent of the legislatures of such States shall also be necessary to its admission. If the admission be consented to, the new States shall be admitted on the same terms with the original States. But the legislature may make conditions with the new States concerning the public debt which shall be then subsisting."

Mr. MORRIS moved to strike out, "If the admission be consented to," &c., to the end of the paragraph, — not wishing to bind Congress to admit the western States on such terms.

Mr. MADISON insisted that the "western States neither would nor ought to submit to a union which degraded them from an equal rank with the other States."

Mr. SHERMAN was for equality among the States.

Mr. WILLIAMSON was for leaving the terms to Congress.

Mr. MORRIS having modified his motion, it was adopted in the following form: —

"New States may be admitted by the legislature into the Union; but no new State shall be erected within the limits of any of the present States, without the consent of the legislature of such State, as well as of the general legislature."

On motion of Mr. DICKINSON, the clause in regard to the junction of two or more States was added, and the clause was referred to the committee of style and revision.

ARTICLE IV.

SECTION III.

Clause 2.—The Congress shall have power to dispose of and make all needful rules and regulations respecting the territory or other property belonging to the United States; and nothing in this Constitution shall be so construed as to prejudice any claims of the United States, or of any particular State.

Mr. MADISON proposed the following additional powers to be vested in Congress.

"To dispose of the unappropriated lands of the United States.

"To institute temporary governments for new States arising therein."

Referred to a general committee.

The subject of the admission of new States being under consideration,—

Mr. CARROLL moved the following:—

"*Provided*, nevertheless, that nothing in this Constitution shall be construed to affect the claim of the United States to vacant lands ceded to them by the treaty of peace."

Mr. WILSON.—"There was nothing in the Constitution

affecting, one way or the other, the claims of the United States, and it was best to insert nothing, leaving every thing on that litigated subject *in statu quo*."

Mr. MADISON "considered the claim of the United States as in fact favored by the jurisdiction of the judicial power of the United States over controversies to which they should be parties. He thought it best to be silent on the subject. He did not view the proviso of Mr. Carroll as dangerous; but to make it neutral and fair, it ought to go further and declare that the claims of particular States also should not be affected."

Mr. SHERMAN and Mr. BALDWIN favored the proviso, with Mr. Madison's amendment.

Mr. CARROLL modified his amendment so as to read:—

"Nothing in this constitution shall be construed to alter the claims of the United States or of the individual States to the western territory; but all such claims shall be examined into by the Supreme Court of the United States."

Mr. G. MORRIS proposed as a substitute the following:—

"The legislature shall have power to dispose of, and make all needful rules and regulations respecting the territory or other property belonging to the United States; and nothing in this Constitution contained shall be so construed as to prejudice any claims, either of the United States or of any particular State."

Mr. L. MARTIN moved to add:—

"But all such claims may be examined into and decided upon, by the Supreme Court of the United States."

Mr. MORRIS thought the addition unnecessary, as the Supreme Court was already invested with jurisdiction in all cases where the United States were a party.

Mr. MARTIN'S amendment was rejected, and the proposition of Mr. Morris agreed to, Maryland alone voting in the negative.

Mr. MADISON, in connection with his amendment to authorize Congress "to institute temporary governments for new States," remarked that the Congress of the Confederation had been embarrassed by the want of power to institute territorial governments in that portion of the territory of the United States outside of the territorial jurisdictions of the State authorities; and had been compelled to usurp the power to organize such governments. He thought the power should be specifically given to the legislature of the United States. The committee, to whom his motion was referred, made no report on the subject, and it does not seem to have attracted any further attention.

Judicial Constructions. — The term *territory*, in this clause, is merely descriptive of one kind of property, and is equivalent to the term lands. U. S. *v.* Gratiot, 14 Pet. 537.

This clause applies only to territory within the chartered limits of some one of the States, when they were colonies of Great Britain. It does not apply to territory acquired by the present federal government, by treaty or conquest from a foreign nation. Dred Scott *v.* Sanford, 19 How. 395.

The right to govern would seem to be the inevitable consequence of the right to acquire territory. Am. Ins. Co. *v.* Canter, 1 Pet. 542; U. S. *v.* Gratiot, 14 Pet. 537; Cross *v.* Harrison, 16 How. 194.

The United States, under the present Constitution, cannot acquire territory to be held as a colony, to be governed at its will and pleasure. But it may acquire territory which, at the time, has not a population that fits it to become a State, and may govern it as a territory, until it has a population which, in the judgment of Congress, entitles it to be admitted as a State of the Union. During the time it remains a territory, Congress may legislate over it, within the scope of its constitutional powers, in relation to citizens of the United States, — and may establish a territorial government — and the form of this local government must be regulated by the discretion of Congress, — but with powers not exceeding those which Congress itself, by the Constitution, is authorized to exercise over citizens of the United States, in respect to their rights of persons or rights of property. The territory thus acquired is acquired by the people of the United States, for their common and equal benefit; and every citizen has a right to take with him into the territory any article of property, including his slaves; which the Constitution recognizes as property, and pledges the federal government for its protection. Dred Scott *v.* Sanford, 19 How. 395.

ARTICLE IV.

SECTION IV.

The United States shall guaranty to every State in this Union a republican form of government, and shall protect each of them against invasion, and, on application of the legislature, or of the Executive (when the legislature cannot be convened), against domestic violence.

Mr. RANDOLPH'S PLAN. — "That a republican government and the territory of each State, except in the instance of a voluntary junction of government and territory, ought to be guarantied by the United States to each State."

Mr. PINCKNEY'S PLAN. — "On the application of the legislature of a State, the United States shall protect it against domestic insurrection."

On these propositions the committee of the whole house reported: —

"That a republican constitution and its existing laws ought to be guarantied to each State by the United States."

On motion by Mr. WILSON, the following was substituted: —

"That a republican form of government shall be guarantied to each State; and that each State shall be protected against foreign and domestic violence." In this form it was referred to the committee on detail, who reported the two following clauses: —

Congress shall have the power — "to subdue a rebellion in any State, on the application of its legislature."

2. "The United States shall guaranty to each State a republican form of government; and shall protect each State against foreign invasions, and, on the application of its legislature, against domestic violence."

Motions to strike out — "on the application of its legislature against," and to substitute "insurrections," for "domestic violence," were rejected.

On motion by Mr. Dickinson, "or executive" after "legislature," was added.

ARTICLE V.

The Congress, whenever two thirds of both Houses shall deem it necessary, shall propose amendments to this Constitution, or, on the application of the legislatures of two thirds of the several States, shall call a convention for proposing amendments, which in either case shall be valid, to all intents and purposes, as part of this Constitution, when ratified by the legislatures of three fourths of the several States, or by conventions in three fourths thereof, as the one or the other mode of ratification may be proposed by the Congress; provided that no amendment which may be made prior to the year one thousand eight hundred and eight shall in any manner affect the first and fourth clauses in the ninth section of the first article; and that no State without its consent, shall be deprived of its equal suffrage in the Senate.

Articles of Confederation. — " And the articles of this confederation shall be inviolably observed by every State, and the Union shall be perpetual; nor shall any alteration at any time hereafter be made in any of them, unless such alteration be agreed to in a Congress of the United States, and be afterwards confirmed by the legislature of every State."

Mr. RANDOLPH'S PLAN. — "That provision ought to be made for the amendment of the articles of Union whensoever it shall seem necessary; and that the assent of the national legislature ought not to be required thereto."

Mr. PINCKNEY'S PLAN. — "If two thirds of the legislatures of the States apply for the same, the legislature of the United States shall call a convention for the purpose of amending the Constitution; or should Congress, with the consent of two thirds of each house, propose to the States amendments to the same, the agreement of two thirds of the legislatures of the States shall be sufficient to make the said amendments parts of the Constitution."

On these propositions the committee of the whole reported, "That provision ought to be made for the amendment of the articles," which was agreed to, and referred to the committee on detail, who gave it the following form: —

"On the application of the legislatures of two thirds of the States in the Union, for an amendment of this Constitution, the legislature of the United States shall call a convention for that purpose."

Mr. SHERMAN proposed to amend the report by adding the following: — "Or the legislature may propose amendments to the several States for their approbation; but no amendments shall be binding until consented to by the several States."

Mr. WILSON moved to amend the amendment so as to make it competent for three fourths of the States to make amendments, which was agreed to. Mr. MADISON then offered the following substitute: —

"The legislature of the United States, whenever two thirds of both houses shall deem necessary, or on the application of two thirds of the legislatures of the several

States, shall propose amendments to this Constitution, which shall be valid, to all intents and purposes, as part thereof, when the same shall have been ratified by three fourths at least of the legislatures of the several States, or by conventions in three fourths thereof, as one or the other mode of ratification may be proposed by the legislature of the United States."

Mr. RUTLEDGE "said he never would agree to give a power by which the articles relating to slaves might be altered by the States not interested in that property, and prejudiced against it."

To obviate this objection, the following was added: —

"Provided that no arrangements which may be made prior to the year 1808, shall in any manner affect the fourth and fifth sections of the seventh article."

In this form the substitute was adopted.

Mr. SHERMAN proposed, as an additional proviso, "that no State should be affected in its internal police, or deprived of its equality in the Senate."

Mr. MADISON opposed this motion, and it was lost; but on the manifestation of very decided dissatisfaction on the part of Connecticut, New Jersey, and Delaware, Mr. MORRIS renewed so much of Mr. Sherman's motion as related to the equal suffrage in the Senate, and it was agreed to without a division.

Mr. RANDOLPH offered the following, and remarked that if it were not adopted, it would be impossible for him to sign the instrument: —

"That amendments to the plan might be offered by the State conventions, which should be submitted to, and finally decided on by another general convention."

On this proposition, all the States voted in the negative.

ARTICLE VI.

Clause 1. — All debts contracted and engagements entered into before the adoption of this Constitution, shall be as valid against the United States under this Constitution, as under the confederation.

Articles of Confederation. — "All bills of credit emitted, moneys borrowed, and debts contracted, by or under the authority of Congress, before the assembling of the United States, in pursuance of the present confederation, shall be deemed and considered a charge against the United States, for payment and satisfaction, whereof the said United States, and the public faith, are hereby solemnly pledged."

Mr. RUTLEDGE — the subject having given rise to considerable discussion — moved the appointment of a grand committee "to consider the necessity and expediency of the United States assuming all the State debts." The committee was ordered. Yeas — Massachusetts, Connecticut, Virginia, North Carolina, South Carolina, Georgia, 6. Nays — New Hampshire, New Jersey, Delaware, Maryland, 4.

Gov. LIVINGSTON reported, from the committee the following: "The legislature of the United States shall have power to fulfil the engagements which have been entered into by Congress, and to discharge, as well the debts of the United States, as the debts incurred by the several States during the late war, for the common defence and general welfare."

Mr. SHERMAN and Mr. WILLIAMSON proposed that provision should be made for settling the war accounts upon the principle adopted for the ratio of taxation and representation.

Mr. ELLSWORTH thought it unnecessary specially to confer the power to fulfil the public engagements, as the United States were already bound to do so.

Mr. RANDOLPH and Mr. MADISON thought that, although the United States would be bound, the new government would have no authority in the case, unless it was specially given.

Mr. GERRY regarded it essential that specific provision should be made "so that no pretext might remain for getting rid of the public engagements."

Mr. G. MORRIS moved the following substitute: —

"The legislature *shall* discharge the debts and fulfil the engagements of the United States." This was carried unanimously. But subsequently, on motion of Mr. RANDOLPH, the above clause of the Constitution was substituted.

ARTICLE VI.

Clause 2. — This Constitution, and the Laws of the United States which shall be made in pursuance thereof, and all treaties made, or which shall be made, under the authority of the United States, shall be the supreme law of the land; and the judges in every State shall be bound thereby, any thing in the Constitution or laws of any State to the contrary notwithstanding.

Articles of Confederation. — "Every State shall abide by the determinations of the United States in Congress assembled, on all questions which, by this confederation, are submitted to them. And the articles of this confederation shall be inviolably observed by every State, and the Union shall be perpetual."

Mr. Patterson's Plan. — "That all acts of the United States in Congress, made by virtue and in pursuance of the powers hereby, and by the Articles of Confederation vested in them, and all treaties made and ratified under the authority of the United States, shall be the supreme law of the respective States, so far forth as those acts or treaties shall relate to the said States or their citizens; and that the judiciary of the several States shall be bound thereby in their decisions, any thing in the respective laws of the individual States to the contrary notwithstanding."

The clause in Mr. Randolph's resolutions, giving Congress power "to negative all laws passed by the several States contravening, in the opinion of the national legislature, the articles of union or any treaty subsisting under the authority of the Union; and to call forth the force of the Union against any member of the Union failing to fulfil its duty under the articles thereof," being under consideration, —

Mr. LUTHER MARTIN moved as a substitute, the above clause of Mr. Patterson's plan, which was agreed to. This was finally modified, on motion of Mr. RUTLEDGE, so as to read nearly as it stands in the Constitution.

Judicial Constructions.—Whenever a right grows out of, or is protected by a treaty, it is sanctioned against all the laws and judicial decisions of the States; and whoever has this right, it is to be protected. Owings *v.* Nor. Les. 5 Cranch, 348.

But though a treaty is the law of the land, and its provisions must be regarded by the courts as equivalent to an act of the legislature, when it operates directly on a subject, yet if it be merely a stipulation for future legislation by Congress, it addresses itself to the political and not to the judicial department, and the latter must await the action of the former. Foster *v.* Neilson, 2 Pet. 253.

A treaty duly ratified is the supreme law of the land, and the courts have no power to examine into the authority of the persons by whom it was entered into on behalf of the foreign nation. Doe *v.* Braden, 16 How. 635.

Though a treaty is the law of the land, under the Constitution, Congress may repeal it, so far as it is a municipal law, provided its subject-matter be within the legislative power. Taylor *v.* Morton, 2 Curt. C. C. 454.

ARTICLE VI.

Clause 3. — The Senators and Representatives before mentioned, and the members of the several State legislatures, and all executive and judicial officers, both of the United States and of the several States, shall be bound by oath or affirmation to support this Constitution; but no religious test shall ever be required as a qualification to any office or public trust under the United States.

Mr. RANDOLPH'S PLAN. — "That the legislative, executive, and judiciary powers, within the several States, ought to be bound by oath, to support the articles of Union."

Mr. WILLIAMSON suggested that a reciprocal oath should be required from the national officers, to support the governments of the States.

On motion of Mr. GERRY, "*and officers of the national government*," was inserted after the words "several States."

Mr. PINCKNEY moved to add, "No religious test or qualification shall ever be annexed to any oath of office under the authority of the United States."

These several propositions having been agreed to and referred to the committee of detail, were reported in the following form: —

"The members of the legislatures and the executive and

judicial officers of the United States, and of the several States, shall be bound by oath to support this Constitution."

Mr. C. Pinckney renewed his motion in regard to religious tests, and it was agreed to, and the clause was sent to the committee of style and arrangement.

ARTICLE VII.

The ratification of the conventions of nine States, shall be sufficient for the establishment of this Constitution between the States so ratifying the same.

The articles of confederation were ratified by the State legislatures.

Mr. RANDOLPH'S PLAN. — "That the amendments which shall be offered to the confederation by the convention ought, at a proper time or times, after the approbation of Congress, to be submitted to an assembly or assemblies of representatives, recommended by the several legislatures to be expressly chosen by the people, to consider and decide thereon."

Mr. ELLSWORTH moved its reference "to the legislatures of the States;" and Mr. G. MORRIS, "to a general convention to be chosen by the people, and authorized to consider, amend, and establish the plan," neither of which was received with favor.

Mr. SHERMAN expressed the opinion that the assent of Congress and the subsequent ratification of the several State legislatures would give the Constitution the proper sanction.

Mr. MADISON regarded it as essential that the direct action of the people should be had; and that the new Constitution should be ratified in the most unexceptionable form by the supreme authority of the people themselves.

Mr. GERRY was apprehensive that the Constitution would be defeated if it should be subjected to the direct action of the people.

Mr. WILSON "hoped the provision for ratifying would be put on such a footing as to admit of a partial union, with a door open for the accession of the rest."

Mr. PINCKNEY proposed, that if nine States should ratify it it should be put into operation between such States.

These several propositions were sent to the committee on detail, who reported the following: —

"The ratifications of the conventions of —— States shall be sufficient for organizing this Constitution."

Mr. WILSON proposed to fill the blank with "seven."

Mr. SHERMAN named "ten," as the present articles required unanimity to make changes.

Mr. RANDOLPH thought "nine" the proper number, "being a respectable majority."

Mr. MADISON remarked that, "if the blank should be filled with 'seven,' 'eight,' or 'nine,' the Constitution as it stands might be put in force over the whole body of the people, though less than a majority of them should ratify it."

Mr. WILSON. — "As the Constitution stands, the States only which ratify it can be bound."

Mr. BUTLER was for filling the blank with "nine." "He revolted at the idea that one or two States should restrain the rest from consulting their safety."

Mr. CARROLL moved "thirteen" — "unanimity being necessary to dissolve the existing confederacy."

On motion of Mr. KING the words "between said States" were added.

Mr. MADISON moved to fill the blank with the following: — "Any seven or more States entitled to thirty-three members at least, in the House of Representatives, according to the allotment made in the third section of the fourth article," thus requiring the concurrence of a majority both of the States and people.

The questions were then taken on filling the blank, and "thirteen" and "ten" were severally rejected. The question being on "nine" —

Col. MASON remarked that he was for preserving ideas familiar to the people. Nine States had been required in all great cases under the Confederation, and that number, on that account, was preferable.

On the question for this number — the vote was, yeas 8, nays 3, Virginia, North Carolina, South Carolina, voting in the negative.

AMENDMENTS.

ARTICLE I.

Congress shall make no law respecting an establishment of religion, or prohibiting the free exercise thereof; or abridging the freedom of speech, or of the press; or the right of the people peaceably to assemble, and to petition the government for a redress of grievances.

Mr. CHARLES PINCKNEY'S PLAN of a Federal Constitution, submitted to the Convention, contained the following: —

"The legislature of the United States shall pass no law on the subject of religion, nor touching or abridging the liberty of the press."

The New Hampshire convention, in adopting the Constitution, proposed the following amendment: —

"Congress shall make no laws touching religion, or to infringe the rights of conscience."

The Virginia and North Carolina conventions recommended the following: —

"That the people have a right peaceably to assemble

together to consult for the common good, or to instruct their representatives; and every citizen has a right to petition or to apply to the legislature for a redress of grievances.

"That the people have a right to freedom of speech, and of writing and publishing their sentiments; that the freedom of the press is one of the greatest bulwarks of liberty and ought not to be violated.

"That no particular religious society ought to be favored or established by law in preference to others."

In the House of Representatives, Mr. TUCKER, of South Carolina, moved to add after "grievances"—and "to instruct their representatives."

Mr. GERRY, of Massachusetts, advocated, and Mr. MADISON opposed the amendment, and it was rejected, yeas 10, nays 41.

Judicial Construction.—The legislature may enact laws more effectually to enable all sects to accomplish the great objects of religion by giving them corporate rights for the management of property, &c. 6 Cranch, 43.

ARTICLE II.

A well-regulated militia being necessary to the security of a free State, the right of the people to keep and bear arms shall not be infringed.

The Virginia and New York conventions, for adopting the Constitution, proposed the following amendment:—

"That the people have a right to keep and bear arms; that a well-regulated militia, composed of the body of the people, trained to arms, is the proper, natural, and safe defence of a free State," and "that any person religiously scrupulous of bearing arms, ought to be exempted, upon payment of an equivalent to employ another in his stead."

The New Hampshire convention proposed:—

"Congress shall never disarm any citizen, unless such as are or have been in actual rebellion."

ARTICLE III.

No soldier shall, in time of peace, be quartered in any house without the consent of the owner, nor in time of war but in a manner to be prescribed by law.

Mr. PINCKNEY, in the Constitutional Convention, proposed the following: —

"No soldier shall be quartered in any house, in time of peace, without consent of the owner."

The Virginia and North Carolina conventions, for adopting the Constitution, proposed the above clause as an amendment.

ARTICLE IV.

The right of the people to be secure in their persons, houses, papers, and effects, against unreasonable searches and seizures, shall not be violated, and no warrants shall issue but upon probable cause, supported by oath or affirmation, and particularly describing the place to be searched, and the persons or things to be seized.

The Virginia and North Carolina conventions proposed, as an amendment:—

"That every freeman has a right to be secure from all unreasonable searches and seizures of his person, his papers, and his property," &c.

Judicial Constructions.—This refers only to processes to be issued under the authority of the United States. Smith *v.* Maryland, 18 How. 71. And it has no applications to proceedings for the recovery of debts. Murray's Lessee *v.* Hob. Land & Ins. Co. 18 How. 272. See also Exparte Burford, 3 Cr. 448.

ARTICLE V.

No person shall be held to answer for a capital or otherwise infamous crime, unless on a presentment or indictment of a grand jury, except in cases arising in the land or naval forces, or in the militia when in actual service, in time of war or public danger; nor shall any person be subject for the same offence to be twice put in jeopardy of life or limb; nor shall be compelled in any criminal case to be a witness against himself; nor be deprived of life, liberty, or property, without due process of law; nor shall private property be taken for public use without just compensation.

The Massachusetts and New Hampshire conventions recommended the following amendment:—

"That no person shall be tried for any crime, by which he may incur an infamous punishment, or loss of life, until he be first indicted by a grand jury, except in such cases as may arise in the government and regulation of the land and naval forces."

The Virginia and North Carolina conventions, recommended by way of amendments a bill of rights; among which were the following:—

"That in all capital and criminal prosecutions a man

hath a right to demand the cause and nature of his accusation, to be confronted with his accusers and witnesses, to call for evidence, and be allowed counsel in his favor, and to a fair and speedy trial by an impartial jury of the vicinage, without whose unanimous consent he cannot be found guilty (except in the government of the land and naval forces); nor can he be compelled to give evidence against himself."

"That no freeman ought to be taken, imprisoned, or disseized of his freehold, liberties, privileges, or franchises, or outlawed, or exiled, or in any manner destroyed, or deprived of his life, liberty, or property, but by the law of the land."

Judicial Constructions. — The court may discharge a jury from giving a verdict without the consent of the prisoner, whenever in their opinion there is a manifest necessity for such an act, or the ends of public justice would be otherwise defeated. U. S. *v.* Perez, 9 Wheat. 579. See also, 18 How. 276.

The last clause of this article is only a limitation to the power of the general government; it has no application to the legislation of the several States. Barron *v.* Mayor of Baltimore, 7 Pet. 243.

These amendments to the Constitution are exclusively restrictions upon the federal power, intended to prevent interference with the rights of the States and of their citizens. Fox *v.* Ohio, 5 How. 434.

ARTICLE VI.

In all criminal prosecutions the accused shall enjoy the right to a speedy and public trial, by an impartial jury of the State and district wherein the crime shall have been committed, which district shall have been previously ascertained by law; and to be informed of the nature and cause of the accusation; to be confronted with the witnesses against him; to have compulsory process for obtaining witnesses in his favor; and to have the assistance of counsel for his defence.

[See recommendation of Virginia under the preceding article.]

Judicial Constructions. — It is only intended that this right of trial by jury shall be secured for those charged with crimes which, by our former laws and customs, had been tried by jury. U. S. *v.* Duane, Wall, 106.

Any person charged with a crime in the courts of the United States, has a right before as well as after indictment, to the process of the court to compel the attendance of his witnesses. 1 Burr's Trial, 179.

ARTICLE VII.

In suits at common law, where the value in controversy shall exceed twenty dollars, the right of trial by jury shall be preserved, and no fact tried by a jury shall be otherwise reëxamined in any court of the United States, than according to the rules of the common law.

ARTICLE VIII.

Excessive bail shall not be required, nor excessive fines imposed, nor cruel and unusual punishments inflicted.

ARTICLE IX.

The enumeration in the Constitution of certain rights shall not be construed to deny or disparage others retained by the people.

The Virginia and North Carolina conventions recommend the following amendment: —

"That excessive bail ought not to be required, nor excessive fines imposed, nor cruel and unusual punishments inflicted."

Judicial Constructions. — This includes not merely modes of proceeding known to the common law, but all suits, not of equity or admiralty jurisdiction, in which legal rights are to be settled and determined. Parsons *v.* Bulford, 3 Pet. 433; United States *v.* La Vengeance, 3 Dall. 297; Webster *v.* Reid, 11 How. 437.

The right of the trial by jury is for the benefit of the parties litigating, and may be waived by them. United States *v.* Rathbone, 2 Paine, 578.

The circuit courts have no power to order a peremptory nonsuit against the will of the plaintiff. Elmore *v.* Grimes, 1 Pet. 469. See also, 6 Pet. 598.

The common law, alluded to, is not the common law of any individual State, but the common law of England; according to which, facts once tried by a jury, are never reëxamined, unless a new trial be granted in the discretion of the court before which the suit is depending, for good cause shown, or unless the judgment of such court be reversed by a superior tribunal, &c. United States *v.* Wonson, 1 Gall. 20.

ARTICLE X.

The powers not delegated to the United States by the Constitution, nor prohibited by it to the States, are reserved to the States respectively, or to the people.

The Massachusetts and New Hampshire conventions recommended the following amendment: —

"That it be explicitly declared that all powers not expressly delegated by the aforesaid Constitution, are reserved to the several States to be by them exercised."

The South Carolina convention "*Resolved*, that no section or paragraph of the said Constitution warrants a construction that the States do not retain every power not expressly relinquished by them and vested in the general government of the Union."

The Virginia convention proposed: —

"That each State in the Union shall respectively retain every power, jurisdiction, and right, which is not by this Constitution delegated to the Congress of the United States, or to the departments of the Federal Government."

ARTICLE XI.

The judicial power of the United States shall not be construed to extend to any suit in law or equity, commenced or prosecuted against one of the United States by citizens of another State, or by citizens or subjects of any foreign State.

Judicial Constructions. — If the State be not necessarily a defendant, though its interests may be affected by the decision, the courts of the United States are bound to exercise jurisdiction. Lon. R. R. Co. *v.* Letson, 2 How. 550.

A State by becoming interested with others in a banking or trading corporation, or by owning all the capital stock, does not impart to that corporation any of its privileges or prerogatives. It lays down its sovereignty, so far as respects the transactions of the corporation. Bank of the United States *v.* Planters Bank of Ga. 9 Wheat. 904; Dorrington *v.* Bank of Alabama, 13 How. 12.

ARTICLE XII.

The electors shall meet in their respective States, and vote by ballot for President and Vice-President, one of whom at least shall not be an inhabitant of the same State with themselves; they shall name in their ballots the person voted for as President, and in distinct ballots the person voted for as Vice-President; and they shall make distinct lists of all persons voted for as President, and of all persons voted for as Vice-President, and of the number of votes for each; which lists they shall sign and certify, and transmit sealed to the seat of the government of the United States, directed to the President of the Senate. The President of the Senate shall, in the presence of the Senate and House of Representatives, open all the certificates, and the votes shall then be counted; the person having the greatest number of votes for President shall be the President, if such number be a majority of the whole number of electors appointed; and if no person have such majority, then from the persons having the highest numbers, not exceeding three, on the list of those voted for as President, the House of Representatives shall choose immediately by ballot the President. But in choosing the President, the votes shall be taken by States, the representation from each State having one vote; a quorum for this purpose shall consist of a member or members from two thirds of the States, and a majority of all the States shall be necessary to a choice. And if the House of Representatives shall not choose a President whenever the right of choice shall devolve upon them, before the fourth day of March next following, then the Vice-President shall act as President as in the case of the death or other constitutional disability of the President.

The person having the greatest number of votes as Vice-President shall be the Vice-President, if such number be a majority of the whole number of electors appointed; and if no person have a majority, then, from the two highest numbers on the list, the Senate shall choose the Vice-President: a quorum for the purpose shall consist of two thirds of the whole number of Senators, and a majority of the whole number shall be necessary to a choice.

But no person constitutionally ineligible to the office of President, shall be eligible to that of Vice-President of the United States.

By the Constitution, as originally adopted, each of the "electors" was required to vote for two persons, without designating which of them it was intended should be President or which to be vice-president; and the candidate receiving the largest number of votes, being a majority of the whole number, was to be President, and the next highest, vice-president.

In the presidential election of 1800, Thomas Jefferson and Aaron Burr were the candidates of the republican party, and John Adams and C. C. Pinckney of the federal party. Jefferson and Burr received seventy-three votes each, and Mr. Adams sixty-five. No person had received the *highest* number of votes, and consequently the election devolved on the House of Representatives. Although there was not the slightest doubt as to which of the candidates was the actual choice of the people, when the House of Representatives proceeded to the election, eight States voted for Jefferson, six for Burr, and two were divided, and it was not until the thirty-fifth ballot that a choice was effected. This bold attempt by a party in the House of Representatives, to counteract and resist the clearly expressed will of the people, led to the adoption of this amendment.

NOTE. — The time for the meeting of the electors is the first Wednesday in December — and the time for counting the votes is the second Wednesday in February. 1 Stat. 239.

CLOSING PROCEEDINGS

OF THE CONVENTION AND OF THE CONGRESS.

In Convention, Monday, September 17, 1787.— Present: The States of New Hampshire, Massachusetts, Connecticut, Mr. Hamilton from New York, New Jersey, Pennsylvania, Delaware, Maryland, Virginia, North Carolina, South Carolina, and Georgia.

Resolved, That the preceding Constitution be laid before the United States in Congress assembled, and that it is the opinion of this Convention that it should afterwards be submitted to a Convention of delegates, chosen in each State by the people thereof, under the recommendation of its legislature, for their assent and ratification; and that each Convention, assenting to and ratifying the same, should give notice thereof, to the United States in Congress assembled.

Resolved, That it is the opinion of this Convention, that as soon as the Conventions of nine States shall have ratified this Constitution, the United States in Congress assembled should fix a day on which electors should be appointed by the States which shall have ratified the same, and a day on which the electors should assemble to vote for the President, and the time and place for commencing proceedings under this Constitution. That after such publication the electors should be appointed, and the senators and representatives elected; that the electors should meet on the day fixed for the election of the President, and should transmit their votes certified, signed, sealed, and directed, as the Constitution requires, to the

Secretary of the United States in Congress assembled; that the senators and representatives should convene at the time and place assigned; that the senators should appoint a president of the Senate, for the sole purpose of receiving, opening, and counting the votes for President; and that, after he shall be chosen, the Congress, together with the President, should without delay, proceed to execute this Constitution.

By the unanimous order of the Convention.

GEORGE WASHINGTON, *President.*

WILLIAM JACKSON, *Secretary.*

In Convention, September 17, 1787.— Sir: We have now the honor to submit to the consideration of the United States in Congress assembled, that Constitution which has appeared to us the most advisable.

The friends of our country have long seen and desired that the power of making war, peace, and treaties, that of levying money and regulating commerce, and the correspondent executive and judicial authorities, should be fully and effectually vested in the general government of the Union; but the impropriety of delegating such extensive trust to one body of men is evident: hence results the necessity of a different organization.

It is obviously impracticable, in the federal government of these States, to secure all rights of independent sovereignty to each, and yet provide for the interest and safety of all. Individuals entering into society must give up a share of liberty to preserve the rest. The magnitude of the sacrifice must depend as well on situation and circumstance as on the object to be obtained. It is at all times difficult to draw with precision the line between those rights which must be surrendered and those which may be reserved; and on the present occasion this difficulty was increased by a difference among the several States as to their situation, extent, habits, and particular interests.

In all our deliberations on this subject, we kept steadily in our view that which appears to us the greatest interest of every true American — the consolidation of our Union — in which is involved our prosperity, felicity, safety, perhaps our national existence. This important consideration, seriously and deeply impressed on o r minds, led each State in the Convention to be less rigid on points of inferior magnitude than might have been otherwise expected; and thus the Constitution which we now present is the result of a spirit of amity, and of that mutual deference and concession which the peculiarity of our political situation rendered indispensable.

That it will meet the full and entire approbation of every State, is not, perhaps, to be expected; but each will doubtless consider that, had her interest been alone consulted, the consequences might have been particularly disagreeable or injurious to others; that it is liable to as few exceptions as could reasonably have been expected, we hope and believe; that it may promote the lasting welfare of that country so dear to us all, and secure her freedom and happiness, is our most ardent wish.

With great respect, we have the honor to be, sir, your excellency's most obedient humble servants.

By unanimous order of the Convention.

GEORGE WASHINGTON, *President.*

His Excellency the *President of Congress.*

United States in Congress Assembled.

Friday, September 28, 1787. — Present: New Hampshire, Massachusetts, Connecticut, New York, New Jersey, Pennsylvania, Delaware, Virginia, North Carolina, South Carolina, and Georgia, and from Maryland, Mr. Ross.

Congress having received the report of the Convention lately assembled in Philadelphia,—

Resolved, unanimously, That the said report, with the resolutions and letter accompanying the same, be transmitted to the several legislatures, in order to be submitted to a convention of delegates chosen in each State by the people thereof, in conformity to the resolves of the Convention made and provided in that case.

The United States in Congress Assembled.

Saturday, September 13, 1788.—Congress assembled. Present: New Hampshire, Massachusetts, Connecticut, New York, New Jersey, Pennsylvania, Virginia, North Carolina, South Carolina, and Georgia; and from Rhode Island, Mr. Arnold, and from Delaware, Mr. Kearny.

On the question to agree to the proposition which was yesterday postponed by the State of Delaware, the yeas and nays being required by Mr. Gilman—

State	Member	Vote	State vote
New Hampshire	Mr. Gilman,	ay	ay
	Wingate,	ay	
Massachusetts	Mr. Dana,	ay	ay
	Thatcher,	ay	
Connecticut	Mr. Huntington,	ay	ay
	Wadsworth,	ay	
New York	Mr. Hamilton,	ay	ay
	Gansevoort,	ay	
New Jersey	Mr. Clarke,	ay	ay
	Dayton,	ay	
Pennsylvania	Mr. Irwine,	ay	ay
	Meredith,	ay	
	Armstrong,	ay	
	Read,	ay	
Virginia	Mr. Griffin,	ay	ay
	Madison,	ay	
	Carrington,	ay	
	Lee,	ay	
South Carolina	Mr. Parker,	ay	ay
	Tucker,	ay	
Georgia	Mr. Few,	ay	ay
	Baldwin,	ay	

So it was resolved in the affirmative, as follows: —

Whereas the Convention assembled in Philadelphia, pursuant to the resolution of Congress of the 21st of February, 1787, did, on the 17th of September in the same year, report to the United States in Congress assembled a Constitution for the people of the United States; whereupon Congress, on the 28th of the same September, did resolve, unanimously, "That the said report, with the resolutions and letter accompanying the same, be transmitted to the several legislatures, in order to be submitted to a Convention of delegates, chosen in each State by the people thereof, in conformity to the resolves of the Convention made and provided in that case:" And whereas the Constitution so reported by the Convention, and by Congress transmitted to the several legislatures, has been ratified in the manner therein declared to be sufficient for the establishment of the same, and such ratifications, duly authenticated, have been received by Congress, and are filed in the office of the Secretary; therefore —

Resolved, That the first Wednesday in January next be the day for appointing electors in the several States, which, before the said day, shall have ratified the said Constitution; that the first Wednesday in February next be the day for the electors to assemble in their respective States, and vote for a President; and that the first Wednesday in March next be the time, and the present seat of Congress (New York) the place, for commencing the proceedings under the said Constitution.

DOCUMENTS

CONNECTED WITH THE

PROCEEDINGS OF THE FEDERAL CONVENTION.

[TAKEN FROM THE MADISON PAPERS.]

1. LETTER of Mr. MADISON to Mr. RANDOLPH, suggesting his views of a Federal Constitution.
2. Mr. RANDOLPH'S PLAN, contained in his resolutions submitted to the FEDERAL CONVENTION, on the opening of its proceedings, 29th May, 1787.
3. Mr. PATTERSON'S PLAN, for amending the Articles of Confederation, offered as a substitute for Mr. Randolph's resolutions.
4. Mr. PINCKNEY'S PLAN of a Federal Government, submitted to the Federal Convention, May 29, 1787.
5. General HAMILTON'S PLAN — read as the conclusion of his speech, but not offered to the Convention.
6. GENERAL RESOLUTIONS; agreed to by the Convention and referred to the Committee on Detail, on the 26th July.
7. DRAFT OF THE CONSTITUTION, reported by the Committee on Detail, Aug. 6, 1798.
8. EXTRACTS FROM THE DEBATES ON THE SEVERAL GENERAL PROPOSITIONS.

LETTER

Of James Madison to Edmund Randolph, suggesting his Views of a Federal Constitution.

New York, April 8, 1787.

Dear Sir, — . . . . I am glad to find that you are turning your thoughts towards the business of May next. My despair of your finding the necessary leisure, as signified in one of your letters, with the probability that some leading propositions, at least, would be expected from Virginia, had engaged me in a closer attention to the subject than I should otherwise have given, I will just hint the ideas that have occurred, leaving explanations for an interview.

I think with you, that it will be well to retain as much as possible of the old confederation, though I doubt whether it may not be best to work the valuable articles into the new system, instead of engrafting the latter on the former. I am also perfectly of your opinion, that, in framing a system, no material sacrifices ought to be made to local or temporary prejudices. An explanatory address must, of necessity, accompany the result of the Convention on the main object.

I am not sure that it will be practicable to present the several parts of the reform in so detached a manner to the States, as that a partial adoption will be binding. Particular States may view different articles as conditions of each other, and would only ratify them as such. Others might ratify them as independent propositions. The consequence would be that the ratifications of both would go for nothing. I have not, however, examined this point thoroughly. In truth, my ideas of a reform strike so deeply at the old confederation, and lead to such a systematic change, that they scarcely admit of the expedient.

I hold it as a fundamental point, that an individual independence of the States is utterly irreconcilable with the idea of an aggregate sovereignty. I think, at the same time, that a consolidation of the States into a simple republic is not less unattainable than it would be inexpedient. Let it be tried, then, whether any middle ground can be taken, which will, at once support a due supremacy of the national authority, and leave in force the local authorities, so far as they can be subordinately useful.

The first step to be taken is, I think, a change in the principle of representation. According to the present form of the Union, an equality of suffrage, if not just towards the larger members of it, is at least safe to them, as the liberty they exercise of rejecting or executing the acts of Congress, is uncontrollable by the nominal sovereignty of Congress. Under a system which would operate without the intervention of the States, the case would be materially altered. A vote from Delaware would have the same effect as one from Massachusetts or Virginia.

Let the national government be armed with a positive and complete authority in all cases where uniform measures are necessary, as in trade, &c. Let it also retain the powers which it now possesses.

Let it have a negative, in all cases whatsoever, on the legislative acts of the States, as the king of Great Britain heretofore had. This I conceive to be essential, and the least possible abridgment of the State sovereignties. Without such a defensive power, every positive power that can be given on paper will be unavailing. It will also give internal stability to the States. There has been no moment since the peace at which the federal assent would have been given to paper-money, &c.

Let this national supremacy be extended also to the judiciary department. If the judges in the last resort depend on the States, and are bound by their oaths to them and not to the Union, the intention of the law and the interests of the nation may be defeated by the obsequiousness of the tribunals to the policy or prejudices of the States. It seems at least essential that an appeal should lie to some national tribunals in all cases which concern foreigners, or inhabitants of other States. The admiralty jurisdiction may be fully submitted to the national government.

A government formed of such extensive powers ought to be well organized. The legislative department may be divided into two branches. One of them to be chosen every —— years by the legislature or the people at large; the other to consist of a more select number, holding their appointments for a longer term and going out in rotation. Perhaps the negative on the State laws may be most conveniently lodged in this branch. A council of revision may be superadded, including the great ministerial officers.

A national executive will also be necessary. I have scarcely ventured to form my own opinion yet, either of the manner in which it ought to be constituted, or of authorities with which it ought to be clothed.

An article ought to be inserted expressly guaranteeing the tranquillity of the States against internal as well as external dangers.

To give the new system its proper energy, it will be desirable to have it ratified by the authority of the people, and not merely by that of the legislature. I am afraid you will think this project, if not extravagant, absolutely unattainable and unworthy of being attempted. Conceiving it myself to go no further than is essential, the objections drawn from this source are to be laid aside. I flatter myself, however, that they may be less formidable on trial than in contemplation. The change in the principle of representation will be relished by a majority of the States, and those too of most influence. The northern States will be reconciled to it by the *actual* superiority of their populousness; the southern, by their *expected* superiority on this point. This principle established, the repugnance of the large States to part with power will in a great degree subside, and the smaller States must ultimately yield to the predominant will. It is also already seen by many, and must by degrees be seen by all, that, unless the Union be organized efficiently on republican principles, innovations of a much more objectionable form may be obtruded, or in the most favorable event, the partition of the empire, into rival and hostile confederacies will ensue.

MR. RANDOLPH'S PLAN.

Resolutions submitted to the Constitutional Convention on the 29th May, 1787.

1. *Resolved,* That the Articles of Confederation ought to be so corrected and enlarged as to accomplish the objects proposed by their institution, namely, "common defence, security of liberty, and general welfare." *

2. *Resolved,* therefore, that the right of suffrage in the national legislature, ought to be proportioned to the quotas of contribution or to the number of free inhabitants, as the one or the other rule may seem best in different cases.

3. *Resolved,* That the national legislature ought to consist of two branches.

4. *Resolved,* That the members of the first branch of the national legislature, ought to be elected by the people of the several States every —— for the term of ——; to be of the age of —— years, at least; to receive liberal stipends by which they may be compensated for the devotion of their time to the public service; to be ineligible to any office established by a particular State, or under the authority of the United States, except those peculiarly belonging to the functions of the first branch, during the term of service and for the space of —— after its expiration; to be incapable of reëlection, for the space of —— after the expiration of their term of service, and to be subject to recall.

* Subsequently modified by him so as to read,—*Resolved,* That a national government ought to be established, consisting of a supreme legislative, executive, and judiciary.

5. *Resolved,* That the members of the second branch of the national legislature ought to be elected by those of the first, out of a proper number of persons nominated by the individual legislatures, to be of the age of —— years, at least; to hold their offices for a term sufficient to insure their independency; to receive liberal stipends by which they may be compensated for the devotion of their time to the public service; and to be ineligible to any office established by a particular State, or under the authority of the United States, except those peculiarly belonging to the functions of the second branch, during the term of service; and for the space of —— after the expiration thereof.

6. *Resolved,* That each branch ought to possess the right of originating acts; that the national legislature ought to be empowered to enjoy the legislative rights vested in Congress by the Confederation, and moreover, to legislate in all cases to which the separate States are incompetent, or in which the harmony of the United States may be interrupted by the exercise of individual legislation; to negative all laws passed by the several States contravening, in the opinion of the national legislature, the Articles of Union, or any treaty subsisting under the authority of the Union; and to call forth the force of the Union against any member of the Union failing to fulfil its duty under the articles thereof.

7. *Resolved,* That a National Executive be instituted; to be chosen by the national legislature, for the term of ——; to receive punctually, at stated times, a fixed compensation for the services rendered, in which no increase or diminution shall be made so as to affect the magistracy existing at the time of increase or diminution; and to be ineligible a second time; and that besides a general authority to execute the national laws, it ought to enjoy the executive rights vested in Congress by the Confederation.

8. *Resolved,* That the Executive and a convenient number of the national judiciary, ought to compose a council of revision, with authority to examine every act of the national legislature, before it shall operate, and every act of a particular legislature, before a negative thereon shall be final; and that the dissent of said council shall amount to a rejection, unless the act of the national legisla-

ture be again passed, or of a particular legislature be again negatived by —— of the members of each branch.

9. *Resolved,* That a national judiciary be established; to consist of one or more supreme tribunals, and of inferior tribunals, to be chosen by the national legislature; to hold their offices during good behavior, and to receive punctually, at stated times, fixed compensation for their services, in which no increase or diminution shall be made, so as to affect the persons actually in office at the time of such increase or diminution. That the jurisdiction of the inferior tribunals shall be to hear and determine in the first instance, and of the supreme tribunal to hear and determine in the *dernier resort,* all piracies and felonies on the high seas; captures from an enemy; cases in which foreigners or citizens of other States, applying to such jurisdictions, may be interested; or which respect the collection of the national revenue; impeachments of any national officers; and questions which may involve the national peace and harmony.

10. *Resolved,* That provision ought to be made for the admission of States lawfully arising within the limits of the United States, whether from a voluntary junction of government and territory or otherwise, with the consent of a number of votes of the national legislature less than the whole.

11. *Resolved,* That a republican government, and the territory of each State, except in the instance of a voluntary junction of government and territory, ought to be guaranteed by the United States to each State.

12. *Resolved,* That provision ought to be made for the continuance of Congress and their authorities and privileges, until a given day after the reform of the articles of Union shall be adopted, and for the completion of all their engagements.

13. *Resolved,* That provision ought to be made for the amendment of the articles of Union whensoever it shall be necessary, and that the assent of the national legislature ought not to be required thereto.

14. *Resolved,* That the legislative, executive, and judiciary powers, within the several States, ought to be bound by oath to support the articles of Union.

15. *Resolved,* That the amendments which shall be offered to the Confederation, by the Convention, ought, at a proper time or times, after the approbation of Congress, to be submitted to an assembly or assemblies of representatives, recommended by the several legislatures, to be expressly chosen by the people to consider and decide thereon.

MR. PATTERSON'S PLAN,

FOR AMENDING THE ARTICLES OF CONFEDERATION; OFFERED AS A SUBSTITUTE FOR MR. RANDOLPH'S RESOLUTIONS.

1. *Resolved*, That the Articles of Confederation ought to be so revised, corrected, and enlarged, as to render the Federal Constitution adequate to the exigencies of government and the preservation of the Union.

2. *Resolved*, That in addition to the powers vested in the United States, in Congress, by the present existing Articles of Confederation, they be authorized to pass acts for raising a revenue, by levying a duty or duties on all goods or merchandises of foreign growth or manufacture, imported into any port of the United States; by stamps on paper, vellum, or parchment; and by a postage on all letters or packages passing through the general post-office; to be applied to such federal purposes as they shall deem proper and expedient; to make rules and regulations for the collection thereof; and the same, from time to time to alter and amend in such manner as they shall think proper; to pass acts for the regulation of trade and commerce, as well with foreign nations as with each other; provided that all punishments, fines, forfeitures, and penalties, to be incurred for contravening such acts, rules, and regulations, shall be adjudged by the common law judiciaries of the State in which any offence, contrary to the true intent and meaning of such acts, rules, and regulations, shall have been committed and perpetrated, with liberty of commencing in the first instance all suits and prosecutions for that purpose in the superior common law judiciary in such State; subject, nevertheless, for the correction of all errors, both in law and fact, in rendering judgment, to an appeal to the judiciary of the United States.

3. *Resolved*, That whenever requisitions shall be necessary, in-

stead of the rules for making requisitions mentioned in the Articles of Confederation, the United States, in Congress, be authorized to make such requisitions, in proportion to the whole number of white and other free inhabitants, of every age, sex, and condition, including those bound to service for a term of years, and three fifths of all other persons not comprehended in the foregoing description, except Indians not paying taxes; that if such requisitions be not complied with, in the time specified therein, to direct the collection thereof in the non-complying States, and for that purpose to devise and pass acts directing and authorizing the same; provided that none of the powers hereby vested in the United States in Congress, shall be exercised without the consent of at least —— States; and in that proportion if the number of confederated States shall hereafter be increased or diminished.

4. *Resolved,* That the United States in Congress be authorized to elect a federal executive, to consist of —— persons, to continue in office for the term of —— years; to receive punctually, at stated times, a fixed compensation for their services, in which no increase or diminution shall be made so as to affect the persons composing the executive at the time of such increase or diminution; to be paid out of the federal treasury; to be incapable of holding any other office or appointment during their time of service, and for —— years thereafter; to be ineligible a second time, and removable by Congress, on application by a majority of the executives of the several States; that the executive, besides their general authority to execute the federal acts, ought to appoint all federal officers, not otherwise provided for, and to direct all military operations, provided that none of the persons composing the federal executive shall, on any occasion, take command of any troops, so as personally to conduct any military enterprise, as general or in any other capacity.

5. *Resolved,* That a Federal Judiciary be established, to consist of a supreme tribunal, the judges of which to be appointed by the executive, and to hold their offices during good behavior, to receive punctually, at stated times, a fixed compensation for their services, in which no increase or diminution shall be made so as to affect the persons actually in office at the time of such increase or diminu-

tion. That the judiciary so established shall have authority to hear and determine, in the first instance, on all impeachments of federal officers; and by way of appeal, in the *dernier resort*, in all cases touching the rights of ambassadors; in all cases of captures from an enemy; in all cases of piracies and felonies on the high seas; in all cases in which foreigners may be interested; in the construction of any treaty or treaties, or which may arise on any of the acts for the regulation of trade, or the collection of the federal revenue; that none of the judiciary shall, during the time they remain in office, be capable of receiving or holding any other office or appointment during the term of service or for —— thereafter.

6. *Resolved*, That all acts of the United States in Congress, made by virtue and in pursuance of the powers hereby, and by the Articles of Confederation, vested in them, and all treaties made and ratified under the authority of the United States, shall be the supreme law of the respective States, so far forth as those acts or treaties shall relate to the said States or their citizens; and that the judiciary of the several States shall be bound thereby in their decisions, any thing in the respective laws of the individual States to the contrary notwithstanding; and that if any State, or any body of men in any State, shall oppose or prevent the carrying into execution such acts or treaties, the federal executive shall be authorized to call forth the power of the confederated States, or so much thereof as may be necessary, to enforce and compel an obedience to such acts, or an observance of such treaties.

7. *Resolved*, That provision be made for the admission of new States into the Union.

8. *Resolved*, That the rule of naturalization ought to be the same in every State.

9. *Resolved*, That a citizen of one State committing an offence in another State of the Union, shall be deemed guilty of the same offence, as if it had been committed by a citizen of a State in which it was committed.

MR. CHARLES PINCKNEY'S PLAN OF A FEDERAL GOVERNMENT.

SUBMITTED TO THE CONSTITUTIONAL CONVENTION, MAY 29, 1787.

We, the people of New Hampshire, &c. [naming all the States] do ordain, declare, and establish the following Constitution for the government of ourselves and our posterity.

ARTICLE I. The style of this government shall be The United States of America, and the government shall consist of supreme legislative, executive, and judicial powers.

ART. II. The legislative power shall be vested in a Congress, to consist of two separate houses; one to be called the House of Delegates, and the other the Senate, who shall meet on the —— day of —— in every year.

ART. III. The members of the House of Delegates shall be chosen every —— year by the people of the several States, and the qualification of the electors shall be the same as those of the electors of the several States for their legislatures. Each member shall have been a citizen of the United States for —— years; and shall be of —— years of age, and a resident of the State he is chosen for. Until a census of the people shall be taken in the manner hereinafter mentioned, the House of Delegates shall consist of —— members, to be chosen by the different States, in the following proportions: for New Hampshire ——, &c.; and the legislature shall hereafter regulate the number of delegates, by the number of inhabitants, according to the provisions hereinafter made, at the rate of one for every —— thousand. All money bills of every kind shall originate in the House of Delegates, and shall not be altered by the Senate. The House of Delegates shall exclusively possess the power of impeachment, and shall choose its own officers; and vacancies therein shall be supplied by the executive authority of the State in the representation from which they shall happen.

Art. IV. The Senate shall be elected and chosen by the House of Delegates; which house immediately after their meeting, shall choose by ballot —— senators from among the citizens and residents of New Hampshire; —— from among those of Massachusetts; —— [and so on through the States, to be divided into three classes to go out in succession]. Each senator shall be of —— years of age, at least, and shall have been a citizen of the United States for four years before his election; and shall be a resident of the State he is chosen from. The Senate shall choose its own officers.

Art. V. Each State shall prescribe the time and manner of holding elections by the people for the House of Delegates; and the House of Delegates shall be the judges of the elections, returns, and qualifications of its members.

In each house a majority shall constitute a quorum to do business. Freedom of speech and debate in the legislature shall not be impeached, or questioned in any place out of it; and the members of both houses shall, in all cases except for treason, felony, or breach of the peace, be free from arrest during their attendance on Congress, and in going to and returning from it. Both houses shall keep journals of their proceedings, and publish them, except on secret occasions; and the yeas and nays may be entered thereon, at the desire of —— of the members present. Neither house without the consent of the other, shall adjourn for more than —— days, nor to any place but where they are sitting.

The members of each house shall not be eligible or capable of holding any office under the Union, during the time for which they have been respectively elected, nor the members of the Senate for one year after. The members of each house shall be paid for their services by the States which they represent. Every bill which shall have passed the legislature, shall be presented to the President of the United States for his revision; if he approves it, he shall sign it; but if he does not approve it, he shall return it, with his objections to the house it originated in; which house, if two thirds of the members present, notwithstanding the President's objections, agree to pass it, shall send it to the other house, with the President's objections; where, if two thirds of the members also agree to pass it, the same shall become a law; and all bills sent to the President and not returned by him within —— days, shall be laws, unless the legislature by adjournment, prevent their return, in which case they shall not be laws.

Art. VI. The legislature of the United States shall have the power to lay and collect taxes, duties, imposts, and excises;

To regulate commerce with all nations and among the several States;

To borrow money and emit bills of credit;

To establish post-offices;

To raise armies; — to build and equip fleets;

To pass laws for arming, organizing, and disciplining the militia of the United States;

To subdue a rebellion in any State, on application of its legislature;

To coin money, and regulate the value of all coins; and fix the standard of weights and measures;

To provide such dock-yards and arsenals, and erect such fortifications as may be necessary for the United States; and to exercise exclusive jurisdiction therein;

To appoint a treasurer by ballot;

To constitute tribunals inferior to the Supreme Court;

To establish post and military roads;

To establish and provide for a National University at the seat of the government of the United States;

To establish uniform rules of naturalization;

To provide for the establishment of a seat of government for the United States not exceeding —— miles square, in which they shall exercise exclusive jurisdiction;

To make rules concerning captures from an enemy;

To declare the law and punishment of piracies, and felonies at sea, and of counterfeiting coin, and of all offences against the laws of nations;

To call forth the aid of the militia to execute the laws of the Union, enforce treaties, suppress insurrections, and repel invasions;

And to make all laws for carrying the foregoing powers into execution.

The legislature of the United States shall have the power to declare the punishment of treason, which shall consist only in levying war against the United States or any of them, or adhering to their enemies. No person shall be convicted of treason but by the testimony of two witnesses.

The proportion of direct taxes shall be regulated by the whole number of inhabitants of every description; which number shall, within —— years after the first meeting of the legislature, and within the term of every —— year after, be taken in the manner to be prescribed by the legislature.

No tax shall be levied on articles exported from the States; nor capitation tax, but in proportion to the census before directed.

All laws regulating commerce shall require the assent of two thirds of the members present in each house. The United States shall not grant any title of nobility. The legislature of the United States shall pass no law on the subject of religion; nor touching or abridging the liberty of the press; nor shall the privilege of the writ of *habeas corpus* ever be suspended, except in case of rebellion or invasion.

All acts made by the legislature of the United States, pursuant to the Constitution, and all treaties made under the authority of the United States, shall be the supreme law of the land, and all judges shall be bound to consider them as such in their decisions.

Art. VII. The Senate shall have the sole and exclusive power to declare war; and to make treaties; and to appoint ambassadors and other ministers to foreign nations, and judges of the Supreme Court.

They shall have exclusive power to regulate the manner of deciding all disputes and controversies now existing, or which may arise between the States, respecting jurisdiction or territory.

Art. VIII. The executive power of the United States shall be vested in a President of the United States of America, which shall be his style, and his title shall be His Excellency. He shall be elected for —— years, and shall be reëligible.

He shall from time to time give information to the legislature, of the state of the Union, and recommend to their consideration the measures he may think necessary. He shall take care that the laws of the United States be duly executed. He shall commission all the officers of the United States; and except as to ambassadors, other ministers, and judges of the Supreme Court, he shall nominate, and with the consent of the Senate, appoint all other officers of the United States. He shall receive public ministers from foreign nations; and may correspond with the executives of the different States. He shall have power to grant pardons and reprieves, except in impeachments. He shall be Commander-in-Chief of the army and navy of the United States, and of the militia of the several States; and shall receive a compensation which shall not be increased or diminished during his continuance in office. At entering on the duties of his office, he shall take an oath faithfully to execute the duties of a President of the United States. He shall be removed from his office on impeachment by the House of Delegates, and conviction in the Supreme Court of treason, bribery, or corruption. In the case of his removal, death, resignation, or disability, the president of the Senate shall exercise the duties of his office until another President be chosen. And in case of the president of the Senate, the speaker of the House of Delegates shall do so.

Art. IX. The legislature of the United States shall have the power, and it shall be their duty, to establish courts of law, equity, and admiralty, as shall be necessary.

The judges of the courts shall hold their offices during good behavior; and receive compensation, which shall not be increased or diminished during their continuance in office. One of these courts shall be termed the Supreme Court; whose jurisdiction shall extend to all cases arising under the laws of the United States, or affecting ambassadors, other public ministers, and consuls; to the trial of impeachment of officers of the United States; to all cases of admiralty and maritime jurisdiction. In cases of impeachment affecting ambassadors, and other public ministers, this jurisdiction shall be original; in all other cases appellate.

All criminal offences, except in cases of impeachment, shall be tried in the State where they shall be committed. The trials shall be open and public, and shall be by jury.

ART. X. Immediately after the first census of the people of the United States, the House of Delegates shall apportion the Senate by electing for each State, out of the citizens resident therein, one Senator for every —— members each State shall have in the House of Delegates. Each State shall be entitled to at least one member of the Senate.

ART. XI. No State shall grant letters of marque and reprisal, or enter into treaty or alliance, or confederation; nor grant any title of nobility; nor without the consent of the legislature of the United States, lay any imposts on imports; nor keep troops or ships of war in time of peace; nor enter into compacts with other States or foreign powers; nor emit bills of credit; nor make any thing but gold and silver or copper a tender in payment of debts; nor engage in war, except for self-defence when actually invaded, or the danger of invasion be so great as not to admit of a delay until the government of the United States can be informed thereof. And to render these prohibitions effectual, the legislature of the United States shall have the power to revise the laws of the several States, that may be supposed to infringe the powers exclusively delegated by this Constitution to Congress, and to negative and annul such as do.

ART. XII. The citizens of each State shall be entitled to all privileges and immunities of citizens in the several States. Every person charged with crimes in any State, fleeing from justice to another, shall, on demand of the executive of the State from which he fled, be delivered up and removed to the State having jurisdiction of the offence.

ART. XIII. Full faith shall be given, in each State, to the acts of the legislature, and to the records and judicial proceedings of the courts and magistrates of every State.

ART. XIV. The legislature shall have power to admit new States into the Union, on the same terms with the original States provided two thirds of the members present in both Houses agree.

ART. XV. On the application of the legislature of a State, the United States shall protect it against domestic insurrection.

ART. XVI. If two thirds of the legislatures of the States apply for the same, the legislature of the United States shall call a convention for the purpose of amending the Constitution; or should Congress, with the consent of two thirds of each House, propose to the States amendments to the same, the agreement of two thirds of the legislatures of the States shall be sufficient to make the said amendments parts of the Constitution.

The ratification of the —— conventions of —— States shall be sufficient for organizing this Constitution.

GENERAL HAMILTON'S PLAN.

ART. I. The supreme legislative power of the United States of America to be vested in two different bodies of men; the one to be called the Assembly, the other the Senate; who together shall form the legislature of the United States, with power to pass all laws whatsoever, subject to the negative hereafter mentioned.

ART. II. The Assembly to consist of persons elected by the people to serve for three years.

ART. III. The Senate to consist of persons elected to serve during good behavior; their election to be made by electors chosen for that purpose by the people. In order to this, the States to be divided into election districts. On the death, removal, or resignation of any Senator, his place to be filled out of the district from which he came.

ART. IV. The supreme executive authority of the United States to be vested in a governor, to be elected to serve during good behavior; the election to be made by electors chosen by the people, in the election districts aforesaid. The authorities and functions of the executive to be as follows: To have a negative on all laws about to be passed, and the execution of all laws passed; to have the direction of war, when authorized or begun; to have, with the advice and approbation of the Senate, the power of making all treaties; to have the sole appointment of the heads or chief officers of the departments, of finance, war, and foreign affairs; to have the nomination of all other officers (ambassadors to foreign nations included), subject to the approbation or rejection of the Senate; to have the power of pardoning all offences, except treason, which he shall not pardon, without the approbation of the Senate.

ART. V. On the death, resignation, or removal of the governor, his authorities to be exercised by the president of the Senate, till a successor be appointed.

Art. VI. The Senate to have the sole power of declaring war; the power of advising and approving all treaties; the power of approving or rejecting all appointments of officers, except the heads or chiefs of the departments of finance, war, and foreign affairs.

Art. VII. The supreme judicial authority to be vested in judges, to hold their offices during good behavior, with adequate and permanent salaries. This court to have original jurisdiction in all causes of capture, and an appellate jurisdiction in all causes in which the revenues of the general government or the citizens of foreign nations, are concerned.

Art. VIII. The legislature of the United States to have power to institute courts in each State for the determination of all matters of general concern.

Art. IX. The governor, senators, and all officers of the United States, to be liable to impeachment for mal-, and corrupt conduct; and upon conviction, to be removed from office, and disqualified for holding any place of trust or profit; all impeachments to be tried by a court to consist of the chief——, or judge of the superior court of law, of each State, provided such judge shall hold his place during good behavior and have a permanent salary.

Art. X. All laws of the particular States contrary to the Constitution or laws of the United States to be utterly void; and the better to prevent such laws being passed, the governor or president of each State shall be appointed by the general government, and shall have a negative upon the laws about to be passed in the State of which he is the governor or president.

Art. XI. No State to have any forces, land or naval, and the militia of all the States to be under the sole or exclusive direction of the United States, the officers of which to be appointed or commissioned by them.

GENERAL RESOLUTIONS.

After a session of two months, on the 26th of July, the Convention referred the following resolutions to the committee of detail, with instructions to prepare and report a constitution in conformity with them. The Convention then adjourned to the 6th of August, to afford the committee time to perform their duty.

This committee was chosen by ballot, and consisted of Messrs. Rutledge, Randolph, Gorham, Ellsworth, and Wilson.

1. *Resolved*, That the government of the United States ought to consist of a supreme legislative, judiciary, and executive.

2. *Resolved*, That the legislature consist of two branches.

3. *Resolved*, That the members of the first branch of the legislature ought to be elected by the people of the several States for the term of two years; to be paid out of the public treasury; to receive an adequate compensation for their services; to be of the age of twenty-five years at least; to be ineligible to, and incapable of holding, any office under the authority of the United States (except those peculiarly belonging to the functions of the first branch), during the term of service of the first branch.

4. *Resolved*, That the members of the second branch of the legislature of the United States ought to be chosen by the individual legislatures; to be of the age of thirty years at least; to hold their offices for six years, one third to go out biennially; to receive a compensation for the devotion of their time to the public service; to be ineligible to, and incapable of holding, any office under the authority of the United States (except those peculiarly belonging to the functions of the second branch), during the term for which they were elected, and for one year thereafter.

5. *Resolved,* That each branch ought to possess the right of originating acts.

6. *Resolved,* That the national legislature ought to possess the legislative rights vested in Congress by the Confederation; and moreover to legislate in all cases for the general interests of the Union, and also in those to which the States are separately incompetent, or in which the harmony of the United States may be interrupted by the exercise of individual legislation.

7. *Resolved,* That the legislative acts of the United States, made by virtue and in pursuance of the articles of Union, and all treaties made and ratified under the authority of the United States, shall be the supreme law of the respective States, as far as those acts or treaties shall relate to the said States, or their citizens or inhabitants; and that the judiciaries of the several States shall be bound thereby in their decisions, any thing in the respective laws of the individual States notwithstanding.

8. *Resolved,* That in the original formation of the legislature of the United States, the first branch thereof shall consist of sixty-five members; of which number,

New Hampshire	shall	send	three,
Massachusetts	"	"	eight,
Rhode Island	"	"	one,
Connecticut	"	"	five,
New York	"	"	six,
New Jersey	"	"	four,
Pennsylvania	"	"	eight,
Delaware	"	"	one,
Maryland	"	"	six,
Virginia	"	"	ten,
North Carolina	"	"	five,
South Carolina	"	"	five,
Georgia	"	"	three.

But as the present situation of the States may probably alter in the number of their inhabitants, the legislature of the United States shall be authorized, from time to time, to apportion the number of representatives; and in case any of the States shall hereafter be divided, or enlarged by addition of territory, or any two or more States united, or any new States created within the limits of the United States, the legislature of the United States shall possess authority to regulate the number of representatives, in any of the foregoing cases, upon the principle of their number of inhabitants, according to the principles hereafter mentioned, namely, — Provided always, that the representation ought to be proportioned to direct taxation. And in order to ascertain the alteration in the direct taxation, which may be required from time to time, by the changes in the relative circumstances of the States, —

9. *Resolved*, That a census be taken within six years from the first meeting of the legislature of the United States, and once within the term of every ten years afterwards, of all the inhabitants of the United States, in the manner and according to the ratio recommended by Congress in their resolution of the 18th of April, 1783; and that the legislature of the United States shall proportion the direct taxation accordingly.

10. *Resolved*, That all bills for raising or appropriating money, or for fixing the salaries of the officers of the government of the United States, shall originate in the first branch of the legislature of the United States, and shall not be altered or amended by the second branch; and that no money shall be drawn from the public treasury, but in pursuance of appropriations to be originated in the first branch.

11. *Resolved*, That in the second branch of the legislature of the United States, each State shall have an equal vote.

12. *Resolved*, That a national executive be instituted, to consist of a single person; to be chosen by the national legislature, for the term of seven years, to be ineligible a second time; with power to carry into execution the national laws; to appoint to offices in cases not otherwise provided for; to be removable on impeachment, and conviction of mal-practice or neglect of duty; to receive a fixed compensation for the devotion of his time to the public service, to be paid out of the national treasury.

13. *Resolved*, That the national executive shall have the right

to negative any legislative act; which shall not be afterwards passed, unless by two third parts of each branch of the national legislature.

14. *Resolved,* That a national judiciary be established, to consist of one supreme tribunal, the judges of which shall be appointed by the second branch of the national legislature; to hold their offices during good behavior; to receive punctually, at stated times, a fixed compensation for their services, in which no diminution shall be made so as to affect the persons actually in office at the time of such diminution.

15. *Resolved,* That the national legislature be empowered to appoint inferior tribunals.

16. *Resolved,* That the jurisdiction of the national judiciary shall extend to cases arising under laws passed by the general legislature; and to such other questions as involve the national peace and harmony.

17. *Resolved,* That provision ought to be made for the admission of States lawfully arising within the limits of the United States, whether from a voluntary junction of government and territory, or otherwise, with the consent of a number of voices in the national legislature less than the whole.

18. *Resolved,* That a republican form of government shall be guaranteed to each State; and that each State shall be protected against foreign and domestic violence.

19. *Resolved,* That provision ought to be made for the amendment of the articles of union, whenever it shall be deemed necessary.

20. *Resolved,* That the legislative, executive, and judiciary powers, within the several States, and of the national government, ought to be bound, by oath, to support the articles of union.

21. *Resolved,* That the amendments which shall be offered to the Confederation by the Convention ought, at proper time or times, after the approbation of Congress, to be submitted to an assembly or assemblies of representatives, recommended by the several legislatures, to be expressly chosen by the people to consider and decide thereon.

22. *Resolved,* That the representation in the second branch of the legislature of the United States shall consist of two members from each State, who shall vote *per capita.*

23. *Resolved,* That it be an instruction to the committee, to whom were referred the proceedings of the Convention for the establishment of a national government, to receive a clause or clauses, requiring certain qualifications of property and citizenship in the United States, for the executive, the judiciary, and the members of both branches of the legislature of the United States.

DRAFT OF THE CONSTITUTION

REPORTED BY MR. RUTLEDGE, FROM THE COMMITTEE ON DETAIL, ON THE 6TH OF AUGUST, 1787, IN CONFORMITY WITH THE "GENERAL RESOLUTIONS," PREVIOUSLY AGREED TO BY THE CONVENTION.

ARTICLE I.

The style of the government shall be, "The United States of America."

ARTICLE II.

The government shall consist of a supreme legislative, executive, and judicial powers.

ARTICLE III.

The legislative power shall be vested in a Congress, to consist of two separate and distinct bodies of men, a House of Representatives and a Senate; each of which shall, in all cases, have a negative on the other. The legislature shall meet on the first Monday in December, in every year.

ARTICLE IV.

SECT. 1. The members of the House of Representatives shall be chosen every second year, by the people of the several States comprehended within the Union. The qualifications of the electors shall be the same from time to time, as those of the electors in the several States, of the most numerous branch of their own legislatures.

SECT. 2. Every member of the House of Representatives shall be of the age of twenty-five years at least; shall have been a citizen in the United States for at least three years before his election;

and shall be, at the time of his election, a resident of the State in which he shall be chosen.

SECT. 3. The House of Representatives shall, at its first formation, and until the number of citizens and inhabitants shall be taken in the manner hereinafter described, consist of sixty-five members, of whom three shall be chosen in New Hampshire, eight in Massachusetts, one in Rhode Island, five in Connecticut, six in New York, four in New Jersey, eight in Pennsylvania, one in Delaware, six in Maryland, ten in Virginia, five in North Carolina, five in South Carolina, and three in Georgia.

SECT. 4. As the proportions of numbers in different States will alter from time to time; as some of the States may hereafter be divided; as others may be enlarged by addition of territory; as two or more States may be united; as new States will be erected within the limits of the United States, the legislature shall, in each of these cases, regulate the number of representatives by the number of inhabitants, according to the provisions hereinafter made, at the rate of one for every forty thousand.

SECT. 5. All bills for raising or appropriating money, and for fixing the salaries of officers of government, shall originate in the House of Representatives, and shall not be altered or amended by the Senate. No money shall be drawn from the public treasury, but in pursuance of appropriations that shall originate in the House of Representatives.

SECT. 6. The House of Representatives shall have the sole power of impeachment; it shall choose its speaker and other officers.

SECT. 7. Vacancies in the House of Representatives shall be supplied by writs of election from the executive authority of the State, in the representation from which they shall happen.

ARTICLE V.

SECT. 1. The Senate of the United States shall be chosen by the legislatures of the several States. Each legislature shall choose two members. Vacancies may be supplied by the executive until the next meeting of the legislature. Each member shall have one vote.

SECT. 2. The Senators shall be chosen for six years; but immediately after the first election, they shall be divided by lot into three classes, as nearly as may be, numbered one, two, and three. The seats of the members of the first class shall be vacated at the expiration of the second year; of the second class at the expiration of the fourth year; of the third class at the expiration of the sixth year; so that a third part of the members may be chosen every second year.

SECT. 3. Every member of the Senate shall be of the age of thirty years at least; shall have been a citizen in the United States for at least four years before his election; and shall be, at the time of his election, a resident of the State for which he shall be chosen.

SECT. 4. The Senate shall choose its own president and other officers.

ARTICLE VI.

SECT. 1. The times, and places, and manner of holding the elections of the members of each house, shall be prescribed by the legislature of each State; but their provisions concerning them, may, at any time, be altered by the legislature of the United States.

SECT. 2. The legislature of the United States shall have authority to establish such uniform qualifications of the members of each house, with regard to property, as to the said legislature shall seem expedient.

SECT. 3. In each house, a majority of its members shall constitute a quorum to do business; but a smaller number may adjourn from day to day.

SECT. 4. Each house shall be the judge of the elections, returns and qualifications of its own members.

SECT. 5. Freedom of speech and debate in the legislature shall not be impeached or questioned in any court or place out of the legislature; and the members of each house shall, in all cases, except treason, felony, and breach of the peace, be privileged from arrest during their attendance at Congress, and in going to and returning from it.

SECT. 6. Each house may determine the rules of its proceedings; may punish its members for disorderly behavior; and may expel a member.

SECT. 7. The House of Representatives and the Senate, when it shall be acting in a legislative capacity, shall keep a journal of their proceedings; and shall, from time to time publish them; and the yeas and nays of the members of each house on any question shall, at the desire of one fifth part of the members present, be entered on the journal.

SECT. 8. Neither house, without the consent of the other, shall adjourn for more than three days, nor to any other place than that at which the two houses are sitting. But this regulation shall not extend to the Senate, when it shall exercise the powers mentioned in the —— article.

SECT. 9. The members of each house shall be ineligible to, and incapable of holding, any office under the authority of the United States, during the time for which they shall respectively be elected; and the members of the Senate shall be ineligible to, and incapable of holding any such office for one year afterwards.

SECT. 10. The members of each house shall receive a compensation for their services, to be ascertained and paid by the State in which they shall be chosen.

SECT. 11. The enacting style of the laws of the United States shall be, "Be it enacted, and it is hereby enacted, by the House of Representatives, and by the Senate of the United States, in Congress assembled."

SECT. 12. Each house shall possess the right of originating bills, except in the cases before mentioned.

SECT. 13. Every bill which shall have passed the House of Representatives and the Senate, shall, before it becomes a law, be presented to the President of the United States for his revision. If, upon such revision, he approve of it, he shall signify his approbation by signing it. But if, upon such revision, it shall appear to him improper for being passed into a law, he shall return it, together with his objections against it, to that house in which it shall have originated; who shall enter their objections at large on their journal, and proceed to reconsider the bill. But if, after such reconsideration, two thirds of the house shall, notwithstanding the objections of the President, agree to pass it, it shall, together with his objections, be sent to the other house, by which it shall likewise be reconsidered; and if approved by two thirds of the other house, it shall become a law. But in all such cases, the votes of both houses shall be determined by yeas and nays; and the names of the persons voting for or against the bill, shall be entered on the journal of each house respectively. If any bill shall not be returned by the President within seven days after it shall have been presented to him, it shall be a law, unless the legislature, by their adjournment, prevent its return, in which case it shall not be a law.

ARTICLE VII.

SECT. 1. The legislature of the United States shall have the power to lay and collect taxes, duties, imposts and excises;

To regulate commerce with foreign nations, and among the several States;

To establish an uniform rule of naturalization throughout the United States;

To coin money; to regulate the value of foreign coin;

To fix the standard of weights and measures;

To establish post-offices;

To borrow money, and emit bills on the credit of the United States;

To appoint a treasurer by ballot;

To constitute tribunals, inferior to the Supreme Court;

To make rules concerning captures on land and water;

To declare the law and punishment of piracies and felonies committed on the high seas, and the punishment of counterfeiting the coin of the United States, and of offences against the law of nations;

To subdue a rebellion in any State, on the application of its legislature;

To make war;

To raise armies;

To build and equip fleets;

To call forth the aid of the militia, in order to execute the laws of the Union, enforce treaties, suppress insurrections, and repel invasions;

And to make all laws that shall be necessary and proper for carrying into execution the foregoing powers, and all other powers vested by this Constitution in the government of the United States, or in any department or office thereof.

SECT. 2. Treason against the United States shall only consist in levying war against the United States or any of them; and in adhering to the enemies of the United States, or any of them. The legislature of the United States shall have power to declare the punishment of treason. No person shall be convicted of treason, unless on the testimony of two witnesses. No attainder of treason shall work corruption of blood nor forfeiture, except during the life of the person attainted.

SECT. 3. The proportions of direct taxation shall be regulated by the whole number of white and other free citizens and inhabitants of every age, sex, and condition, including those bound to service for a term of years, and three fifths of all other persons not comprehended in the foregoing description (except Indians not paying taxes); which number shall, within six years after the first meeting of the legislature, and within the term of every ten years afterwards, be taken in such manner as the legislature shall direct.

SECT. 4. No tax or duty shall be laid by the legislature on articles exported from any State; nor on the migration or importation of such persons as the several States shall think proper to admit; nor shall such migration or importation be prohibited.

SECT. 5. No capitation tax shall be laid, unless in proportion to the census herein before directed to be taken.

SECT. 6. No navigation act shall be passed, without the consent of two thirds of the members present in each House.

SECT. 7. The United States shall not grant any title of nobility.

ARTICLE VIII.

The acts of the legislature of the United States made in pursuance of this Constitution, and all treaties made under the authority of the United States shall be the supreme law of the several States, and of their citizens and inhabitants; and the judges in the several States shall be bound thereby in their decisions, any thing in the constitutions or laws of the several States to the contrary notwithstanding.

ARTICLE IX.

SECT. 1. The Senate of the United States shall have power to make treaties, and to appoint ambassadors and judges of the Supreme Court.

SECT. 2. In all disputes and controversies now subsisting, or that may hereafter subsist between two or more States, respecting jurisdiction or territory, the Senate shall possess the following powers:— Whenever the legislature or the executive authority, or lawful agent of any State, in controversy with another, shall by memorial to the Senate, state the matter in question, and apply for a hearing, notice of such memorial or application shall be given by order of the Senate, to the legislature, or executive authority of the other State in controversy. The Senate shall also assign a day for the appearance of the parties, by their agents, before that house. The agents shall be directed to appoint, by joint consent, commissioners or judges to constitute a court for hearing and determining the matter in question. But if the agents cannot agree, the Senate shall name three persons out of each of the several States; and from the list of such persons, each party shall alternately strike out one, until the number shall be reduced to thirteen; and from that number, not less than seven, nor more than nine names, as the Senate shall direct, shall, in their presence, be drawn out by lot; and the persons whose names shall be so drawn, or any five of them, shall constitute commissioners or judges to hear and finally determine the controversy; provided a majority of the judges who shall hear the cause agree in the determination. If either party shall neglect to attend at the day assigned, without showing sufficient reasons for not attending, or being present shall refuse to strike, the Senate shall proceed to nominate three persons out of each State, and the clerk of the Senate shall strike in behalf of the party absent or refusing. If any of the parties shall refuse to submit to the authority of such court, or shall not appear to prosecute or defend their claim or cause, the court shall nevertheless proceed to pronounce judgment. The judgment shall be final and conclusive. The proceedings shall be transmitted to the president of the Senate, and shall be lodged among the public records for the security of the party concerned. Every commissioner shall, before he sit in judgment, take an oath, to be administered by one of the judges of the supreme or superior court of the State where the cause shall be tried, "well and truly to hear and determine the matter in question, according to the best of his judgment, without favor, affection, or hope of reward."

SECT. 3. All controversies concerning land claimed under different grants of two or more States, whose jurisdictions, as they respect such lands, shall have been adjusted or decided subsequently to such grants, or any of them, shall, on application to the Senate, be finally determined, as near as may be, in the same manner as before prescribed for deciding controversies between different States.

ARTICLE X.

SECT. 1. The executive power of the United States shall be vested in a single person. His style shall be, "The President of the United States of America," and his title shall be, "His Excellency." He shall be elected by ballot by the legislature. He shall hold his office during the term of seven years; but shall not be elected a second time.

SECT. 2. He shall, from time to time, give information to the legislature, of the state of the Union. He may recommend such measures as he shall judge necessary and expedient. He may convene them on extraordinary occasions. In case of disagreement between the two houses, with regard to the time of adjournment, he may adjourn them to such time as he thinks proper. He shall take care that the laws of the United States be duly and faithfully executed. He shall commission all the officers of the United States; and shall appoint officers in all cases not otherwise provided for by this Constitution. He shall receive ambassadors, and may correspond with the supreme executives of the several States. He shall have power to grant reprieves and pardons, but his pardon shall not be pleadable in bar of an impeachment. He shall be commander-in-chief of the army and navy of the United States, and of the militia of the several States. He shall, at stated times, receive for his services a compensation, which shall neither be increased nor diminished during his continuance in office. Before he shall enter on the duties of his department, he shall take the following oath or affirmation, "I —— solemnly swear (or affirm) that I will faithfully execute the office of President of the United States of America." He shall be removed from his office on impeachment by the House of Representatives, and conviction in the Supreme Court, of treason, bribery, or corruption. In case of his removal, as aforesaid, death, resignation, or disability to discharge the powers and duties of his office, the president of the Senate shall exercise those powers and duties, until another President of the United States be chosen, or until the disability of the President be removed.

ARTICLE XI.

SECT. 1. The judicial power of the United States shall be vested in one Supreme Court, and in such inferior courts as shall, when necessary, from time to time, be constituted by the legislature of the United States.

SECT. 2. The judges of the Supreme Court, and of the inferior courts, shall hold their offices during good behavior. They shall, at stated times, receive for their services a compensation, which shall not be diminished during their continuance in office.

SECT. 3. The jurisdiction of the Supreme Court shall extend to all cases arising under laws passed by the legislature of the United States; to all cases affecting ambassadors, other public ministers, and consuls; to the trial of impeachments of officers of the United

States; to all cases of admiralty and maritime jurisdiction; to controversies between two or more States (except such as shall regard territory or jurisdiction); between a State and citizens of another State; between citizens of different States; and between a State, or the citizens thereof, and foreign States, citizens or subjects. In cases of impeachment, cases affecting ambassadors, other public ministers and consuls, and those in which a State shall be a party, this jurisdiction shall be original. In all the other cases before mentioned, it shall be appellate, with such exceptions and under such regulations, as the legislature shall make. The legislature may assign any part of the jurisdiction above mentioned (except the trial of the President of the United States), in the manner and under the limitations which it shall think proper, to such inferior courts as it shall constitute from time to time.

SECT. 4. The trial of all criminal offences (except in cases of impeachment) shall be in the State where they shall be committed; and shall be by jury.

SECT. 5. Judgment, in cases of impeachment, shall not extend further than to removal from office, and disqualification to hold and enjoy any office of honor, trust, or profit under the United States. But the party convicted shall nevertheless be liable and subject to indictment, trial, judgment, and punishment according to law.

ARTICLE XII.

No State shall coin money; nor grant letters of marque and reprisal; nor enter into any treaty, alliance, or confederation; nor grant any title of nobility.

ARTICLE XIII.

No State, without the consent of the legislature of the United States, shall emit bills of credit, or make any thing but specie a tender in payment of debts; nor lay imposts or duties on imports; nor keep troops or ships of war in time of peace; nor enter into any agreement or compact with another State, or with any foreign power; nor engage in any war, unless it shall be actually invaded by enemies, or the danger of invasion be so imminent as not to admit of a delay until the legislature of the United States can be consulted.

ARTICLE XIV.

The citizens of each State shall be entitled to all privileges and immunities of citizens in the several States.

ARTICLE XV.

Any person charged with treason, felony, or high misdemeanor in any State, who shall flee from justice, and shall be found in any other State, shall, on demand of the executive power of the State from which he fled, be delivered up and removed to the State having jurisdiction of the offence.

ARTICLE XVI.

Full faith shall be given in each State, to the acts of the legislatures, and to the records and judicial proceedings of the courts and magistrates of every other State.

ARTICLE XVII.

New States lawfully constituted and established within the limits of the United States, may be admitted, by the legislature, into this government; but to such admission the consent of two thirds of the members present in each house shall be necessary. If a new State shall arise within the limits of any of the present States, the consent of the legislatures of such States shall be necessary to the admission. If the admission be consented to, the new States shall be admitted on the same terms with the original States. But the legislature may make conditions with the new States, concerning the public debt which shall be then subsisting.

ARTICLE XVIII.

The United States shall guarantee to each State a republican form of government; and shall protect each State against foreign invasions, and, on the application of its legislature, against domestic violence.

ARTICLE XIX.

On the application of the legislatures of two thirds of the States in the Union, for an amendment to this Constitution, the legislature of the United States shall call a convention for that purpose.

ARTICLE XX.

The members of the legislatures, and the executive and judicial officers of the United States and of the several States, shall be bound by oath to support this Constitution.

ARTICLE XXI.

The ratification of the conventions of —— States shall be sufficient for organizing this Constitution.

ARTICLE XXII.

This Constitution shall be laid before the United States in Congress assembled, for their approbation; and it is the opinion of this Convention, that it should be afterwards submitted to a convention chosen in each State, under the recommendation of its legislature, in order to receive the ratification of such convention.

ARTICLE XXIII.

To introduce this government, it is the opinion of this Convention, that each assenting convention should notify its assent and ratification to the United States in Congress assembled; that Congress, after receiving the assent and ratification of the conventions of —— States, should appoint and publish a day, as early as may be, and appoint a place for commencing proceedings under this Constitution; and after such publication, the legislatures of the several States should elect members of the Senate and direct the election of members of the House of Representatives; and that the members of the legislature should meet at the time and place, assigned by Congress, and should as soon as may be after their meeting, choose the President of the United States and proceed to execute this Constitution.

This report was considered and debated in the Convention from the 6th of August until the 9th of September, during which it received a great variety of modifications and alterations.

On the 9th of September it was referred as amended. to a committee of style and revision, consisting of Messrs. Johnson of Connecticut, Hamilton of New York, Morris of Pennsylvania, Madison of Virginia, and King of Massachusetts.

This committee reported on the 14th September, and after a great variety of motions to amend, of which the record is very imperfect, their draft was adopted, with but slight modifications.

EXTRACTS FROM THE DEBATE

In the Federal Convention, on the respective Plans of Mr. Randolph and Mr. Patterson.

The first resolution of each plan having been read, Mr. Lansing of New York, said: — "The plan of Mr. Patterson sustains the sovereignty of the respective States, that of Mr. Randolph destroys it.

"The plan of Mr. Randolph, in short, absorbs all power, except what may be exercised in the little local matters of the States, which are not objects worthy of the supreme cognizance. He grounded his preference of Mr. Patterson's plan, chiefly on two objections to that of Mr. Randolph, — first, want of power in the Convention to discuss and propose it; secondly, the improbability of its being adopted.

"He was decidedly of opinion that the power of the Convention was restrained to amendments of a Federal nature, and having for their basis the confederacy in being. The acts of Congress, the tenor of the acts of the States, the commissions produced by the several deputations, all proved this. And this limitation of the power to an amendment of the confederacy marked the opinion of the States, that it was unnecessary and improper to go further."

Mr. Patterson said, he preferred his own plan, "because it accorded, — first, with the powers of the Convention; secondly, with the sentiments of the people. If the confederacy was radically wrong, let us return to our States, and obtain larger powers, not assume them ourselves. . . . . If we argue the matter on the supposition, that no confederacy, at present, exists, it cannot be denied, that all the States stand on the footing of equal sovereignty. All, therefore, must concur, before any can be bound. If a proportional representation be right, why do we not vote so here? If we argue on the fact that a federal compact actually exists, and consult the articles of it, we shall find an equal sovereignty to be the basis of it. He read the fifth article of the Confederation, giving each State a vote; and the thirteenth, declaring that no alteration shall be made without unanimous consent. This is the nature of all treaties. What is unanimously done must be unanimously undone."

"If the sovereignty of the States is to be maintained, the representatives must be drawn immediately from the States, not from the people; and we have no power to vary the idea of equal sovereignty. Do the people at large complain of Congress? No. What they wish is that Congress may have more power. If the power now proposed be not enough, the people hereafter will make additions to it. With proper powers, Congress will act with more energy and wisdom than the proposed national legislature; being few in number and more secreted and refined by the mode of election. The plan of Mr. Randolph will also be enormously expensive. Allowing Georgia and Delaware two representatives each in the popular branch, the aggregate number of that branch will be one hundred and eighty. Add to it half as many for the other branch, and you have two hundred and seventy members, coming once at least a year from the most distant as well as the most central parts of the republic. In the present deranged state of our finances, can so expensive a system be seriously thought of?"

Mr. PINCKNEY. — "The whole comes to this, as he conceived. Give New Jersey an equal vote, and she will dismiss her scruples and concur in the national system. He thought the convention authorized to go any length in recommending, which they found necessary to remedy the evils which produced this convention."

Mr. RANDOLPH "was not scrupulous with regard to power. When the salvation of the republic was at stake, it would be treason to our trust, not to propose what we found necessary. He painted in strong colors the imbecility of the existing confederacy, and the danger of delaying a substantial reform. In answer to the objection drawn from the sense of our constituents, as denoted by their acts relating to the convention and the objects of their deliberation, he observed, as each State acted separately in the case, it would have been indecent for it, to have charged the existing constitution with all the vices which it might have perceived in it. . . . . . There are reasons certainly of a peculiar nature, where the ordinary cautions must be dispensed with; and this is certainly one of them. He would not, so far as depended on him, leave any thing that seemed necessary undone. The present moment is favorable, and is probably the last that will offer.

"The true question is whether we will adhere to the federal plan, or introduce the national plan. The insufficiency of the former has been fully displayed by the trial already made. There are but two modes by which the ends of a Federal government can be attained; the first by coercion, as proposed by Mr. Patterson's plan; the second by real legislation, as proposed by the other plan. Coercion he pronounced to be *impracticable, expensive, cruel to individuals.* It tended also to habituate the instruments of it, to shed the blood, and riot in the spoils of their fellow-citizens and consequently trained them up for the service of ambition.

"We must resort, therefore, to a *national legislation over individuals;* for which Congress are unfit. To vest such power in them would be blending the legislative with the executive, contrary to the received maxim on this subject. If the union of these powers, heretofore in Congress has been safe, it has been owing to the general impotency of that body. Congress, moreover, are not elected by the people, but by the legislatures, who retain even a power to recall. They have therefore, no will of their own; they are a mere diplomatic body, and are always obsequious to the views of the States, who are always encroaching on the authority of the United States. A provision for harmony among the States, as in trade, naturalization, &c.; for crushing rebellion, whenever it may rear its crest, and for certain other general benefits, must be made. . . A national government alone, properly constituted, will answer this purpose, and he begged it may be considered that the present is the last moment for establishing one. After this select experiment, the people will despair."

Mr. Hamilton said, he was unfriendly to both plans. "He was

particularly opposed to that from New Jersey, being fully convinced that no amendment of the Confederation, leaving the States in possession of their sovereignty, could possibly answer the purpose. On the other hand, he confessed he was much discouraged by the amazing extent of country, in expecting the desired blessings from any general sovereignty that could be substituted. As to the powers of the convention, he thought the doubts started on that subject had arisen from distinctions and reasonings too subtle.

"A federal government he conceived to mean an association of independent communities into one.

"He agreed with the honorable gentleman from Virginia, that we owed it to our country to do, on this emergency, whatever we should deem essential to its happiness. The States sent us here to provide for the exigencies of the Union. . . . . . The question is, What provision shall we make for the happiness of our country?"

General HAMILTON then read his "plan," which, however, he remarked, he did not mean to offer to the Convention.

Mr. MARTIN said, "he considered that the separation from Great Britain placed the thirteen States in a state of nature towards each other; that they would have remained in that state till this time, but for the confederation; that they entered into the confederation on a footing of equality; that they met now to amend it, on the same footing, and that he could never accede to a plan that would introduce an inequality and lay ten States at the mercy of Virginia, Massachusetts, and Pennsylvania."

Mr. WILSON "could not admit the doctrine, that when the colonies became independent of Great Britain, they became independent also of each other. By the Declaration of Independence, the *United Colonies* were declared to be free and independent States; he inferred that they were independent, not *individually*, but *unitedly*, and that they were confederated, as they were independent States."

Col. MASON. — "The essential difference between the two plans had been clearly stated. The principal objections against that of Mr. Randolph were, the *want of power and the want of practi-*

cability. There can be no weight in the first, as the fiat is not to be here, but in the people. He thought with his colleague (Mr. Randolph) that there were besides, certain crises, in which all the ordinary cautions yielded to public necessity. The *impracticability* of gaining the public concurrence, he thought was still more groundless. . . . He took this occasion to repeat that, notwithstanding his solicitude to establish a national government, he never would agree to abolish the State governments, or render them absolutely insignificant. They were as necessary as the general government, and he would be equally careful to preserve them. He was aware of the difficulty of drawing the line between them, but hoped it was not insurmountable."

Mr. Luther Martin "agreed with Col. Mason as to the importance of the State governments; he would support them at the expense of the general government, which was instituted for the purpose of that support. . . . At the separation from the British empire, the people of America preferred the establishment of themselves into thirteen separate sovereignties, instead of incorporating themselves into one. To these they look up for the security of their lives, liberties, and properties; to these they must look up. The federal government they formed to defend the whole against foreign nations in time of war, and to defend the lesser States against the ambition of the larger."

Mr. Sherman. — "The complaints at present are not that the views of Congress are unwise or unfaithful, but that their powers are insufficient for the execution of their views. The national debt, and the want of power somewhere, to draw forth the national resources, are the great matters that press. All the States were sensible of the defects of power in Congress. . . . For want of a general system, taxes to a due amount had not been drawn from trade, which was the most convenient resource. The disparity of States in point of size, he perceived, was the main difficulty. But the large States had not yet suffered from the inequality of votes enjoyed by the smaller ones. In all the great and general points, the interests of all the States were the same. . . . If the difficulty on the subject of representation cannot otherwise be got over, he would agree to have two branches, and a proportional representation in one of them, provided each State had an equal voice in the other."

Dr. JOHNSON said,—"They [the advocates of the Virginia plan] wished to leave the States in possession of a considerable, though a subordinate jurisdiction. They had not yet, however, shown how this could consist with, or be secured against, the general sovereignty and jurisdiction which they proposed to give to the national government."

Mr. MADISON "was of opinion in the first place, that there was less danger of encroachment from the general government than from the State governments; and in the second place, that the mischiefs from encroachments would be less fatal if made by the former than if made by the latter. All the examples of other confederacies prove the greater tendency, in such systems, to anarchy than to tyranny; to disobedience of the members, than usurpations of the federal head. Our own experience had fully illustrated this tendency. But it will be said, that the proposed change in the principles and form of the Union will vary the tendency; that the general government will have real and greater powers, and will be derived, in one branch at least, from the people, not from the governments of the States. To give full force to this objection, let it be supposed for a moment that indefinite power should be given to the general legislature, and the States reduced to corporations dependent on the general legislature — why should it follow that the general government would take from the States any branch of their power, as far as its operation was beneficial and its continuance desirable to the people? In some of the States, particularly in Connecticut, the townships are incorporated, and have a certain limited jurisdiction, — have the representatives of the people of the townships in the legislation of the State ever endeavored to despoil the townships of any part of their local authority? As far as this local authority is convenient to the people, they are attached to it; and their representatives, chosen by and amenable to them, naturally respect their attachment to this as much as their attachment to any other right or interest. The relation of a general government to State governments is parallel.

"Guards were more necessary against encroachments of the State governments on the general government, than of the latter on the former. The great objection made against an abolition of the State governments was, that the general government could not extend its care to all the minute objects which fall under the cognizance of the local jurisdictions. The objection as stated lay not against the probable abuse of the general power, but against the imperfect use that could be made of it throughout so great an extent of country, and over so great a variety of objects. As far as its operations would be practicable, it would not, in this view, be improper; as far as it would be impracticable, the convenience of the general government itself would concur with that of the people in the maintenance of subordinate governments."

HISTORY

OF THE

COLONIAL CONFEDERATIONS.

INTRODUCTION.

It is my purpose in the following sketch to show how the American system of government came into operation, and briefly to trace the course of events which led to the adoption of the Federal Constitution. I think it will be made to appear that the whole structure of our political institutions is the natural production of the principles laid down by the founders of the several States. As originally planted, each colony or settlement was a distinct community, with a jurisdiction over its own internal affairs, entirely independent of its neighbors. Several of these colonies, as Plymouth, Connecticut, and Rhode Island, established their governments by voluntary association, without any charter or authority but the consent of the governed. The other colonies, although acting under royal charters, exercised the right of local legislation by assemblies, chosen by themselves, and the distance which separated the colonies from the mother country, and the disturbed and revolutionary condition of the British government during much of our colonial existence, greatly favored the development and facilitated the exercise of the principles of self-government. Favored by these circumstances, the infant States early attained a strong and vigorous individuality. Each colony regarded itself as practically a sovereign community, although they all recognized a sort of vague allegiance to the British crown. This idea, after the Declaration of Independence, ripened into the great doctrine of *State Rights.*

The colonies, in the earlier periods of their history, were small and feeble, and surrounded by tribes of jealous aborigines and by rival and often hostile European settlements. As a security against the dangers which threatened them from these sources, and left to their own resources for the means of defence, the expedient of temporary alliances soon gave place to permanent confederacies. These were succeeded by annual Congresses, — by the Confederation which conducted the country through the struggle of the Revolution, — and, finally, by the establishment of the federal government.

In the compilation of the following historical sketch, I have followed, mainly, the authority, and quoted with considerable freedom, the language, of the "History of the United States," by the Hon. George Bancroft, to whom I wish to make proper acknowledgments. I have also consulted many other works, as indicated in the text.

HISTORY.

General Washington commences his first inaugural address to the first Congress of the United States assembled under the Constitution, in the following language: —

"No people can be bound to acknowledge and adore the Invisible Hand which conducts the affairs of men more than the people of the United States. Every step by which they have advanced to the character of an independent nation seems to have been distinguished by some token of providential agency; and in the important revolution just accomplished, in the system of their united government, the tranquil deliberations, and voluntary consent of so many distinct communities from which the event has resulted, cannot be compared with the means by which most governments have been established, without the return of pious gratitude along with an humble anticipation of the future blessings which the past seems to presage."

Among these "steps" so appropriately alluded to by the Father of his country, none are more significant than those which attended the discovery of this continent. History teaches that each of the great divisions of the earth has developed a peculiar and distinctive phase of human civilization. Africa, whose unwritten annals are brought down to us by the pyramids and other enduring monuments of physical power, appears to have produced what may be regarded as physical civilization of a high order. Asia, whose existing fossilized and petrified forms of civil and social institutions have remained nearly stationary from the earliest periods of authentic history, appears to have been the theatre of the second great "step" in the development of human nature.

Europe had been reserved for the development of the next stage of human progress. This was ushered in by the birth of the arts and sciences, of language, literature, poetry, and eloquence of Greece and Rome; and consummated by the establishment of modern Christian civilization.

The Old World was now overspread with institutions differing in their character in the various countries which had given them birth, but all attached to the soil, and as permanently affixed to it as the mountains and valleys over which their influence extended.

Countries and nations have like characteristics with individual man. They have their periods of growth and decay; of youth, manhood, and age. And it is remarkable that no new people or nation has seemed to flourish upon the soil of a preceding one. If a nation has become decrepid and died out, the soil appears to have been exhausted, no phœnix springs from its ashes. The empire of the Ptolemies and the Pharaohs, Persia, Babylon, Syria, Palestine, and even Greece and Rome, are illustrations of this great law. In neither of those countries has a new or powerful people resuscitated the greatness and glory of the departed. It seems to be a law of our nature, that every successive step of progress which marks a distinctive era in the upward development of the human race, must be taken upon a virgin soil.

American civilization is a new civilization. American nationality is not a continuation or an extension of any or all of the European policies, but a new and distinct system of national development. Africa has produced and developed the African; Asia has produced and developed the Asiatic; Europe has fulfilled the same function for the European. America has been reserved to become the theatre of American civilization.

The existence of the western continent was made known to the world through the genius and enterprise of Christopher Columbus, towards the close of the fifteenth century of the Christian era. During the succeeding century, several permanent settlements were made upon the West India Islands and the adjacent main lands. About the same time, the coasts of the United States were discovered by English navigators. It is generally conceded that the American continent was first actually discovered by John and Sebastian Cabot, sailing under the English flag, in the year 1496. The first permanent settlement made within the original limits of the United States, was at Jamestown, Virginia, in 1607. This settlement was made, and a colonial government established under a charter from the English crown.

The colony of Plymouth, the second in order of time, was founded in 1620. Unlike that at Jamestown, the founders of New England had no charter or authority from any established government of the old world. They had long been exiles and outcasts from their native England.

Mr. JOHN QUINCY ADAMS, in a discourse delivered before the Massachusetts Historical Society, in 1843, says: "The Plymouth colony is remarkable for having furnished the first example in modern times, of a social compact or system of government, instituted by voluntary agreement, conformably to the laws of nature, by men of equal rights and about to establish their permanent habitation as a community, in a new country. Upon landing at Plymouth, they had no charter from their king and no right [grant] to the soil upon which they landed." Before they left the deck of the *Mayflower*, they drew up and signed articles of compact, as the basis of their future government. "This social compact was the necessary result of their situation, as men in a state of nature, subject to no human law but that which they consented to impose upon themselves," and it contains the leading principles of those great doctrines which were subsequently announced to the world in the Declaration of Independence.

Within twenty years from the landing of the Pilgrim fathers, colonies were planted and separate jurisdictions established in Massachusetts, Connecticut, New Hampshire, and Rhode Island, and other places. The colonies in Connecticut and Rhode Island, like that at Plymouth, established their own governments, without recourse to royal charters.

As early as 1636, the idea of a confederacy began to be agitated amongst the New England colonies; and in the following year, a conference was held in Boston, between the magistrates and ministers of the colonies of Plymouth and Massachusetts, with the view of forming an alliance offensive and defensive. Mr. Adams, in the discourse before alluded to says, that "the idea of a confederacy seems to have originated with the colony of Plymouth, which submitted the proposition to Massachusetts on the 12th of May, 1637."

Other authorities state that the original movement towards a confederation proceeded from the colonies of Connecticut and New Haven.* But the Connecticut proposition is dated August 21, 1637, more than three months later than that of Plymouth. These movements resulted in the assembling of a convention in Boston for the purpose of agreeing to articles of union, "but the apprehensions of Connecticut dictated such extreme reserve in relation to grants of power to the proposed confederacy, that Massachusetts did not deem it desirable to prosecute the scheme."

The proposition was renewed by Connecticut in 1639, in consequence of the dangers which threatened that colony from the encroachments of their Dutch neighbors, inhabiting the country along the banks of the Hudson river. It was, however, again unsuccessful, the government of Massachusetts "not being satisfied with having an equal vote in the confederacy with the smaller colonies," and the latter firmly adhering to the doctrine of equal colonial dignity.

The breaking out of the civil war in England, and the circumstances which surrounded the colonies at home, seeming to throw them upon their own resources for providing for their common defence against the encroachments of the French and their Indian allies upon the north, and the Dutch upon the west, as well as against the hostile Indian tribes, the General Court of Massachusetts, in 1642, appointed a committee to take into consideration the expediency and practicability of forming a union of the colonies. This committee was instructed to report at the succeeding session of the General Court. As the result of this movement, commissioners from the several colonies assembled in Boston on the 10th of May, 1643. The first difficulty which presented

* Palfrey's History of New England, Vol I. p. 626.

itself in the deliberations of the convention was the question involving the power of the several colonies in the general assembly. Massachusetts was nearly as large and populous, and probably more wealthy, than all the others combined, and insisted upon a relative suffrage in the confederacy. The Plymouth delegates, on the other hand, were under special instructions not to yield the principle of colonial equality in the general body. That colony also required that the articles agreed on, should not be obligatory upon her, until they had been approved by a popular vote.

After a session of nine days, the commissioners agreed upon twelve articles, to constitute the organic law of the new general government.

These articles were, in substance, as follows: namely,*

First. "The colonies of Massachusetts, Plymouth, Connecticut, and New Haven, do agree and conclude that they will hereafter be called and known as the UNITED COLONIES OF NEW ENGLAND."

Second. "The said United Colonies, for themselves and their posterities, do jointly and severally hereby enter into a firm and perpetual league of friendship and amity, for offence and defence, mutual advice and succor upon all just occasions, for their mutual safety and general welfare."

Third. "Each colony retains its distinct and separate jurisdiction and control over its domestic and local affairs, institutions and laws. No two colonies are to be joined in one jurisdiction, nor any other colony admitted into the confederacy, without the consent of the whole."

Fourth. "The charge of all wars, offensive and defensive, and other general expenses, shall be borne in proportion to the number of male inhabitants between sixteen and sixty years of age, in each colony."

Fifth. "Upon due notice from any colony, of an invasion, the other colonies shall immediately furnish and send forward their respective quotas of troops," &c.

* Hazard's Historical Collections, Vol. I. p. 1.

Sixth. The general assembly of the united colonies was to consist of two commissioners from each colony, and to meet annually on the first Monday of September. This body had power to hear, examine, weigh, and determine all affairs of war or peace, and other matters pertaining to the general welfare — "*but not to intermeddle with the local affairs of the colonies.*" The concurrence of two thirds of the body was sufficient authority to carry into effect any proposed measure, but if less than two thirds concurred, a majority could submit the measure to the consideration of the respective governments for decision.

Seventh. Provides for the annual election of the President.

Eighth. The assembled commissioners are authorized to frame and establish general regulations of a civil nature for preserving the general peace and preventing occasions for war; to regulate intercourse with Indian tribes.

Ninth. "It is also agreed, that if any servant shall run away from his master, into any other of these confederated jurisdictions, that in such case, upon the certificate of one magistrate in the jurisdiction out of which the said servant fled, or upon other due proof, the said servant shall be delivered either to his master or to any other that pursues and brings such certificate or proof."

Tenth. Provides against hasty or inconsiderate wars being entered into or fomented by any of the colonies.

Eleventh. Makes provision for extraordinary meetings of the general assembly.

Twelfth. It is agreed that this confederacy shall be perpetual, and if any of the confederates shall violate or fail to comply with the articles of the confederacy, the breach and consequent injury shall be duly considered and adjudged by the commissioners of the other colonies, "so that the peace and the confederation shall be entirely preserved without violation."

An examination of this confederation and of the principles involved in its inception and development, will show that it involves the exercise of sovereign power in its highest attributes. By it, provision is made for a government to which is committed the control of the foreign relations of the confederacy, and authority over other matters of great and general concern, while local powers and objects of government are carefully reserved to the local jurisdictions.

The New England confederacy of 1643, was the model and prototype of the North American confederacy of 1756, and of the continental Congress of 1774.

The almost incessant wars which grew out of the constant struggles of England and France for ascendency on this continent, and in which the colonies warmly sympathized, finally led to the meeting of a general Congress of the colonies at New York in 1690.

On the 8th February, 1696, WILLIAM PENN submitted to the board of trade in London, a plan for a union of the American colonies. He proposed that "the several colonies do meet once a year, and oftener, if need be, during war, and once in two years in peace, by stated deputies, to debate and resolve of such measures as are most advisable for their better understanding and the public tranquillity and safety."

When the information of the passage of the stamp act, by the British Parliament, reached the colonies, indicating the fixed purpose of that government to tax America, without her consent, a general determination to resist its execution, was manifested. The General Court of Massachusetts, which, Mr. Bancroft says, "is certainly the parent of the American Union," immediately extended an invitation to the other colonies to meet in general Congress. In pursuance of this invitation, the colonies met in New York in October, 1765. Delegates were present from Massachusetts, Rhode Island, Connecticut, New York, New Jersey, Pennsylvania, Delaware, Maryland, and South Carolina.

This Congress adopted a declaration of rights, asserting that the sole power of taxation resided in the people of the colonies, and adopted other energetic measures.

In 1751, Archibald Kennedy proposed that provision should be made, by act of Parliament, for an annual meeting of commissioners from all the colonies, to be held at New York, for the purpose of providing means of defence against the French and Indians.

In 1752, an article appeared in a Philadelphia newspaper, understood to have been from the pen of Dr. Franklin, in which a voluntary union, originating in the colonies themselves, and under their exclusive control and management, was advocated as preferable to one imposed by Parliament. The writer thought it would be very strange, if six nations of ignorant savages should be capable of forming a scheme for such a union, and be able to execute it in such a manner as that it has subsisted for ages, and that yet a like union should be impracticable for ten or a dozen English colonies, to whom it was more necessary and must be more advantageous.

In accordance with these and other similar suggestions, commissioners from several of the colonies, including Virginia and all the colonies north of it, assembled at Albany in the summer of 1754, to which Dr. Franklin submitted a *project* of union.

Hitherto all the propositions for a union of the colonies, looked mainly to a means of common defence against the hostile demonstrations of the aborigines and the threatened and attempted encroachments of the French. But the conquest of Canada by the united arms of England and America, ushered in a new era of our history. The French power had substantially disappeared from the continent, and the Indians, weakened and exhausted by their long struggles with the superior race, were disposed to peace. But instead of the repose which the colonies might have reasonably anticipated from the retirement of their natural and ancient enemies, they were immediately precipitated into a still more severe and momentous struggle with their mother country. They had contended with the savage for the right to occupy the continent and turn its wilderness into fruitful fields — and with the French for the right of growth and expansion. They were now to contend with the more formidable power of the mother country for existence as a free people. From their earliest settlement the colonies had recognized a *quasi* allegiance to the British crown, but they had, at the same time, claimed and exercised the right of substantial self-government. While the French power hovered over their northern border, this right, although repeatedly threatened, was successfully maintained. But no sooner had the British government, by the aid of the colonies, triumphed over their rival, than they instituted a series of measures for the subjugation of the colonies themselves. These led to what may be properly regarded as the first "*American Congress.*"

On the 6th of June, 1765, James Otis introduced into the House of Delegates of Massachusetts, a proposition "for calling an *American Congress*, which should come together without asking the consent of the king, and should consist of committees from each of the thirteen colonies, to be appointed directly by the delegates of the people without regard to the other branches of the legislature." The immediate object was to concert measures for a general resistance to the stamp act. The measure was adopted, and letters were sent to all the colonies, inviting the meeting of the Congress in the following October.

Nine colonies, represented by twenty-eight delegates, assembled in the city of New York on the 7th of that month.

After the examination of the credentials of the members, they proceeded by ballot to the election of president, and TIMOTHY RUGGLES, of Massachusetts, was declared to be duly elected, and conducted to the chair.

This was unquestionably the signal gun which aroused the continent, and called to a concentration of its energies for the great struggle of the Revolution. Before, however, these proceedings could have become known in the sister colonies, they were aroused to simultaneous action. The celebrated resolutions of Patrick Henry were passed in the House of Burgesses of Virginia on the last day of May.

The hope of OTIS, the originator of the movement, was, that a Union would be formed, which in its result, would "knit and work into the very blood and bones of the original system, *every region as fast as settled.*" How fully has this aspiration been realized! And the magnanimous Gadsden of South Carolina said, in his opening speech—"We should stand upon the broad common ground of those natural rights that we all feel and know as men. There ought to be no New England man, no New Yorker, known on the continent, but all of us Americans."

The immediate result of this movement was a complete triumph of the colonies, in the repeal of the obnoxious law — but the ultimate result is yet to be developed by the progress and destiny of the American Union. The idea of a union of the colonies for mutual support and defence, had become the pervading sentiment of the popular mind. They began to speak of each other as "sister colonies," and regard for the common interests became interwoven with all their ideas of patriotism. "If Boston suffered, Charleston rushed to her relief, with the unselfish and prodigal zeal of a sister's love."

In 1766, Mayhew of Boston, suggested whether "it would not be decorous for our Assembly to send circulars to all the rest, expressing a desire to cement union among ourselves? A good foundation for this," he adds, "has been laid by the Congress at New York." And in 1768, the House of Representatives of Massachusetts directed a circular letter, drafted by Samuel Adams, to be despatched to each House of Representatives or of Burgesses, on the continent, with that object in view. When intelligence of this proceeding reached England, it was regarded by the ministry as a movement to prepare the country for rebellion and revolution; and it was determined that immediate measures must be taken to curb the independent spirit of the offending province. Orders were sent to the governors of the other twelve colonies, warning them to give no countenance to the "seditious paper." The Burgesses of Virginia, regardless of these warnings, responded to the call of Massachusetts, assured her of their applause and support, and directed their speaker "to write to the respective speakers of all the assemblies on the continent, to make known their proceedings and to intimate how necessary they thought it that the colonies should unite." The Assembly of South Carolina, "sitting with its doors locked, unanimously directed its speaker to signify to both provinces its entire approbation" of the course they had adopted. The other colonies manifested the same determination to make common cause in defence of the "liberties of America."

In 1769, the House of Burgesses of Virginia passed resolutions, claiming for that body "the sole right of imposing taxes on the inhabitants" of that dominion, and "asserted the lawfulness and expediency of procuring a concert of the colonies in case of the violated rights of America." These resolutions were directed to be communicated "to every legislature in America," asking their concurrence. Encouraged by this bold and manly position of the Old Dominion, the other colonies adopted the same or similar resolutions.

The assembly of New York took one step in advance of the positions assumed by the other colonies, by passing resolutions inviting each province, without waiting for further aggressions, to elect delegates at once, to a general congress, "which should exercise legislative power for them all." Virginia concurred in the proposition, but the other colonies were not prepared for so bold and decided a step at that time.

Towards the close of the year 1772 was brought into operation that great institution, which has been declared to have included the whole Revolution, "THE COMMITTEE OF CORRESPONDENCE." Simple and unostentatious in its organization, it became the germ of a power which not only conducted the American colonies to independence and established a republic which already extends from ocean to ocean, and controls the destiny of one half the world; but which, by force of example, overturned the most ancient and powerful thrones of the other hemisphere, and annihilated the feudal institutions which had enslaved the peoples of Europe for ten centuries. This powerful engine of the popular will was called into being by the fertile intellect and fervid patriotism of SAMUEL ADAMS, a name not unworthy to be inscribed upon the same imperishable tablet of the American heart, with that of GEORGE WASHINGTON.

On the 2d of November, 1772, the citizens of Boston were assembled in *town-meeting*, to take into consideration the "rights of the colonists," and "the infringements and violations thereof." They had been warned by the royal governor, that the law did not authorize *town-meetings* to meddle with such matters. They, however, resolved that they "had and ought to have, a right" to consider their "grievances," "and to communicate their sentiments to other towns."

To this mass meeting of the citizens of Boston, assembled for consultation upon the great questions involved in the controversy waged between themselves and their country on one side, and the British government on the other, touching the "rights of America," and the aggressions of England, SAMUEL ADAMS, the representative man of the time, submitted the following resolution: —

Resolved, "That a COMMITTEE OF CORRESPONDENCE be appointed, to consist of twenty-one persons, to state the rights of the colonists of this province in particular, as men, as Christians, and as subjects, to communicate and publish the same," &c.

The object was to secure a concert of action among the towns of the province, so that their delegates to the general assembly might be prepared, at their approaching session, to extend an invitation to the other colonies, to take measures for the assembling of another general congress.

This was a movement in the right direction, and based upon the fundamental principles of civil government. It contemplated the establishment of a government emanating immediately and directly from the will of the people, without the intervention of any of the preëxisting forms of law or government. Its result was, to repel the foreign domination with which they were threatened, by superseding the existing forms of authority, which were so interwoven with foreign elements as to be incompatible with the full enjoyment of their natural rights. It was the inauguration of a new era in the gradual development of American institutions.

"The flame caught," and in a short time all the principal towns were organized, with their committees of correspondence, acting in harmonious concert with that of Boston, and the breath of life was breathed into the "COMMONWEALTH OF MASSACHUSETTS." It ceased forever to be a dependency of a foreign jurisdiction.

In their first report submitted to the TOWN-MEETING held in Faneuil Hall, on the 20th of November, the Committee enumerate, among the natural rights of the colonists, "the right to life, to liberty, and to property — the right to support and defend these — and the right to change their allegiance for their sake;" thus distinctly announcing the great doctrines of the Declaration of Independence, and foreshadowing its approach.

On the meeting of the Assembly, in January, 1773, the speaker transmitted to Richard Henry Lee, of Virginia, the proceedings in Boston and other towns of Massachusetts through their committees of correspondence, and suggested the organization of provincial committees, for the purpose of inaugurating a continental confederacy. The fate of the proposition depended upon the decision of the Old Dominion. The Burgesses met on the fourth of March, and the proceedings in Massachusetts were laid before them. Virginia did not hesitate. A series of resolutions for a system of intercolonial committees of correspondence was introduced and unanimously adopted, and the committee was at once appointed on the part of that colony. They sent their resolves to the other colonies and asked concurrence in that great measure which was to realize the idea of an American Union. The colonies one after another responded with zeal and alacrity; and thus an inchoate organization was effected, competent to convene a Congress on any emergency.

During the autumn of 1773, there appeared in the "Boston Gazette" a series of articles advocating "an annual Congress of American States," to form and provide for the maintenance of a bill of rights; and in case of the continued attempts of the British government to subvert their liberties, "to form an independent State — an *American commonwealth.*"

In March, 1774, the Massachusetts committee of correspondence despatched a circular to the other colonies, explaining why that colony had been under the necessity of proceeding so far of itself, and asking for its future guidance, the benefit of the councils of the whole country. They concluded by suggesting that a general Congress of all the colonies on the continent should be convened.

In the mean time, the British government were busily engaged in maturing their measures for reducing the colonies to obedience. The town of Boston was first to feel the iron grasp. The Boston port bill, as the leading measure of the ministry, and the special favorite of the king, was introduced by Lord North on the 18th

March. "The town of Boston," said one of the leading advocates of the measure, "ought to be knocked about their ears and destroyed. *Delenda est Carthago.* You will never have proper obedience to the laws of this country, until you have destroyed that nest of locusts." "Put an end to their *town-meetings*," exclaimed another. "What passed in Boston," said a third, "is the last overt act of high treason." And on signing the bill, the king is said to have made the significative remark, that "Boston has now no option but to claim entire independence or approach the throne as a penitent." Boston had no difficulty in making her choice.

The second penal bill for Massachusetts contained a clause abolishing *town-meetings*, except for the choice of town-officers, or on the special permission of the governor.

The course of events and the force of circumstances had compelled Massachusetts, and especially the town of Boston, to take the lead, and to unfurl the banner of the American Revolution. But when its ample folds were given to the breeze, the whole people of the continent were impelled by one general and all-pervading impulse, to the accomplishment of the great destiny opening before them. "As the earth bursts forth into new life at the bidding of the sun and showers of spring," the great heart of the Anglo-American colonies was expanded by a common fire of patriotic devotion to the common cause.

In this early stage of the struggle, it was the evident purpose of the British ministry to insulate Massachusetts from her sister colonies, and they even hoped to confine the contest to her refractory capital. Hence they commenced their operations by closing that port with the view of starving its inhabitants into submission. The act was received on the 10th of May, 1774, and the Boston committee of correspondence, immediately met and invited the committees of the neighboring towns to a conference "on the critical state of public affairs." The committee met in the "Cradle of Liberty" on the 12th of May, and while they were in session, as if by a miraculous interposition, they received intelligence, that in answer to the recent circular, all the thirteen colonies had come to the unanimous resolution to accede to the UNION.

The next day a *town*-meeting was called, and the port act was read and discussed. The people resolved not to be intimidated into submission, but "to maintain to the utmost of our abilities, the *rights of America*." They adopted an appeal to the "*sister colonies*, promising to suffer for America with becoming fortitude," but "entreating not to be left to suffer alone."

The New York committee anticipated the appeal of Boston. Having received a copy of the "port act" directly from England, they held a meeting and adopted resolutions recommending the holding of a "general Congress," which they immediately forwarded to the other colonies. "This prompt and decisive action sent a thrill of joy through the hearts of the suffering Bostonians, and assured them of the sympathy of the continent."

The Boston circular was adopted on the 12th of May, and before the close of the month nearly all of the colonies had concurred in the suggestion for a general Congress, and adopted the cause of Boston as their own. Virginia and South Carolina took immediate action, on the arrival of the Boston messenger, for a united resistance. The committee of Connecticut entreated Massachusetts to appoint a time and place for the meeting of the Congress without delay.

In June, the assembly of Massachusetts met in regular annual session. The eyes of the continent were fixed upon them. It had been universally conceded, that from them was to proceed the call, fixing the time and place for assembling of the American Congress. Gen. Gage, at the head of a formidable military force, had just entered upon the government of that colony. He was armed with despotic power, and specially authorized to arrest and bring to justice Samuel Adams and other ringleaders. Adams was a member of the legislature and of the committee of nine, on the condition of the colony. After secret consultation with a sufficient number of his colleagues to insure success, on Friday the 17th June, the assembly having ordered the doors to be closed and "locked," Mr. Adams reported the proposition for the meeting of the CONTINENTAL CONGRESS at Philadelphia on the first of September. The measure was carried through the house, dele gates elected, a tax levied to defray the expenses.

In the mean time, the governor becoming alarmed at these unusual proceedings, sent his secretary with a message, dissolving the assembly. But he knocked in vain for admission, until the House had accomplished its great object, appealed to the "towns" to sustain their proceedings and to provide for the relief of their suffering fellow-citizens, and submitted their cause to God and their sister colonies. But so universally were the fires of liberty already kindled throughout the length and breadth of the land, that Rhode Island had already anticipated these proceedings and elected her delegates, and before a knowledge of them had reached the Brandywine, a convention of the people of Maryland had assembled at Annapolis and elected delegates to the Congress.

Nothing is more characteristic of the spirit which pervaded the country, than the fact, that contributions of provisions poured into Boston from the remotest settlements. South Carolina, North Carolina, Virginia, and Maryland vied with each other in the liberality of their contributions. Washington presided at a meeting for this purpose and headed the subscription with fifty pounds. From the interior valley of Virginia, beyond the Blue Ridge, through which wagon roads were not yet constructed, a portion of the rich harvests of the pioneer farmers was packed on horses to Fredericksburg and thence forwarded to the suffering Bostonians — "as a free-will offering upon the altar of liberty and fraternity."

In the midst of these proceedings in the colonies, the British government took another step, which, although it was aimed directly at Massachusetts only, could not but be regarded as striking at the foundation of all pretence at liberty in any of the colonies. This was what was called the *regulating act.* This act abolished in effect the charter of Massachusetts, which, in most of its essential principles had existed from the original settlement, and concentrated all the powers of government in the hands of the king or his representative and appointee, the governor. The council, judges, jurors, and other officers were to be appointed by and hold their places at the will of the executive. It uprooted one of the dearest institutions of New England, then and now regarded as the cradle and nursery of democratic principles, namely; the *town-*

meeting. In short, it subjected the colony to the condition of a penal province. The sister colonies were not deceived by the local application of this act. They did not fail to see that the principles upon which it was based, would make it equally applicable to them, whenever it might suit the caprice of a British ministry to subject them to its provisions. They therefore, with a sagacious forecast, hastened to meet the issue with united counsels, upon the soil of Massachusetts. If the charter, laws and customs of that colony could be abrogated by the British Parliament, so might those of all the others. A sense of common danger was, therefore, now added to all the other ties which tended to cement the "Union of America." "Every grievance of any colony must be held as a grievance to the whole" had become the common sentiment, and pervaded alike the fishermen along the coasts of Maine, and the planters scattered over the broad savannas of the Carolinas and Georgia.

The Congress, which, in the language of Patrick Henry, "was the first in a never-ending succession of Congresses," assembled at Carpenter's Hall, Philadelphia, on the 5th of September, 1774. Having organized, by the selection of PEYTON RANDOLPH as president and Charles Thompson as secretary, the first question which arose was in relation to the method of voting. It was a question of the greatest magnitude, in its bearing upon the future political organization of the country. Patrick Henry, speaking for Virginia, thought "it would be unjust for a little colony to weigh as much in the councils of America as a great one." Mr. Sullivan from New Hampshire, responded that "a little colony had its all at stake as well as a great one,"—thus announcing, in the outset, the great doctrine of the equality of the States as independent communities. John Adams concurred in the reasoning of Mr. Henry, but inclined to a compromise. Without determining the question, the Congress adjourned. The next day the discussion was resumed. Mr. Henry argued "that British oppression had effaced the boundaries of the several colonies." That they were no longer Virginians and New Yorkers and New Englanders, but all Americans. Mr. Lynch and Mr. Rutledge of South Carolina, concurred substantially with Messrs. Henry, Harrison, and Bland in favor of a proportional vote, while Mr. Gadsden of South Carolina, and Richard Henry Lee, were disposed to acquiesce in the principle of the equality of the colonies. They saw "no way of voting but by colonies."

The first American precedent was, that of the "United Colonies of New England" formed in 1643, in which each colony had an equal vote. That principle was finally adopted, and it was resolved, that, in taking questions, "each colony shall have one vote."

The wheels of the Revolution were now in motion, and all efforts at a reconciliation between the crown and the colonies were unavailing. But the Congress proceeded with great caution and deliberation. They sent addresses respectively to the king, the parliament, and the people of Great Britain, in which they calmly argued the justice of their cause. Nearly two years passed in this state of *quasi* independence, before the final act of separation was accomplished.

On the 2d of July, 1776, the Continental Congress passed the following resolution, namely: —

"*Resolved*, That these United Colonies are and of right ought to be free and independent States; that they are absolved from all allegiance to the British crown; and that all political connection between them and the State of Great Britain is and ought to be totally dissolved."

On the passage of the resolution, a special committee was appointed to prepare a preamble or declaration of the reasons and causes which had led to its adoption, to accompany its promulgation to the world. On the *fourth of July*, Mr. JEFFERSON, in behalf of the committee, reported the original draft of the Declaration of Independence, which, after some amendments and modifications, received the unanimous sanction of the Congress, and was signed by each member.

The Congress having been originally assembled without any charter or form of legal authority, was without any organic law by which its proceedings could be regulated, or any rules by which they could be governed. While their duty was merely advisory, no great difficulty was experienced, but when, by the progress of events, it became to be the supreme authority of a nation, the necessity of definite organic principles became apparent. It had been agreed at the commencement of the proceedings, that as they had no means of ascertaining the relative population of the colonies, each should have an equal vote in determining questions. But as the importance of their proceedings increased in magnitude, the larger colonies urged their right to a relative vote.

The first resolution passed, after the organization of Congress, was the following, passed September 6, 1774: —

"*Resolved*, That in determining questions in Congress, each colony or province shall have one vote; the Congress not being possessed of, or at present able to procure proper materials for ascertaining the importance of each colony."

The main objects of the Congress of 1774 were to harmonize the views and cement the union of the colonies, and to prepare addresses to the king, the parliament, and the people, respectively, of Great Britain; defining and defending the rights, liberties, and purposes of the colonies, and demanding their recognition and security.

On the 20th of October, the following preamble and resolutions were adopted, namely: —

"We do for ourselves and the inhabitants of the several colonies whom we represent, firmly agree and associate, under the sacred ties of virtue, honor, and love of our country, as follows: —

"*First*, That from and after the first day of December next we will not import into British America any goods, &c. from Great Britain or Ireland.

"*Second*, That we will neither import nor purchase any slave imported after the first day of December next; after which time we will wholly discontinue the slave-trade, and will neither be concerned in it ourselves, nor will we hire our vessels nor sell our commodities or manufactures to those who are concerned in it."

The first of these propositions appears to have originated with a convention of delegates of Suffolk county, Mass.

But as the course of events indicated no reasonable probability of a reconciliation between the colonies and the British government, when the Congress assembled in the following year, the necessity of adopting some definite plan of union of a permanent character became apparent. To meet this necessity Doctor FRANKLIN, on the 21st July, 1775, submitted the following sketch of

ARTICLES OF CONFEDERATION AND PERPETUAL UNION.

ART. I. The name of this Confederacy shall henceforth be "*The United Colonies of North America.*"

ART. II. The said United Colonies severally enter into a firm league of friendship with each other, binding on themselves and their posterity, for the common defence against their enemies, for the securities of their liberties and properties, the safety of their persons and families, and their mutual and general welfare.

ART. III. Each colony shall enjoy and retain as much as it may think fit, its present laws, &c., and may amend its constitution.

ART. IV. —— delegates shall be annually elected in each colony to meet in general Congress, at such times and places as shall be agreed on in the next preceding Congress, &c.

ART. V. That the power and duty of Congress shall extend to the determining on war and peace; the sending and receiving ambassadors, and entering into alliances; the settling all disputes and differences between colony and colony, &c., and the *planting new colonies* when proper. The Congress shall also make such general ordinances as, though necessary to the general welfare, particular assemblies cannot be competent to, namely, those that may relate to our general commerce or general currency; the establishment of ports and the regulation of our common forces. The Congress shall also have the appointment of all general officers, civil and military, &c.

ART. VI. All charges of wars and all other general expenses to be incurred for the common welfare, shall be defrayed out of a common treasury, which is to be supplied by each colony in proportion to its number of male polls between sixteen and sixty years of age.

ART. VII. The number of delegates to be elected and sent to Congress by each colony shall be regulated by the number of such polls returned; so as that one delegate be allowed for every 5,000 polls.

ART. VIII. One half to constitute a quorum.

ART. IX. An executive council shall be appointed by the Congress out of its own body, consisting of twelve persons — one third to go out annually. [This council to perform usual executive duties.]

ART. X. No colony to engage in offensive war without the consent of Congress.

ART. XI. The general Congress are authorized to prepare amendments, to be ratified by a majority of the colonial assemblies.

These articles, and particularly the seventh, gave rise to much debate and conflict of opinion. The less populous colonies insisted upon their equality with the others, as distinct and independent political communities, and persistently refused to listen to any compromise on that point; while the larger colonies, especially Virginia and Massachusetts, contended that the vote in Congress should be in proportion to the amount contributed to the general treasury. The authority of precedent being in favor of the political equality of the colonies, that principle maintained its position. The consequence was, that no articles of confederation were finally agreed on until the 15th of November, 1777, a year and a half subsequently to the Declaration of Independence, and during the fourth year of the operations of the Congress. These articles were not finally ratified by all the colonies until March, 1781, when Maryland was induced, by the earnest representations of leading statesmen of the country, of the necessity that the States should present to foreign countries an aspect of union and harmony amongst themselves, in order to secure the confidence of the European governments, and facilitate the recognition of our independence and the negotiation of favorable treaties of friendship and commerce, to yield her objections and ratify the articles of union.

The greatest and most constantly recurring difficulty which Congress had to encounter from the commencement of their operations, was the means and the manner of supplying the money required to carry on the war. On the 29th of July, 1775, the following resolution was adopted, namely: —

"*Resolved*, That the proportion of quota for each colony be determined according to the number of inhabitants of all ages, including negroes and mulattoes in each colony."

This resolution continued in force until the adoption of the Articles of Confederation, November, 1777, which provided by the 8th article, that "all charges of war and all other expenses that shall be incurred for the common defence and general welfare, and allowed by the United States in Congress assembled, shall be defrayed out of a common treasury, which shall be supplied by the several States, in proportion to the value of all land, within each State, granted to or surveyed for any person, as such land and the buildings and improvements thereon shall be estimated according to such mode as the United States in Congress assembled, shall from time to time direct and appoint." These taxes were to be levied and collected by the authority of each State, thus leaving Congress entirely dependent upon the ability, patriotism, and good faith of the respective States, to enable them to sustain the army and defray the expenses of government. The unreliability of this mode of supply, the insuperable difficulties which attended its practical operation, as well as its unequal bearing upon the different sections of the country and the disparity between the proportion of taxation and representation, soon led to efforts to remedy its defects. This mode of fixing the quotas of the States upon the value of land, instead of that based upon population, was adopted in consequence of the disagreement as to the proper mode of reckoning slaves. The southern States would have agreed to base the proportion of taxation upon numbers with a provision that two slaves should be counted as one freeman; but the northern States insisted that all persons should count equally. All efforts to effect a more satisfactory arrangement of the subject proved unsuccessful until the termination of the war. But as soon as the country was relieved from the pressure of a foreign enemy, the attention of Congress and of the country was turned to the means of remedying the radical defects of the Articles of Confederation, namely: — those relating to the revenues and to the proportion of representation in Congress. The resources of the States had become exhausted by the long-continued struggle for independence, and they failed to furnish their quotas to the national treasury, which was consequently left without the means to meet the public engagements.

In the spring of 1783, a proposition was introduced into Congress to substitute, for the mode of ascertaining the quotas of the States, as fixed by the Articles of Confederation, the following, namely: —

"That the common treasury should be supplied by the several States in proportion to the whole number of inhabitants of every age, sex, and condition, except Indians, not paying taxes, in each State. . . . *Provided*, that no persons shall be included who are bound to service for life, according to the laws of the States to which they belong, other than such as may be between the ages of —— years." The purpose was to fill the blank, so as to count such slaves only as had attained an age to be efficient and profitable laborers. In the discussion of this proposition, it was generally conceded that it would be better to fix the ratio by absolute numbers, than by making a distinction of ages. The proposition was finally referred to a committee, who reported, on the 7th of March, "that two blacks be rated as one freeman." Mr. WOLCOTT, of Connecticut, moved to amend the report, by requiring "that *four blacks be counted as three freemen.*"

Mr. CARROLL, of Maryland, proposed that *four negroes be counted as one freeman.*

Mr. WILLIAMSON, of North Carolina, objected to counting negroes at all. He regarded them as an incumbrance to the State, instead of increasing its ability to pay taxes.

Mr. RUTLEDGE, of South Carolina, would consent that slaves should be rated at half their number, as had been originally proposed at the formation of the Articles of Confederation, but he thought that was really rating them too high. The proportion of three to one he thought more just.

Mr. MADISON, of Virginia, was anxious that a reasonable compromise of these conflicting opinions and interests should be effected; and in order to accomplish this patriotic object he proposed, "*that five negroes be rated as three.*"

On this proposition of Mr. Madison, the States of New Hampshire, New Jersey, Pennsylvania, Maryland, Virginia, North Carolina, and South Carolina (7), voted in the affirmative, and Rhode Island and Connecticut (2), in the negative. The delegation of Massachusetts was equally divided.

Thus was fixed the rule for computing the political value of slaves, which was subsequently adopted into the federal Constitution as an element in determining the proportion of members to which the States are entitled in the House of Representatives. In its original adoption, it had no reference to slaves, as an element of political power. It only regarded them as subjects of taxation. The States, therefore, in which they were principally found, contended that they should be regarded as property and not as persons or as a portion of the population, while the States in which the institution was becoming extinct, claimed that, in federal estimation, all should be alike counted. It will be seen, that in the federal Convention, both parties changed positions, but ultimately met upon the same ground.

But this change in the mode of ascertaining the proportion which each State should be required to furnish to the common treasury, did not remedy the great evils under which the country was suffering in consequence of the deplorable condition of its finances. Congress possessed no power to enforce the collection of the taxes, or their payment into the treasury when collected, or any other means of securing a revenue. The power to regulate commerce, and by that means to secure a revenue by means of duties on imports, remained with the States.

The necessity of having this power, in some form and to some extent, conferred upon Congress, both as an available and efficient means of replenishing the treasury and restoring the credit of the United States, and of promoting the general interests of commerce, continued to attract the earnest consideration of public men.

Mr. MADISON, in the Federalist (p. 36, vol. 1), accords to the State of New York the honor of having first officially taken measures which lead to the assembling of the constitutional convention.

On the 21st day of July, 1782, the legislature of that State passed a series of resolutions in reference to the condition and necessities of the confederacy, amongst which is the following: —

"*Resolved*, That in the opinion of this legislature, the radical source of most of our embarrassments, is the want of sufficient power in Congress to effectuate that ready and perfect coöperation of the different States, on which their immediate safety and future happiness depend. That experience has demonstrated the confederation to be defective in several essential points, particularly in not vesting the federal government either with a power of providing revenue for itself, or with ascertained and productive funds, secured by a sanction so solemn and general, as would inspire the fullest confidence in them, and make them a substantial basis of credit. That these defects ought to be, without loss of time repaired; the powers of Congress extended; a solid security established for the payment of debts already incurred, and competent means provided for future credit, and for supplying the future demands of the war."

"*Resolved*, That it appears to this legislature, that the aforegoing important ends can never be attained by partial deliberations of the States separately; but that it is essential to the common welfare, that there should be, as soon as possible, a conference of the whole on the subject; and that it would be advisable for this purpose, to propose to Congress to recommend, and to each State to adopt the measure of assembling a general convention of the States, specially authorized to revise and amend the confederation, reserving to the respective legislatures a right to ratify their deliberations."

At the following session of Congress, Mr. HAMILTON gave notice, that it was his intention, in pursuance of instructions from his constituents, to bring forward a plan to provide for the meeting of a general convention to revise the Articles of Confederation.

Mr. GORHAM of Massachusetts, in the course of some remarks on the necessity of general laws for the regulation of commerce, made in Congress in April, 1783, said that, "the eastern States, on an invitation of the legislature of Massachusetts, were, with New York, about to form a convention for regulating matters of common concern." The object was expressed to be, principally, to guard against an interference of taxes amongst adjacent States — but not to interfere with proper federal authority.

Mr. MADISON, and other members from Virginia, expressed strong disapprobation of these partial conventions, as improper and of dangerous tendency.

Governor BOWDOIN, in his annual message to the legislature of Massachusetts in May, 1785, suggested the expediency of a general convention of delegates from all the States, to consider and determine what further powers ought to be vested in Congress. In compliance with this suggestion, the legislature passed a resolution recommending that such a convention should be called, to take into consideration "the state of the federal union."

These proceedings of the executive and legislature of Massachusetts, have been regarded as the first State action which led to the meeting of the constitutional convention. But it can hardly be denied that the proceedings in the legislature of New York, three years earlier, looked to the same result.

Numerous attempts had been made during the war, to procure from the States authority for Congress, to levy duties on imports, but the assent of all the States could not be procured. It has been already seen that the States of New York and Massachusetts had recommended a convention to remedy this difficulty. On the 12th of February, 1783, Congress resolved, "That the establishment of permanent and adequate funds, or taxes, or duties throughout the United States, was indispensable to do justice to public creditors." They recommended to the States to vest in Congress the authority to levy certain duties for a period of five years. An attempt was also made to procure authority to levy taxes for the Union, separately from the State taxes. General Washington, impressed with the absolute necessity of a more perfect union of the States, uses the following language, in a circular letter to the governors of the several States, shortly prior to his retirement from the army: — "Unless the States will suffer Congress to exercise those prerogatives they are undoubtedly vested with by the Constitution, every thing must very rapidly tend to anarchy and confusion. It is indispensable to the happiness of the individual States, that there should be lodged somewhere, a supreme power to regulate and govern the general concerns of the confederated republic." "Whatever measures," he adds, "have a tendency to dissolve the Union, or contribute to violate or lessen its sovereign authority, ought to be considered hostile to the liberty and independence of America, and the authors of them treated accordingly."

Notwithstanding the strength of these appeals, the States refused to yield the power required. It does not appear that the proposed convention of the New England States and New York ever assembled. In 1785, commissioners were appointed by the legislatures of Virginia and Maryland, for the purpose of agreeing upon some common regulations relative to the navigation of the Chesapeake Bay and its tributary streams. Finding their powers too restricted to accomplish any valuable purpose, the commissioners adjourned, after adopting a recommendation, to be reported to their respective legislatures, for the assembling of a more general convention, with power to provide for a local navy and a tariff of duties upon imports. The Maryland commissioners deemed the concurrence of Delaware and Pennsylvania as assential to the proposed measures, and proposed that they should be invited to send delegates.

At the time this report came before the legislature of Virginia, a resolution was pending in that body, inviting a meeting of delegates from all the States as follows:—

"*Resolved*, That Edmund Randolph, James Madison, Jr., Walter Jones, St. George Tucker, and M. Smith, Esqrs., be appointed commissioners, who, or any three of whom, shall meet such commissioners as may be appointed in the other States of the Union, at a time and place to be agreed on, to take into consideration the trade of the United States; to examine the relative situations and trade of said States; to consider how far a uniform system in their commercial relations may be necessary to their common interests and their permanent harmony; and to report to the several States, such an act, relative to this great object, as, when unanimously ratified by them, will enable the United States in Congress, effectually to provide for the same."

As the result of this movement, delegates from five States assembled at Annapolis, on the 11th day of September, 1786. This convention, like its predecessor, finding its powers too restricted to accomplish any valuable purpose, and that less than half the States were represented, declined to attempt the execution of the task assigned to it; but, instead of attempting to frame a navigation act, to be submitted to the several States, they adopted a report from the pen of Alexander Hamilton, recommending the appointment of commissioners from all the States, "to meet at Philadelphia on the second Monday in May next, to take into consideration the situation of the United States; to devise such further provisions as shall appear to them necessary to render the Constitution of the federal government adequate to the exigencies of the Union." When this report reached Virginia, it found the legislature in session. The proposition was favorably received; and on the 23d November an act was passed for the appointment of the delegates as recommended. This act authorized the deputies from Virginia "to meet such deputies as may be appointed and authorized by other States, to assemble in convention at Philadelphia as above recommended, and to join with them in devising and discussing all such alterations and further provisions as may be necessary to render the federal Constitution adequate to the exigencies of the Union; and in reporting such an act for that purpose to the United States in Congress, as when agreed to by them, and duly confirmed by the several States, will effectually provide for the same."

On the 30th of December, the legislature of Pennsylvania passed an act appointing delegates from that State, with power to join "in devising, deliberating on, and discussing all such alterations and further provisions as may be necessary to render the federal Constitution fully adequate to the exigencies of the Union." All the other States, except the State of Rhode Island, appointed deputies, with powers nearly identical with those above described. The delegates from Delaware were, however, restrained from agreeing to any modification of the fifth article of Confederation, which secures to each State an equal vote.

The Convention accordingly met in the city of Philadelphia, on the 14th day of May, 1787; but a majority of States did not appear, by their delegates, until the 25th, on which day the Convention was organized, by the unanimous election of George Washington, as its President.

ORIGIN

OF

THE FEDERAL CONVENTION.

PUBLIC PROCEEDINGS,

SHOWING THE NECESSITY OF A MORE PERFECT UNION, AND LEADING TO THE MEETING OF THE FEDERAL CONVENTION.

Articles of Confederation and Perpetual Union between the States of New Hampshire, Massachusetts Bay, Rhode Island and Providence Plantations, Connecticut, New York, New Jersey, Pennsylvania, Delaware, Maryland, Virginia, North Carolina, South Carolina, and Georgia.

ARTICLE I. The style of this Confederacy shall be "The United States of America."

ART. II. Each State retains its sovereignty, freedom, and independence, and every power, jurisdiction, and right, which is not by this confederation expressly delegated to the United States, in Congress assembled.

ART. III. The said States hereby severally enter into a firm league of friendship with each other, for their common defence, the security of their liberties, and their mutual and general welfare, binding themselves to assist each other, against all force offered to, or attacks made upon them, or any of them, on account of religion, sovereignty, trade, or any other pretence whatever.

ART. IV. The better to secure and perpetuate mutual friendship and intercourse among the people of the different States in this Union, the free inhabitants of each of these States, paupers, vagabonds, and fugitives from justice excepted, shall be entitled to all privileges and immunities of free citizens in the several States; and the people of each State shall have free ingress and regress to and from any other State, and shall enjoy therein all the privileges of trade and commerce, subject to the same duties, impositions, and restrictions as the inhabitants thereof respectively, provided that such restriction shall not extend so far as to prevent the removal of property imported into any State to any other State of which the owner is an inhabitant; provided also that no imposition, duties, or restriction shall be laid by any State, on the property of the United States, or either of them.

If any person guilty of, or charged with treason, felony, or other high misdemeanor in any State, shall flee from justice, and be found in any of the United States, he shall upon demand of the governor or executive power of the State from which he fled, be delivered up and removed to the State having jurisdiction of his offence.

Full faith and credit shall be given in each of these States to the records, acts, and judicial proceedings of the courts and magistrates of every other State.

Art. V. For the more convenient management of the general interest of the United States, delegates shall be annually appointed in such manner as the legislature of each State shall direct, to meet in Congress on the first Monday in November, in every year, with a power reserved to each State, to recall its delegates, or any of them, at any time within the year, and to send others in their stead, for the remainder of the year.

No State shall be represented in Congress by less than two, nor by more than seven members; and no person shall be capable of being a delegate for more than three years in any term of six years; nor shall any person, being a delegate, be capable of holding any office under the United States, for which he, or another for his benefit receives any salary, fees, or emolument of any kind.

Each State shall maintain its own delegates in any meeting of the States, and while they act as members of the committee of the States.

In determining questions in the United States, in Congress assembled, each State shall have one vote.

Freedom of speech and debate in Congress shall not be impeached or questioned in any Court, or place out of Congress, and the members of Congress shall be protected in their persons from arrests and imprisonments, during the time of their going to and from, and attendance on Congress, except for treason, felony or breach of the peace.

ART. VI. No State without the consent of the United States in Congress assembled, shall send any embassy to, or receive any embassy from, or enter into any conference, agreement, alliance, or treaty with any king, prince, or State; nor shall any person holding any office of profit or trust under the United States, or any of them, accept of any present, emolument, office, or title of any kind whatever from any king, prince, or foreign State; nor shall the United States in Congress assembled, or any of them, grant any title of nobility.

No two or more States shall enter into any treaty, confederation, or alliance whatever between them, without the consent of the United States in Congress assembled, specifying accurately the purposes for which the same is to be entered into, and how long it shall continue.

No State shall lay any imposts or duties, which may interfere with any stipulations in treaties, entered into by the United States in Congress assembled, with any king, prince, or State, in pursuance of any treaties already proposed by Congress, to the courts of France and Spain.

No vessels of war shall be kept up in time of peace by any State, except such number only, as shall be deemed necessary by the United States in Congress assembled, for the defence of such State, or its trade; nor shall any body of forces be kept up by any State, in time of peace, except such number only, as in the judgment of the United States, in Congress assembled, shall be deemed requisite to garrison the forts necessary for the defence of such State; but every State shall always keep up a well-regulated and disciplined militia, sufficiently armed and accoutred, and shall provide and have constantly ready for use, in public stores, a due number of field-pieces and tents, and a proper quantity of arms, ammunition, and camp equipage.

No State shall engage in any war without the consent of the United States in Congress assembled, unless such State be actually invaded by enemies, or shall have received certain advice of a resolution being formed by some nation of Indians to invade such State, and the danger is so imminent as not to admit of a delay, till the United States in Congress assembled can be consulted: nor shall any State grant commission to any ships or vessels of war, nor letters of marque or reprisal, except it be after a declaration of war by the United States in Congress assembled, and then only against the kingdom or State and the subjects thereof, against which war has been so declared, and under such regulations as shall be established by the United States in Congress assembled, unless such State be infested by pirates, in which case vessels of war may be fitted out for that occasion, and kept so long as the danger shall continue, or until the United States in Congress assembled shall determine otherwise.

Art. VII. When land forces are raised by any State for the common defence, all officers of or under the rank of colonel, shall be appointed by the legislature of each State respectively by whom such forces shall be raised, or in such manner as such State shall direct, and all vacancies shall be filled up by the State which first made the appointment.

Art. VIII. All charges of war, and all other expenses that shall be incurred for the common defence or general welfare, and allowed by the United States in Congress assembled, shall be defrayed out of a common treasury, which shall be supplied by the several States, in proportion to the value of all land within each State, granted to or surveyed for any person, as such land and the buildings and improvements thereon shall be estimated according to such mode as the United States in Congress assembled, shall from time to time direct and appoint. The taxes for paying that proportion shall be laid and levied by the authority and direction of the legislatures of the several States, within the time agreed upon by the United States in Congress assembled.

Art. IX. The United States in Congress assembled, shall

have the sole and exclusive right and power of determining on peace and war, except in the cases mentioned in the 6th article — of sending and receiving ambassadors — entering into treaties and alliances, provided that no treaty of commerce shall be made whereby the legislative power of the respective States shall be restrained from imposing such imposts and duties on foreigners, as their own people are subjected to, or from prohibiting the exportation or importation of any species of goods or commodities whatsoever — of establishing rules for deciding in all cases, what captures on land or water shall be legal, and in what manner prizes taken by land or naval forces in the service of the United States shall be divided or appropriated — of granting letters of marque and reprisal in times of peace — appointing courts for the trial of piracies and felonies committed on the high seas, and establishing courts for receiving and determining finally appeals in all cases of captures, provided that no member of Congress shall be appointed a judge of any of the said courts.

The United States in Congress assembled shall also be the last resort on appeal in all disputes and differences now subsisting, or that hereafter may arise between two or more States concerning boundary, jurisdiction, or any other cause whatever; which authority shall always be exercised in the manner following. Whenever the legislative or executive authority or lawful agent of any State in controversy with another shall present a petition to Congress, stating the matter in question and praying for a hearing, notice thereof shall be given by order of Congress to the legislative or executive authority of the other State in controversy, and a day assigned for the appearance of the parties by their lawful agents, who shall then be directed to appoint by joint consent, commissioners or judges to constitute a court for hearing and determining the matter in question: but if they cannot agree, Congress shall name three persons out of each of the United States, and from the list of such persons each party shall alternately strike out one, the petitioners beginning, until the number shall be reduced to thirteen; and from that number not less than seven, nor more than nine names as Congress shall direct, shall in the presence of Congress be drawn out by lot, and the persons whose names shall be so drawn or any five of them, shall be commissioners or judges, to hear and finally determine the controversy, so always as a major part of the judges who shall hear the cause shall agree in the determination: and if either party shall neglect to attend at the day appointed, without showing reasons, which Congress shall judge sufficient, or being present shall refuse to strike, the Congress shall proceed to nominate three persons out of each State, and the secretary of Congress shall strike in behalf of such party absent or refusing; and the judgment and sentence of the court to be appointed, in the manner before prescribed, shall be final and conclusive; and if any of the parties shall refuse to submit to the authority of such court, or to appear or defend their claim or cause, the court shall nevertheless proceed to pronounce sentence, or judgment, which shall in like manner be final and decisive, the judgment or sentence and other proceedings being in either case transmitted to Congress, and lodged among the acts of Congress for the security of the parties concerned; provided that every commissioner, before he sits in judgment, shall take an oath to be administered by one of the judges of the supreme or superior court of the State, where the cause shall be tried, "well and truly to hear and determine the matter in question, according to the best of his judgment, without favor, affection, or hope of reward:" provided also that no State shall be deprived of territory for the benefit of the United States.

All controversies concerning the private right of soil claimed under different grants of two or more States, whose jurisdictions as they may respect such lands, and the States which passed such grants are adjusted, the said grants or either of them being at the same time claimed to have originated antecedent to such settlement of jurisdiction, shall on the petition of either party to the Congress of the United States, be finally determined as near as may be in the same manner as is before prescribed for deciding disputes respecting territorial jurisdiction between different States.

The United States in Congress assembled shall also have the sole and exclusive right and power of regulating the alloy and value of coin struck by their own authority, or by that of the respective States — fixing the standard of weights and measures throughout the United States — regulating the trade and managing all affairs with the Indians, not members of any of the States, provided that the legislative right of any State within its own limits be not infringed or violated — establishing or regulating post-offices from one State to another, throughout all the United States, and exacting such postage on the papers passing through the same as may be requisite to defray the expenses of the said office — appointing all officers of the land forces, in the service of the United States, excepting regimental officers — appointing all the officers of the naval forces, and commissioning all officers whatever in the service of the United States — making rules for the government and regulation of the said land and naval forces, and directing their operations.

The United States in Congress assembled shall have authority to appoint a committee, to sit in the recess of Congress, to be denominated "A Committee of the States," and to consist of one delegate from each State; and to appoint such other committees and civil officers as may be necessary for managing the general affairs of the United States under their direction — to appoint one of their number to preside, provided that no person be allowed to serve in the office of president more than one year in any term of three years; to ascertain the necessary sums of money to be raised for the service of the United States, and to appropriate and apply the same for defraying the public expenses — to borrow money, or emit bills on the credit of the United States, transmitting every half year to the respective States an account of the sums of money so borrowed or emitted — to build and equip a navy — to agree upon the number of land forces, and to make requisitions from each State for its quota, in proportion to the number of white inhabitants in such State; which requisition shall be binding, and thereupon the legislature of each State shall appoint the regimental officers, raise the men, and clothe, arm and equip them in a soldier-like manner, at the expense of the United States; and the officers and men so clothed, armed and equipped, shall march to the place appointed, and within the time agreed on by the United States in Congress assembled: but if the United States in Congress assembled shall, on consideration of circumstances judge proper that any State should not raise men, or should raise a smaller number than its quota, and that any other State should raise a greater number of men than the quota thereof, such extra number shall be raised, officered, clothed, armed and equipped, in the same manner as the quota of such State, unless the legislature of such State shall judge that such extra number cannot be safely spared out of the same, in which case they shall raise, officer, clothe, arm and equip, as many of such extra number as they judge can be safely spared. And the officers and men so clothed, armed and equipped, shall march to the place appointed, and within the time agreed on by the United States in Congress assembled.

The United States in Congress assembled shall never engage in a war, nor grant letters of marque and reprisal in time of peace, nor enter into any treaties or alliances, nor coin money, nor regulate the value thereof, nor ascertain the sums and expenses necessary for the defence and welfare of the United States, or any of them, nor emit bills, nor borrow money on the credit of the United States, nor appropriate money, nor agree upon the number of vessels of war, to be built or purchased, or the number of land or sea forces to be raised, nor appoint a commander-in-chief of the army or navy, unless nine States assent to the same: nor shall a question on any other point, except for adjourning from day to day be determined, unless by the votes of a majority of the United States in Congress assembled.

The Congress of the United States shall have power to adjourn to any time within the year, and to any place within the United States, so that no period of adjournment be for a longer duration than the space of six months, and shall publish the journal of their proceedings monthly, except such parts thereof relating to treaties, alliances or military operations, as in their judgment require secrecy; and the yeas and nays of the delegates of each State on any question shall be entered on the journal, when it is desired by any delegate; and the delegates of a State, or any of them, at his or their request shall be furnished with a transcript of the said journal, except such parts as are above excepted, to lay before the legislatures of the several States.

Art. X. The committee of the States, or any nine of them, shall be authorized to execute, in the recess of Congress, such of the powers of Congress as the United States in Congress assembled, by the consent of nine States, shall from time to time think expedient to vest them with; provided that no power be delegated to the said committee, for the exercise of which, by the Articles of Confederation, the voice of nine States in the Congress of the United States assembled is requisite.

Art. XI. Canada acceding to this Confederation, and joining in the measures of the United States, shall be admitted into, and entitled to all the advantages of this Union; but no other colony shall be admitted into the same, unless such admission be agreed to by nine States.

Art. XII. All bills of credit emitted, moneys borrowed, and debts contracted by, or under the authority of Congress, before the assembling of the United States, in pursuance of the present Confederation, shall be deemed and considered as a charge against the United States, for payment and satisfaction whereof the said United States and the public faith are hereby solemnly pledged.

Art. XIII. Every State shall abide by the determinations of the United States in Congress assembled, on all questions which by this Confederation is submitted to them. And the Articles of this Confederation shall be inviolably observed by every State, and the union shall be perpetual; nor shall any alteration at any time hereafter be made in any of them; unless such alteration be agreed to in a Congress of the United States, and be afterwards confirmed by the legislatures of every State.

RESOLUTIONS OF THE STATE OF NEW YORK.

Sunday, July 21, 1782.

Resolved, That it appears to this legislature, after full and solemn consideration of the several matters communicated by the honorable the committee of Congress, relating to the present posture of our affairs, foreign and domestic, and contained in a letter from the secretary for foreign affairs respecting the former, as well as of the representations from time to time made by the superintendent of the finances of the United States, relative to his particular department; that the situation of these States is in a peculiar manner critical, and affords the strongest reason to apprehend, from a continuance of the present Constitution of the continental government, a subversion of public credit, and consequences highly dangerous to the safety and independence of these States.

Resolved, That while this legislature are convinced by the before-mentioned communications, that, notwithstanding the generous intentions of an ally from whom we have experienced, and doubtless shall still experience, all possible support, exigencies may arise to prevent our receiving pecuniary succors hereafter, in any degree proportioned to our necessities. They are also convinced, from facts within their own knowledge, that the provisions made by the respective States for carrying on the war, are not only inadequate to the end, but must continue to be so, while there is an adherence to the principles which now direct the operation of public measures.

Resolved, That it is also the opinion of this legislature, that the present plan instituted by Congress for the administration of their finances, is founded in wisdom and sound policy. That the salutary effects of it have already been felt in an extensive degree; and that after so many violent shocks sustained by the public credit, a failure in this system, for want of the support which the States are able to give, would be productive of evils too pernicious to be hazarded.

Resolved, That it appears to this legislature, that the present British ministry, with a disposition not less hostile than that of their predecessors, taught by experience to avoid their errors, and assuming the appearance of moderation, are pursuing a scheme calculated to conciliate in Europe, and seduce in America. That the economical arrangements they appear to be adopting are adapted to enlarging the credit of their government, and multiplying its resources at the same time that they serve to confirm the prepossessions and confidence of the people; and that the plan of a defensive war on this continent, while they direct all their attention and resources to the augmentation of their navy, is that which may be productive of consequences ultimately dangerous to the United States.

Resolved, That it is the opinion of this legislature, that the present system of these States exposes the common cause to a precarious issue, and leaves us at the mercy of events over which we have no influence, a conduct extremely unwise in any nation, and at all times, and to a change of which we are impelled at this juncture, by reason of peculiar and irresistible weight; and that it is the natural tendency of the weakness and disorders in our national measures, to spread diffidence and distrust among the people, and prepare their minds to receive the impressions the enemy wish to make.

Resolved, That the general state of European affairs, as far as they have come to the knowledge of this legislature, affords, in their opinion, reasonable ground of confidence, and assures us, that with judicious and vigorous exertion on our part, we may rely on the final attainment of our object; but, far from justifying indifference and security, calls upon us by every motive of honor, good faith, and patriotism, without delay to unite in some system more effectual for producing energy, harmony, and consistency of measures than that which now exists, and more capable of putting the common cause out of the reach of contingencies.

Resolved, That in the opinion of this legislature, the radical source of most of our embarrassments, is the want of sufficient power in Congress, to effectuate that ready and perfect coöperation of the different States, on which their immediate safety and future happiness depend. That experience has demonstrated the Confederation to be defective in several essential points, particularly in not vesting the federal government either with a power of providing revenue for itself, or with ascertained and productive funds, secured by a sanction so solemn and general, as would inspire the fullest confidence in them, and make them a substantial basis of credit. That these defects ought to be without loss of time repaired; the powers of Congress extended, a solid security established for the payment of debts already incurred, and competent means provided for future credit, and for supplying the future demands of the war.

Resolved, That it appears evident to this legislature, that the annual income of these States, admitting the best means were adopted for drawing out their resources, would fall far short of the annual expenditure; and that there would be a large deficiency to be supplied on the credit of these States, which, if it should be inconvenient for those powers to afford, on whose friendship we justly rely, must be sought for from individuals, to engage whom to lend, satisfactory securities must be pledged for the punctual payment of interest, and the final redemption of the principal.

Resolved, That it appears to this legislature, that the aforegoing important ends can never be attained by partial deliberations of the States separately; but that it is essential to the common welfare, that there should be, as soon as possible, a conference of the whole on the subject; and that it would be advisable for this purpose, to propose to Congress to recommend, and to each State to adopt the measure of assembling a general convention of the States, specially authorized to revise and amend the Confederation, reserving a right to the respective legislatures to ratify their determinations.

RESOLUTION OF THE STATE OF VIRGINIA.

21ST JANUARY, 1786.

Resolved, That Edmund Randolph, James Madison, junior, Walter Jones, Saint George Tucker, Meriwether Smith, David Ross, William Ronald, and George Mason, esquires, be appointed commissioners, who, or any five of whom, shall meet such commissioners as may be appointed by the other States in the Union, at a time and place to be agreed on, to take into consideration the trade of the United States; to examine the relative situations and trade of the said States; to consider how far an uniform system in their commercial regulations may be necessary to their common interest and their permanent harmony; and to report to the several States such an act relative to this great object, as, when unanimously ratified by them, will enable the United States in Congress assembled effectually to provide for the same: that the said commissioners shall immediately transmit to the several States copies of the preceding resolution, with a circular letter requesting their concurrence therein, and proposing a time and place for the meeting aforesaid.

REPORT OF THE COMMISSIONERS

Who met at Annapolis, Maryland, September 11, 1786.

To the honorable the Legislatures of Virginia, Delaware, Pennsylvania, New Jersey, and New York, the commissioners from the said States, respectively, assembled at Annapolis, humbly beg leave to report: —

That, pursuant to their several appointments, they met at Annapolis, in the State of Maryland, on the 11th day of September instant, and having proceeded to a communication of their powers, they found that the States of New York, Pennsylvania, and Virginia, had, in substance, and nearly in the same terms, authorized their respective commissioners "to meet such commissioners as were or might be appointed by the other States in the Union, at such time and place as should be agreed upon by the said commissioners, to take into consideration the trade and commerce of the United States, to consider how far an uniform system in their commercial intercourse and regulation might be necessary to their common interest and permanent harmony, and to report to the several States such an act relative to this great object, as when unanimously ratified by them, would enable the United States in Congress assembled effectually to provide for the same."

That the State of Delaware had given similar powers to their commissioners, with this difference only, that the act to be framed in virtue of these powers is required to be reported "to the United States in Congress assembled, to be agreed to by them, and confirmed by the legislatures of every State."

That the State of New Jersey had enlarged the object of their appointment, empowering their commissioners "to consider how far an uniform system in their commercial regulations and *other important matters* might be necessary to the common interest and permanent harmony of the several States;" and to report such an act on the subject as, when ratified by them, "would enable the United States in Congress assembled effectually to provide for the exigencies of the Union."

That appointments of commissioners have also been made by the States of New Hampshire, Massachusetts, Rhode Island, and North Carolina, none of whom, however, have attended; but that no information has been received by your commissioners of any appointment having been made by the States of Connecticut, Maryland, South Carolina, or Georgia.

That the express terms of the powers to your commissioners supposing a deputation from all the States, and having for object the trade and commerce of the United States, your commissioners did not conceive it advisable to proceed on the business of their mission under the circumstance of so partial and defective a representation.

Deeply impressed, however, with the magnitude and importance of the object confided to them on this occasion, your commissioners cannot forbear to indulge an expression of their earnest and unanimous wish that speedy measures may be taken to effect a general meeting of the States, in a future convention for the same and such other purposes as the situation of public affairs may be found to require.

If, in expressing this wish, or in intimating any other sentiment, your commissioners should seem to exceed the strict bounds of their appointment, they entertain a full confidence that a conduct dictated by an anxiety for the welfare of the United States will not fail to receive an indulgent construction.

In this persuasion, your commissioners submit an opinion, that the idea of extending the powers of their deputies to other objects than those of commerce, which has been adopted by the State of New Jersey, was an improvement on the original plan, and will deserve to be incorporated into that of a future convention. They are the more naturally led to this conclusion, as, in the course of their reflections on the subject, they have been induced to think that the power of regulating trade is of such comprehensive extent, and will enter so far into the general system of the federal government, that to give it efficacy, and to obviate questions and doubts concerning its precise nature and limits, may require a correspondent adjustment of other parts of the federal system.

That there are important defects in the system of the federal government, is acknowledged by the acts of all those States which have concurred in the present meeting; that the defects, upon a closer examination, may be found greater and more numerous than even these acts imply, is at least so far probable, from the embarrassments which characterize the present state of our national affairs, foreign and domestic, as may reasonably be supposed to merit a deliberate and candid discussion, in some mode which will unite the sentiments and councils of all the States. In the choice of the mode, your commissioners are of opinion that a convention of deputies from the different States, for the special and sole purpose of entering into this investigation, and digesting a plan for supplying such defects as may be discovered to exist, will be entitled to a preference, from considerations which will occur without being particularized.

Your commissioners decline an enumeration of those national circumstances on which their opinion respecting the propriety of a future convention, with more enlarged powers, is founded, as it would be an useless intrusion of facts and observations, most of which have been frequently the subject of public discussion, and none of which can have escaped the penetration of those to whom they would in this instance be addressed. They are, however, of a nature so serious, as in the view of your commissioners, to render the situation of the United States delicate and critical, calling for an exertion of the united virtue and wisdom of all the members of the confederacy.

Under this impression, your commissioners, with the most respectful deference, beg leave to suggest their unanimous conviction, that it may essentially tend to advance the interests of the Union, if the States, by whom they have been respectively delegated, would themselves concur, and use their endeavors to procure the concurrence of the other States in the appointment of commissioners, to meet at Philadelphia on the second Monday in May next, to take into consideration the situation of the United States, to devise such further provisions as shall appear to them necessary to render the Constitution of the federal government adequate to the exigencies of the Union; and to report such an act for that purpose to the United States in Congress assembled, as, when agreed to by them, and afterwards confirmed by the legislatures of every State, will effectually provide for the same.

Though your commissioners could not with propriety address these observations and sentiments to any but the States they have the honor to represent, they have nevertheless concluded, from motives of respect, to transmit copies of this report to the United States in Congress assembled, and to the executives of the other States.

By order of the Commissioners.

Dated at Annapolis, September 14, 1786.

Resolved, That the chairman sign the aforegoing report in behalf of the commissioners.

Then adjourned without day.

NEW YORK.

Egbert Benson,
Alexander Hamilton.

NEW JERSEY.

Abra. Clark,
Wm. Ch. Houston,
James Schureman.

PENNSYLVANIA.

Tench Coxe.

DELAWARE.

George Read,
John Dickinson,
Richard Bassett.

VIRGINIA.

Edmund Randolph,
James Madison, jun.
St. George Tucker.

IN THE CONGRESS OF THE CONFEDERATION.

WEDNESDAY, FEBRUARY 21, 1787.

The report of a Grand Committee, consisting of Mr. Dane, Mr Varnum, Mr. S. M. Mitchell, Mr. Smith, Mr. Cadwallader, Mr Irvine, Mr. N. Mitchell, Mr. Forrest, Mr. Grayson, Mr. Blount, Mr. Bull, and Mr. Few, to whom was referred a letter of 14th September, 1786, from J. Dickinson, written at the request of commissioners from the States of Virginia, Delaware, Pennsylvania, New Jersey, and New York, assembled at the city of Annapolis, together with a copy of the report of the said commissioners to the legislatures of the States by whom they were appointed, being an order of the day, was called up, and which is contained in the following resolution, namely:—

"Congress having had under consideration the letter of John Dickinson, Esq., chairman of the commissioners who assembled at Annapolis during the last year; also the proceedings of the said commissioners; and entirely coinciding with them, as to the inefficiency of the federal government, and the necessity of devising such further provisions as shall render the same adequate to the exigencies of the Union, do strongly recommend to the different legislatures to send forward delegates, to meet the proposed convention, on the second Monday in May next, at the city of Philadelphia."

The delegates for the State of New York thereupon laid before Congress instructions which they had received from their constituents, and, in pursuance of the said instructions, moved to postpone the further consideration of the report, in order to take up the following propositions, namely:—

"That it be recommended to the States composing the Union,

that a convention of representatives from the said States respectively, be held at , on , for the purpose of revising the articles of confederation and perpetual union between the United States of America, and reporting to the United States in Congress assembled, and to the States respectively, such alterations and amendments of the said articles of confederation, as the representatives met in such convention shall judge proper and necessary to render them adequate to the preservation and support of the Union."

On the question to postpone, for the purpose above-mentioned, the yeas and nays being required by the delegates for New York,

Massachusetts	Mr. King,	ay	ay
	Dane,	ay	
Connecticut	Mr. Johnson,	ay	div.
	S. Mitchell,	no	
New York	Mr. Smith,	ay	ay
	Benson,	ay	
New Jersey	Mr. Cadwallader,	ay	no
	Clarke,	no	
	Schureman,	no	
Pennsylvania	Mr. Irvine,	no	no
	Meredith,	ay	
	Bingham,	no	
Delaware	Mr. N. Mitchell,	no	*
Maryland	Mr. Forrest,	no	*
Virginia	Mr. Grayson,	ay	ay
	Madison,	ay	
N. Carolina	Mr. Blount,	no	no
	Hawkins,	no	
S. Carolina	Mr. Bull,	no	no
	Kean,	no	
	Huger,	no	
	Parker,	no	
Georgia	Mr. Few,	ay	div.
	Pierce,	no	

So the question was lost.

A motion was then made by the delegates for Massachusetts, to postpone the further consideration of the report, in order to take into consideration a motion which they read in their place; this being agreed to, the motion of the delegates for Massachusetts was taken up, and, being amended, was agreed to, as follows: —

Whereas there is provision in the articles of confederation and perpetual union, for making alterations therein, by the assent of a Congress of the United States, and of the legislatures of the several States; and whereas experience hath evinced that there are defects in the present confederation, as a mean to remedy which several of the States, and particularly the State of New York, by express instructions to their delegates in Congress, have suggested a convention for the purposes expressed in the following resolution; and such convention appearing to be the most probable mean of establishing in these States a firm national government:

Resolved, That in the opinion of Congress, it is expedient, that, on the second Monday in May next, a convention of delegates, who shall have been appointed by the several States, be held at Philadelphia, for the sole and express purpose of revising the Articles of Confederation, and reporting to Congress, and the several legislatures, such alterations and provisions therein as shall, when agreed to in Congress, and confirmed by the States, render the Federal Constitution adequate to the exigencies of government, and the preservation of the Union.

EXTRACTS FROM THE ACTS OF THE STATES

AUTHORIZING THE APPOINTMENT OF DELEGATES TO THE CONVENTION AT PHILADELPHIA, SHOWING THE POWERS CONFERRED ON THEM.

VIRGINIA, passed on the 16th of October, 1786 — "To join with [the delegates from the other States] in devising and discussing all such alterations and further provisions as may be necessary to render the federal Constitution adequate to the exigencies of the Union."

NEW JERSEY, passed 23d November, 1786 — "For the purpose of taking into consideration the state of the Union, as to trade and other important objects, and of devising such other provisions as shall appear to be necessary to render the Constitution of the federal government adequate to the exigencies thereof."

PENNSYLVANIA, passed December 30, 1786 — "To join in devising, deliberating on, and discussing all such alterations and further provisions as may be necessary to render the federal Constitution fully adequate to the exigencies of the Union."

DELAWARE, passed February 23, 1787 — "To join with them in devising, deliberating on, and discussing, such alterations and further provisions as may be necessary to render the federal Constitution adequate to the exigencies of the Union . . . . so always, and provided, that such alterations or further provisions, or any of them, do not extend to that part of the fifth article of the confederation of the said States, finally ratified on the first day of March, 1781, which declares that, 'In determining questions in the United States in Congress assembled, each State shall have one vote.'"

NORTH CAROLINA, passed 6th January, 1786 — "To discuss and decide upon the most effectual means to remove the defects of the federal Union, and to procure the enlarged purposes which it was intended to effect."

GEORGIA, passed February 11, 1786—"To join in devising and discussing all such alterations and further provisions as may be necessary to render the federal Constitution adequate to the exigencies of the Union."

NEW YORK, passed February 28, 1787—"For the sole and express purpose of revising the Articles of Confederation and reporting to Congress, and to the several legislatures, such alterations and provisions therein as shall, when agreed to in Congress, and confirmed by the several States, render the federal Constitution adequate to the exigencies of government, and the preservation of the Union."

MASSACHUSETTS, passed 10th March, 1787—"For the sole and express purpose of revising the Articles of Confederation."

SOUTH CAROLINA, passed March 8, 1787—"To join in devising and discussing all such alterations, clauses, articles, and provisions, as may be thought necessary to render the federal Constitution entirely adequate to the actual situation and future good government of the confederated States."

CONNECTICUT, passed May, 1787—"To discuss upon such alterations and provisions, agreeable to the general principles of republican government, as they shall think proper, to render the federal Constitution adequate to the exigencies of government and the preservation of the Union."

MARYLAND, passed May 26, 1787—"To join with them in considering such alterations and further provisions as may be necessary to render the federal Constitution adequate to the exigencies of the Union."

NEW HAMPSHIRE, passed June 27, 1787—"To discuss and decide upon the most effectual means to remedy the defects of our federal Union, and to procure and secure the enlarged purposes which it was intended to effect."

All the acts required that the proceedings of the Convention should be reported to the United States in Congress, and to the respective State legislatures, for final action.

CESSION OF THE WESTERN TERRITORY.

The original settlements upon the portion of the American continent, now constituting the United States, were made along the coast of the Atlantic Ocean. The grants from the British crown to the companies under whose auspices the settlements were commenced, were made with little regard to the actual geography of the country. The conceded territory was generally described as included between certain parallels of latitude, and commencing on the Atlantic Ocean, thence extending westward to the "South Sea," or the Pacific Ocean. Massachusetts, Connecticut, New York, Virginia, the two Carolinas, and Georgia, all claimed by virtue of such grants the right of soil and jurisdiction as far west as the Mississippi river at least. Massachusetts and Connecticut yielded to the paramount right of New York and Pennsylvania to the territory within their appropriate limits, but insisted upon their own rights to the unoccupied territory to the westward of those intervening States.

While the interior of the continent was but little regarded and the eminent domain was admitted to be in the British crown, these claims attracted but little attention. But when the colonies had thrown off their allegiance to the British crown and took the attitude of sovereign and independent States, the value of these western possessions assumed a magnitude and importance of serious import. The blood and treasure of all the colonies were to be expended for the common defence of the sovereignty and independence of the respective States; and it was but just and proper that all should share as equally as practicable in the benefits to be attained. The States, whose western limits were circumscribed by the intervention of other States, and which, therefore, could have no separate claim to any interest in the vast and unoccupied domain to be secured as one of the results of the war, demanded that this domain should be devoted to the purpose of contributing to the general fund required for acquiring and defending the title to it. They called on the States claiming such land as being within their chartered limits, to surrender their respective claims to all unoccupied territory lying beyond a reasonable western limit for their State jurisdictions, to the United States. The failure of the States claiming the territory, to respond to this just demand, created great dissatisfaction on the part of the other States. Maryland refused to ratify the Articles of Confederation, until the claims to these lands should be ceded to the United States. She insisted that the boundaries of the respective States, and especially those claiming, under their charters, the right to extend their jurisdiction to the Mississippi river, or to the "South Sea," should be ascertained and restricted within reasonable limits; and that the unoccupied territory lying west of the proper limits of the States should be held, both as to property and jurisdiction, by the Congress of the United States, for the common benefit. Maryland presented these terms to Congress as the condition of her ratification of the Articles of Confederation, at the time, or soon after they were agreed to in that body. The following instructions of that State to her delegates in Congress, under date of May 21st, 1779, clearly present the views which influenced her action.

Instructions of the General Assembly of Maryland to George Plater, William Paca, William Carmichael, John Henry, James Forbes, and Daniel of St. Thomas Jenifer, Esqs.

GENTLEMEN, — Having conferred upon you a trust of the highest nature, it is evident we place great confidence in your integrity, abilities, and zeal to promote the general welfare of the United States, and the particular interest of this State, where the latter is not incompatible with the former; but, to add greater weight to your proceedings in Congress, and take away all suspicion that the opinions you there deliver, and the votes you give, may be the mere opinions of individuals, and not resulting from your knowledge of the sense and deliberate judgment of the State you repre sent, we think it our duty to instruct as followeth on the subject of the confederation, — a subject in which, unfortunately, a supposed difference of interest has produced an almost equal division of sentiments among the several States composing the Union. We say a supposed difference of interests; for if local attachments and prejudices and the avarice and ambition of individuals, would give way to the dictates of a sound policy, founded on the principles of justice (and no other policy but what is founded on those immutable principles deserves to be called sound), we flatter ourselves this apparent diversity of interests would soon vanish, and all the States would confederate on terms mutually advantageous to all; for they would then perceive that no other confederation than one so formed can be lasting. Although the pressure of immediate calamities, the dread of their continuance from the appearance of disunion, and some other peculiar circumstances, may have induced some States to accede to the present confederation, contrary to their own interests and judgments, it requires no great share of foresight to predict, that, when those causes cease to operate, the States which have thus acceded to the confederation will consider it as no longer binding, and will eagerly embrace the first occasion of asserting their just rights, and securing their independence. Is it possible that those States who are ambitiously grasping at territories to which, in our judgment, they have not the least shadow of exclusive right, will use with greater moderation the increase of wealth and power derived from those territories when acquired, than what they have displayed in their endeavors to acquire them? We think not. We are convinced the same spirit which hath prompted them to insist on a claim so extravagant, so repugnant to every principle of justice, so incompatible with the general welfare of all the States, will urge them on to add oppression to injustice. If they should not be incited by a superiority of wealth and strength to oppress by open force their less wealthy and less powerful neighbors, yet depopulation, and consequently the impoverishment of those States, will necessarily follow, which, by an unfair construction of the confederation, may be stripped of a common interest and the common benefits derivable from the western country. Suppose, for instance, Virginia indisputably possessed of the extensive and fertile country to which she has set up a claim, what would be the probable consequences to Maryland of such an undisturbed and undisputed possession? They cannot escape the least discerning.

Virginia, by selling on the most moderate terms a small proportion of the lands in question, would draw into her treasury vast sums of money, and in proportion to the sums arising from such sales, would be enabled to lessen her taxes. Lands comparatively cheap, and taxes comparatively low with the lands and taxes of an adjacent State, would quickly drain the State thus disadvantageously circumstanced of its most useful inhabitants; its wealth, and its consequence in the scale of the confederated States would sink of course. A claim so injurious to more than one half, if not to the whole of the United States, ought to be supported by the clearest evidence of the right. Yet what evidences of that right have been produced? What arguments alleged in support either of the evidence or the right? None that we have heard of deserving a serious refutation.

It has been said, that some of the delegates of a neighboring State have declared their opinion of the impracticability of governing the extensive dominion claimed by that State. Hence also the necessity was admitted of dividing its territory, and erecting a new State, under the auspices and direction of the elder, from whom, no doubt, it would receive its form of government, to whom it would be bound by some alliance or confederacy, and by whose councils it would be influenced. Such a measure, if ever attempted, would certainly be opposed by the other States as inconsistent with the letter and spirit of the proposed confederation. Should it take place by establishing a sub-confederacy, *imperium in imperio*, the State possessed of this extensive dominion must then either submit to all the inconveniences of an overgrown and unwieldy government, or suffer the authority of Congress to interpose, at a future time, and to lop off a part of its territory, to be erected into a new and free State, and admitted into a confederation on such conditions as shall be settled by nine States. If it is necessary, for the happiness and tranquillity of a State thus overgrown, that Congress should hereafter interfere and divide its territory, why is the claim to that territory now made, and so pertinaciously insisted on? We can suggest to ourselves but two motives: either the declaration of relinquishing, at some future period, a proportion of the country now contended for, was made to lull suspicion asleep, and to cover the designs of a secret ambition, or, if the thought was seriously entertained, the lands are now claimed to reap an immediate profit from the sale. We are convinced, policy and justice require that a country unsettled at the commencement of this war, claimed by the British crown, and ceded to it by the treaty of Paris, if wrested from the common enemy by the blood and treasure of the thirteen States, should be considered as a common property, subject to be parcelled out by Congress into free, convenient, and independent governments, in such manner and at such times as the wisdom of that assembly shall hereafter direct.

Thus convinced, we should betray the trust reposed in us by our constituents, were we to authorize you to ratify on their behalf the confederation, unless it be further explained. We have coolly and dispassionately considered the subject; we have weighed probable inconveniences and hardships, against the sacrifice of just and essential rights; and do instruct you not to agree to the confederation, unless an article or articles be added thereto in conformity with our declaration. Should we succeed in obtaining such article or articles, then you are hereby fully empowered to accede to the confederation.

That these our sentiments respecting our confederation may be more publicly known, and more explicitly and concisely declared, we have drawn up the annexed declaration, which we instruct you to lay before Congress, to have it printed, and to deliver to each of the delegates of the other States in Congress assembled, copies thereof, signed by yourselves, or by such of you as may be present at the time of delivery; to the intent and purpose that the copies aforesaid may be communicated to our brethren of the United States, and the contents of the said declaration taken into their serious and candid consideration.

Also we desire and instruct you to move, at a proper time, that these instructions be read to Congress by their secretary, and entered on the journals of Congress.

We have spoken with freedom, as becomes freemen; and we sincerely wish that these our representations may make such an impression on that assembly as to induce them to make such addition to the Articles of Confederation as may bring about a permanent union.

New Jersey withheld her ratification to the articles until near the close of 1778, on the same grounds, but finally yielded "in the firm reliance that the candor and justice of the several States will, in due time, remove as far as possible, the inequality which now subsists."

The State of Delaware, in connection with her ratification of the Articles of Confederation in 1779, directed her delegates to present to Congress the following resolutions of the legislature of that State: —

"*Resolved*, That this State thinks it necessary, for the peace and safety of the States to be included in the Union, that a moderate extent of limits should be assigned for such of those States as claim to the Mississippi or South Sea; and that the United States in Congress assembled, should, and ought to have the power of fixing their western limits.

"*Resolved*, That this State consider themselves justly entitled to a right, in common with the members of the Union, to that extensive tract of country which lies westward of the frontiers of the United States, the property of which was not vested in, or granted to, individuals at the commencement of the present war: That the same hath been, or may be gained from Great Britain or the native Indians, by the blood and treasure of all, and ought therefore to be a common estate, to be granted out on terms beneficial to the United States."

The increasing dissatisfaction which continued to manifest itself in the other States at the apparent design of a portion of the confederacy to endeavor to set up and maintain a claim to the western territory, for their own exclusive benefit, to the exclusion of those who were expending their treasures and pouring out their blood in the struggle to defend its possession, finally induced Congress to take the matter into serious consideration.

On the 30th October, 1779, by a vote of eight States in the affirmative to three in the negative, Congress passed the following resolution: —

"Whereas the appropriation of vacant lands by the several States, during the continuance of the war, will, in the opinion of Congress, be attended with great mischiefs; therefore,

"*Resolved*, That it be earnestly recommended to the State of Virginia to reconsider their late act of assembly for opening their land-office; and that it be recommended to the said State, and all other States similarly circumstanced, to forbear selling or issuing warrants for unappropriated lands, or granting the same during the continuance of the present war."

Under these critical and embarrassing circumstances the State of New York, as she had previously done in urging the immediate assembling of a continental Congress on the approach of British aggression in 1774, and as she subsequently did in leading the way for the assembling of the Federal Convention in 1787, magnanimously took the lead in laying her own individual interests and selfish ambition upon the altar of the whole country.

On the 7th of March, 1780, the delegates from that State laid upon the table of Congress the following: —

"An act to facilitate the completion of the Articles of Confederation and perpetual Union among the United States of America.

"Whereas nothing under divine Providence can more effectually contribute to the tranquillity and safety of the United States of America than a federal alliance, on such liberal principles as will give satisfaction to its respective members: And whereas the Articles of Confederation and perpetual Union recommended by the honorable the Congress of the United States of America have not proved acceptable to all the States, it having been conceived that a portion of the waste and uncultivated territory within the limits or claims of certain States ought to be appropriated as a common fund for the expenses of the war: And the people of the State of

New York being on all occasions disposed to manifest their regard for their sister States, and their earnest desire to promote the general interest and security, and more especially to accelerate the federal alliance, by removing, as far as it depends upon them, the before-mentioned impediment to its final accomplishment:

"Be it therefore enacted, by the people of the State of New York, represented in Senate and Assembly, and it is hereby enacted by the authority of the same, That it shall and may be lawful to and for the delegates of this State in the honorable Congress of the United States of America, or the major part of such of them as shall be assembled in Congress, and they, the said delegates, or a major part of them, so assembled, are hereby fully authorized and empowered, for and on behalf of this State, and by proper and authentic acts or instruments, to limit and restrict the boundaries of this State, in the western parts thereof, by such line or lines, and in such manner and form, as they shall judge to be expedient, either with respect to the jurisdiction, as well as the right or preëmption of soil, or reserving the jurisdiction in part, or in the whole, over the lands which may be ceded, or relinquished, with respect only to the right or preëmption of the soil.

"And be it further enacted by the authority aforesaid, That the territory which may be ceded or relinquished by virtue of this act, either with respect to the jurisdiction, as well as the right or preëmption of soil, or the right or preëmption of soil only, shall be and enure for the use and benefit of such of the United States as shall become members of the federal alliance of the said States, and for no other use or purpose whatever.

"And be it further enacted by the authority aforesaid, That all the lands to be ceded and relinquished by virtue of this act, for the benefit of the United States, with respect to property, but which shall nevertheless remain under the jurisdiction of this State, shall be disposed of and appropriated in such manner only as the Congress of the said States shall direct; and that a warrant under the authority of Congress for surveying and laying out any part thereof, shall entitle the party in whose favor it shall issue to cause the same to be surveyed and laid out and returned, according to the directions of such warrant; and thereupon letters patent, under the great seal of this State, shall pass to the grantee for the estate specified in the said warrant; for which no other fee or reward shall be demanded or received than such as shall be allowed by Congress.

"Provided always, and be it further enacted by the authority aforesaid, That the trust reposed by virtue of this act shall not be executed by the delegates of this State, unless at least three of the said delegates shall be present in Congress."

Encouraged by this noble example of New York, and impressed with the urgent necessity of harmonizing and consolidating the Union, in order to secure a successful termination of the war and a foundation for the future peace and prosperity of the country, Congress, at their session in 1780, made further efforts to adjust the matter of the western lands, as will be seen from the following extracts from their proceedings.

WEDNESDAY, September 6, 1780.

Congress took into consideration the report of the committee to whom were referred the instructions of the general assembly of Maryland to their delegates in Congress, respecting the Articles of Confederation, and the declaration therein referred to; the act of the legislature of New York on the same subject, and the remonstrance of the general assembly of Virginia; which report was agreed to, and is in the words following: —

That having duly considered the several matters to them submitted, they conceive it unnecessary to examine into the merits or policy of the instructions or declarations of the general assembly of Maryland, or of the remonstrance of the general assembly of Virginia, as they involve questions, a discussion of which was declined, on mature consideration, when the Articles of Confederation were debated; nor in the opinion of the committee, can such questions be now revived with any prospect of conciliation; that it appears more advisable to press upon those States which can remove the embarrassments respecting the western country, a liberal surrender of a portion of their territorial claims, since they cannot be preserved entire without endangering the stability of the general confederacy; to remind them how indispensably necessary it is to establish the Federal Union on a fixed and permanent basis, and on principles acceptable to all its respective members; how essential to public credit and confidence, to the support of our army, to the vigor of our councils, and success of our measures; to our tranquillity at home, our reputation abroad, to our very existence as a free, sovereign, and independent people; that they are fully persuaded the wisdom of the respective legislatures will lead them to a full and impartial consideration of a subject so interesting to the United States, and so necessary to the happy establishment of the Federal Union; that they are confirmed in these expectations by a review of the before-mentioned act of the legislature of New York, submitted to their consideration; that this act is expressly calculated to accelerate the federal alliance, by removing, as far as depends on that State, the impediment arising from the western country, and for that purpose to yield up a portion of territorial claim for the general benefit; Whereupon,

Resolved, That copies of the several papers referred to the committee be transmitted, with a copy of the report, to the legislatures of the several States, and that it be *earnestly recommended to those States, who have claims to the western country, to pass such laws, and give their delegates in Congress such powers as may effectually remove the only obstacle to a final ratification of the Articles of Confederation;* and that the legislature of Maryland, be earnestly requested to authorize the delegates in Congress to subscribe the said articles.

TUESDAY, October 10, 1780.

Resolved, That the unappropriated lands that may be ceded or relinquished to the United States, by any particular State, pursuant to the recommendation of Congress of the 6th day of September last, shall be disposed of for the common benefit of the United States, and be settled and formed into distinct republican States, which shall become members of the Federal Union, and have the same rights of sovereignty, freedom, and independence, as the other States: that each State which shall be so formed shall contain a suitable extent of territory, not less than one hundred nor more than one hundred and fifty miles square, or as near thereto as circumstances will admit: that the necessary and reasonable expenses which any particular State shall have incurred since the commencement of the present war, in subduing any British posts, or in maintaining forts or garrisons within and for the defence, or in acquiring any part of the territory that may be ceded or relinquished to the United States, shall be reimbursed.

That the said lands shall be granted or settled at such times, and under such regulations, as shall hereafter be agreed on by the United States, in Congress assembled, or any nine or more of them.

As the result of these proceedings, Virginia, in 1784, ceded to the United States, the territory claimed by that State, lying north and west of the Ohio river, with the condition that all the bounties promised to officers of the Revolution, out of her public lands, should be provided for by Congress. The State of Kentucky was subsequently formed out of the western portion of Virginia, with her consent.

The other States claiming title to portions of the western territory, also ceded their claims to the United States.

Compact between the Original States and the People and States to be formed in the Territory North-west of the Ohio River, contained in the Ordinance of 1787.

"It is hereby ordained and declared by the authority [of Congress] that the following articles shall be considered as articles of compact between the original States and the people and States in the said territory, and for ever remain unalterable, unless by common consent, to wit:—

Article I. No person, demeaning himself in a peaceable and orderly manner, shall ever be molested on account of his mode of worship or religious sentiments, in the said territory.

Art. II. The inhabitants of the said territory shall always be entitled to the benefits of the writ of habeas corpus, and of the trial by jury; of a proportionate representation of the people in the legislature, and of judicial proceedings according to the course of the common law. All persons shall be bailable, unless for capital offences, where the proof shall be evident, or the presumption great. All fines shall be moderate, and no cruel or unusual punishments shall be inflicted. No man shall be deprived of his liberty or property, but by the judgment of his peers, or the law of the land, and should the public exigencies make it necessary, for the common preservation, to take any person's property, or to demand his particular services, full compensation shall be made for the same. And, in the just preservation of rights and property, it is understood and declared, that no law ought ever to be made, or have force in the said territory, that shall, in any manner whatever, interfere with, or affect private contracts or engagements, *bona fide*, and without fraud previously formed.

Art. III. Religion, morality, and knowledge, being necessary to good government, and the happiness of mankind, schools and the means of education shall forever be encouraged. The utmost good faith shall always be observed towards the Indians; their lands and property shall never be taken from them without their consent; and in their property, rights, and liberty, they never shall be invaded or disturbed, unless in just and lawful wars authorized by Congress; but laws founded in justice and humanity shall, from time to time, be made, for preventing wrongs being done to them, and for preserving peace and friendship with them.

Art. IV. The said territory, and the States which may be formed therein, shall forever remain a part of this confederacy of the United States of America, subject to the Articles of Confederation, and to such alterations therein as shall be constitutionally made; and to all the acts and ordinances of the United States, in Congress assembled, conformable thereto. The inhabitants and settlers in the said territory shall be subject to pay a part of the federal debts, contracted or to be contracted, and a proportional part of the expenses of government, to be apportioned on them by Congress, according to the same common rule and measure by which apportionments thereof shall be made on the other States; and the taxes for paying their proportion shall be laid and levied by the authority and direction of the legislatures of the district or districts, or new States, as in the original States, within the time agreed upon by the United States, in Congress assembled. The legislatures of those districts, or new States, shall never interfere with the primary disposal of the soil by the United States, in Congress assembled, nor with any regulations Congress may find necessary, for securing the title in such soil, to the *bona fide* purchasers. No tax shall be imposed on lands, the property of the United States; and in no case shall non-resident proprietors be taxed higher than residents. The navigable waters leading into the Mississippi and St. Lawrence, and the carrying places between the same, shall be common highways, and forever free, as well to the inhabitants of the said territory as to the citizens of the United States, and those of any other States that may be admitted into the confederacy, without any tax, impost, or duty therefor.

ART. V. There shall be formed in the said territory, not less than three, nor more than five States; and the boundaries of the States, as soon as Virginia shall alter her act of cession, and consent to the same, shall become fixed and established as follows, to wit: the western State in the said territory shall be bounded by the Mississippi, the Ohio, and the Wabash rivers; a direct line drawn from the Wabash and Post Vincents, due north, to the territorial line between the United States and Canada; and by the said territorial line to the Lake of the Woods and Mississippi. The middle States shall be bounded by the said direct line, the Wabash, from Post Vincents to the Ohio, by the Ohio, by a direct line drawn due north from the mouth of the Great Miami to the said territorial line, and by the said territorial line. The eastern State shall be bounded by the last-mentioned direct line, the Ohio, Pennsylvania, and the said territorial line; provided, however, and it is further understood and declared, that the boundaries of these three States shall be subject so far to be altered, that, if Congress shall hereafter find it expedient, they shall have authority to form one or two States in that part of the said territory which lies north of an east and west line drawn through the southerly bend or extreme of Lake Michigan. And whenever any of the said States shall have sixty thousand free inhabitants therein, such State shall be admitted, by its delegates, into the Congress of the United States, on an equal footing with the original States, in all respects whatever; and shall be at liberty to form a permanent constitution and State government; provided the constitution and government, so to be formed, shall be republican, and in conformity to the principles contained in these articles; and, so far as can be consistent with the general interest of the confederacy, such admission shall be allowed at an earlier period, and when there may be a less number of free inhabitants in the State than sixty thousand.

ART. VI. There shall be neither slavery nor involuntary servitude in the said territory, otherwise than in the punishment of crimes, whereof the party shall have been duly convicted; provided, always, that any person escaping into the same, from whom labor or service is lawfully claimed in any one of the original States, such fugitive may be lawfully reclaimed, and conveyed to the person claiming his or her labor or service as aforesaid.

Be it ordained by the authority aforesaid, That the resolutions of the 23d of April, 1784, relative to the subject of this ordinance, be, and the same are hereby, repealed, and declared null and void.

Done by the United States, in Congress assembled, the 13th day of July, in the year of our Lord 1787, and of their sovereignty and independence the 12th.

CHARLES THOMSON, *Secretary.*

NEW STATES

ADMITTED INTO THE UNION SINCE THE ADOPTION OF THE CONSTITUTION OF THE UNITED STATES.

VERMONT.

The territory of this State was originally claimed as belonging to New Hampshire, and a large portion of the land was granted by the colonial governors of that jurisdiction. It was also claimed as being a part of the colony of New York, and on that account, it was never admitted as a member of the old confederation. The people, however, never submitted to the authority of New York, and resolutely maintained their independence until the 4th of March, 1791, when, with the assent of that State, Vermont was admitted into the Union, by an act of Congress passed on the 18th of February preceding, under her constitution adopted in 1777.

KENTUCKY.

This State originally formed the western portion of the State of Virginia. It was admitted into the Union on the 1st of June, 1792, by virtue of an act of Congress, passed Feb. 4th, 1791.

TENNESSEE.

This State was formed of territory which had been ceded to the United States in 1789, and organized as a territory by act of May 26, 1790. It was admitted into the Union, June 1, 1796.

OHIO

Was a part of the territory ceded to the United States by the States of Virginia and Connecticut, in 1783–4. It constituted a part of the North-west territory, organized under the Ordinance of 1787, and was organized into a separate jurisdiction by act of Congress of May 7, 1800. It became a member of the Union on the 29th of November, 1802, having formed a constitution in compliance with an enabling act, of 30th April of that year.

LOUISIANA.

This State was formed out of a portion of the territory purchased from France in 1803. It was provided with a territorial organization, by the act of 26th March, 1804, under the name of the territory of Orleans. By act of February 20, 1811, it was authorized to form a State constitution, and was admitted by act of 8th April, 1812.

INDIANA.

The second State formed out of the North-west territory, was admitted into the Union by act of Congress of Dec. 11, 1816, having formed its constitution by authority of an act passed April 19, of that year.

MISSISSIPPI.

This State was formed out of territory ceded to the United States by the State of South Carolina, in 1787, and by Georgia in 1802. It was provided with a territorial organization, by acts of 7th April, 1798, May 10, 1800, and March 27, 1804. It was admitted into the Union by act of Dec. 10, 1817, having formed its constitution by authority of the act of March 1st of that year.

ILLINOIS.

The third State formed out of the North-west territory, was admitted into the Union by act of Dec. 3, 1818, having formed a constitution under an act of April 18, of that year.

ALABAMA.

The western portion of the Mississippi territory was erected into a State, by act of December 14, 1819, under the name of Alabama. [See Mississippi.]

MAINE.

Maine, although under the jurisdiction of Massachusetts from an early period of its history until 1820, does not lie contiguous to it. The State of New Hampshire intervenes. It was erected into a separate State, with the concurrence of Massachusetts, and admitted into the Union by act of March 3, 1820.

MISSOURI.

This was the second State formed from the Louisiana purchase. For about a year, this portion of the country ceded by France, was placed under the jurisdiction of the governor and judges of the territory of Indiana, when a separate territorial organization was provided for it. On the 6th of March, 1820, Congress passed "an act to authorize the people of the territory of Missouri to form a constitution and State government, and for the admission of such State into the Union, and to prohibit slavery in certain territories." This act constituted the famous *compromise* of 1820. The people of Missouri proceeded to form their constitution, which was presented to Congress at its succeeding session. After some difficulty between the two houses in regard to the terms upon which Missouri was to be admitted, Mr. Clay, on the 26th February, 1821, reported a resolution in the Senate, providing for the admission of Missouri into the Union, on a certain condition. This resolution passed both houses of Congress, and became a law, March 2, 1821. The State of Missouri accepted the condition, and became a member of the Union, August 10, 1821.

ARKANSAS.

The third State formed out of the Louisiana purchase, was organized as a separate territory, March 2, 1819, having previously constituted a part of the territory of Missouri. It was erected into a State by act of June 15th, 1836. No previous act had been passed, authorizing it to form a constitution.

MICHIGAN

Was the fourth State formed from the North-west territory. It received its separate territorial organization by act of Jan. 11, 1805, and was admitted into the Union, Jan. 26, 1837.

FLORIDA.

The territory of Florida was ceded to the United States, by Spain, by treaty of February 22, 1819. It received its territorial organization by act of March 30, 1822, and was admitted into the Union, by act of March 3, 1845.

TEXAS.

This State was formerly one of the "United Mexican States." Having separated itself from that Republic and established its independence, a treaty was negotiated between its government and that of the United States, for its accession to the Union as one of the United States, on an equal footing with the original States. This treaty was rejected by the Senate, two thirds of the Senators not consenting to it. The following resolutions were subsequently introduced and passed by virtue of which Texas was admitted into the Union.

A joint resolution for annexing Texas to the United States, approved March 1, 1845.

JOINT RESOLUTION FOR ANNEXING TEXAS TO THE UNITED STATES.

Resolved by the Senate and House of Representatives of the United States of America in Congress assembled, That Congress doth consent that the territory properly included within and rightfully belonging to the Republic of Texas may be erected into a new State, to be called the State of Texas, with a republican form of government, to be adopted by the people of said republic, by deputies in convention assembled, with the consent of the existing government, in order that the same may be admitted as one of the States of this Union.

SEC. 2. *And be it further resolved*, That the foregoing consent of Congress is given upon the following conditions, and with the following guarantees, to wit: —

FIRST. Said State to be formed, subject to the adjustment by this government of all questions of boundary that may arise with other governments; and the constitution thereof, with the proper evidence of its adoption by the people of said Republic of Texas, shall be transmitted to the President of the United States, to be laid before Congress for its final action, on or before the first day of January, one thousand eight hundred and forty-six.

SECOND. Said State, when admitted into the Union, after ceding to the United States all public edifices, fortifications, barracks, ports, and harbors, navy and navy-yards, docks, magazines, arms, armaments, and all other property and means pertaining to the public defence belonging to said Republic of Texas, shall retain all the public funds, debts, taxes, and dues of every kind, which may belong to or be due and owing said republic; and shall also retain all the vacant and unappropriated lands lying within its limits, to be applied to the payment of the debts and liabilities of said Republic of Texas; and the residue of said lands, after discharging said debts and liabilities, to be disposed of as said State may direct; but in no event are said debts and liabilities to become a charge upon the government of the United States.

THIRD. New States, of convenient size, not exceeding four in number, in addition to said State of Texas, and having sufficient population, may hereafter, by the consent of said State, be formed out of the territory thereof, which shall be entitled to admission under the provisions of the Federal Constitution. And such States as may be formed out of that portion of said territory lying south of thirty-six degrees thirty minutes north latitude, commonly known as the Missouri compromise line, shall be admitted into the

Union with or without slavery, as the people of each State asking admission may desire. And in such State or States as shall be formed out of said territory north of said Missouri compromise line, slavery, or involuntary servitude (except for crimes), shall be prohibited.

SEC. 3. *And be it further resolved*, That if the President of the United States shall, in his judgment and discretion, deem it most advisable, instead of proceeding to submit the foregoing resolution to the Republic of Texas, as an overture on the part of the United States, for admission, to negotiate with that republic; then,

Be it resolved, That a State, to be formed out of the present Republic of Texas, with suitable extent and boundaries, and with two representatives in Congress, until the next apportionment of representation, shall be admitted into the Union, by virtue of this act, on an equal footing with the existing States, as soon as the terms and conditions of such admission, and the cession of the remaining Texan territory to the United States, shall be agreed upon by the governments of Texas and the United States: That the sum of one hundred thousand dollars be, and the same is hereby, appropriated to defray the expenses of missions and negotiations, to agree upon the terms of said admission and cession, either by treaty to be submitted to the Senate, or by articles to be submitted to the two houses of Congress, as the President may direct.

Approved March 1, 1845.

A joint resolution for the admission of the State of Texas into the Union, approved December, 29, 1845.

JOINT RESOLUTION FOR THE ADMISSION OF THE STATE OF TEXAS INTO THE UNION.

Whereas the Congress of the United States, by a joint resolution approved March the first, eighteen hundred and forty-five, did consent that the territory properly included within and rightfully belonging to the Republic of Texas might be erected into a new State, to be called the State of Texas, with a republican form of government, to be adopted by the people of said republic, by deputies in convention assembled, with the consent of the existing government, in order that the same might be admitted as one of the States of the Union; which consent of Congress was given upon certain conditions specified in the first and second sections of said joint resolution: and whereas the people of the said Republic of Texas, by deputies in convention assembled, with the consent of the existing government, did adopt a constitution, and erect a new State, with a republican form of government, and, in the name of the people of Texas, and by their authority, did ordain and declare that they assented to and accepted the proposals, conditions, and guarantees contained in said first and second sections of said resolution: and whereas the said Constitution, and the proper evidence of its adoption by the people of the Republic of Texas, have been transmitted to the President of the United States, and laid before Congress, in conformity to the provisions of said joint resolution: Therefore,

Resolved by the Senate and House of Representatives of the United States of America in Congress assembled, That the State of Texas shall be one, and is hereby declared to be one, of the United States of America, and admitted into the Union on an equal footing with the original States in all respects whatever.

SEC. 2. *And be it further resolved,* That until the Representatives in Congress shall be apportioned according to an actual enumeration of the inhabitants of the United States, the State of Texas shall be entitled to choose two representatives.

Approved December 29, 1845.

WISCONSIN

Was organized as a territory by act of April 20, 1836; authorized to form a State government by act of 6th August, 1846, and admitted into the Union by act of March 3, 1847.

IOWA

Received a territorial organization by act of June 12, 1838, and was admitted into the Union, in connection with Florida, by act of March 3, 1845.

CALIFORNIA,

Formed out of the territory acquired from Mexico, by the treaty of 2d February, 1848, was admitted into the Union by act of September 9, 1850.

MINNESOTA

Was organized as a territory by act of 3d March, 1849, and admitted into the Union by act of May 11, 1858.

OREGON

Was organized as a territory by act of 14th August, 1848, and admitted into the Union by act of February 14, 1859.

TERRITORIES.

NEW MEXICO
AND
UTAH

Were organized from territory acquired from Mexico, by act of 9th September, 1850.

KANSAS
AND
NEBRASKA

Were organized from territory acquired from France, by the Louisiana purchase, by act of 22d May, 1854.

WASHINGTON

Is that portion of Oregon Territory not embraced in the State of Oregon. Each territory is allowed one delegate in Congress, who has a seat in the House of Representatives, with the right to introduce bills and motions, and to speak upon any subject under debate in the House, but without the right to vote on any question. He receives the same compensation and emoluments as a member of Congress.

DISTRICT OF COLUMBIA.

The framers of the Constitution of the United States regarded it as an important object that the general government should have a fixed and permanent location, and that its jurisdiction over the territory assigned to that purpose, should be exclusive, and secure from the interposition of any conflicting authority. For the attainment of this purpose, they inserted in the Constitution the following provision: " Congress shall have power to exercise exclusive legislation in all cases whatsoever, over such district (not exceeding ten miles square) as may, by cession of particular States, and the acceptance of Congress, become the seat of the government of the United States."

The subject of fixing a permanent location for the seat of government had been several times agitated in Congress prior to the adoption of the Constitution.

In 1784, Congress passed a resolution for the erection of buildings for the permanent use of Congress and the public officers, near the falls of the Delaware, but it failed to be carried into effect. On the 10th of May, 1787, Mr. Lee of Virginia, moved in Congress, a resolution for fixing the permanent seat of the federal government at Georgetown, on the Potomac River (adjoining the present site of Washington), and for the adjournment of Congress to that place as soon as buildings could be erected. The motion was lost.

On the assembling of Congress in the city of New York, under the new Constitution, Mr. White of Virginia, presented to the House of Representatives a resolution of the Virginia legislature, offering to the United States ten miles square of the territory of that State, for the seat of the federal government. Mr. Seney of Maryland, also laid before Congress, an act of that State, offering ten miles square of its territory for the same purpose. Numerous memorials and petitions were also offered, from citizens of Pennsylvania, New Jersey, and Maryland, for the selection of the location for the government in their respective States. On the 5th of September, 1789, a bill passed the House of Representatives "to fix the permanent seat of the government of the United States at some convenient place on the banks of the Susquehanna, in the State of Pennsylvania." On the introduction of this bill, much feeling was manifested by the southern members, and particularly by those from Virginia, who contended that the banks of the Potomac was the most suitable location. Mr. Madison expressed a doubt whether Virginia would have become a party to the Constitution, if they could have foreseen that the government would be located so far north. The bill passed the House of Representatives by a vote of thirty-one to seventeen. It was sent to the Senate, and there amended by changing the location from "the banks of the Susquehanna" to Germantown, near Philadelphia. This amendment was agreed to in the House of Representatives, with an amendment, providing that the laws of Pennsylvania should continue in force in said district until Congress should otherwise direct. This rendered it necessary that the bill should go again to the Senate, where it was postponed until the next session. Germantown, Pennsylvania, was therefore, actually agreed upon, by both houses of Congress, as the permanent seat of the federal government, and the bill failed to become a law, only by a delay brought about by parliamentary management.

At the next session of Congress, Mr. Smith, of Maryland, proposed Baltimore as the location, and as an inducement, stated that the citizens of that place would raise twenty or thirty thousand dollars, as a contribution towards the erection of the public buildings.

In the mean time the legislature of Virginia, on the 3d of December, 1789, passed an act, ceding to Congress a district for the location of the general government, within the limits of that State; and called on the State of Maryland to coöperate with them in an effort to procure the location to be fixed on the banks of the Potomac. In answer to this appeal, Maryland passed a resolution, offering to cede territory and to furnish seventy-two thousand dollars towards the erection of the public buildings. Virginia offered to advance one hundred and twenty thousand dollars for the same purpose.

On the 28th June, 1790, a bill passed the Senate "to fix the permanent seat of Congress and the government of the United States" . . . . "on the river Potomac, at some place between the mouths of the eastern branch and the Connogocheque." When this bill reached the House of Representatives, it produced great excitement. A decided majority of the members had already expressed their preference for a more northern location. But at this particular juncture, another absorbing question, to wit, the funding of the revolutionary State debts, also made its appearance in the House. This measure was generally favored by the eastern members and opposed by the South. In an interview between Mr. Hamilton and Mr. Jefferson (both then members of General Washington's cabinet), on the dangers of secession and disunion in case of the final rejection of the funding system, Colonel Hamilton urged it upon Mr. Jefferson to appeal to the judgment and discretion of his friends to aid in the passage of the latter measure. Mr. Jefferson replied, that he would invite another friend or two to meet Colonel Hamilton at dinner the next day, and he thought it impossible that reasonable men, consulting together coolly, could fail, by some mutual sacrifices of opinion, to "*form a compromise, which was to save the Union.*" The consultation took place, and it was finally agreed, that, whatever importance might be attached to the rejection of the funding bill, the preservation of the Union and of harmony among the States was more important. Mr. Jefferson's friends consented, therefore, to change their votes on that measure; but as "it would be a very bitter pill," they thought some concomitant measure should be adopted to "sweeten it a little to them." It was suggested, that there was a proposition pending to fix the seat of government either at Germantown, near Philadelphia, or at Georgetown, on the Potomac; and it was thought that by giving it to Philadelphia for ten years, and to Georgetown permanently afterwards, this might, as an anodyne, calm, in some degree, the hostility to the other measure. With this understanding, two of the Virginia members, from the Potomac districts, White and Lee, agreed to change their votes in favor of the funding bill, which would secure its passage; and Colonel Hamilton undertook to procure votes enough from his northern friends to secure the passage of the bill for fixing the seat of government on the banks of the Potomac. The compromise was carried out in good faith, — the State debts were assumed and funded by the general government, and the District of Columbia became the seat of government of the United States.

Congress accepted the ten miles square, lying on both sides of the Potomac River, which is the dividing line between the States of Maryland and Virginia, one half of the territory being taken from each State. The cities of Alexandria, in Virginia, and Georgetown, Maryland, were both included in the cession. The city of Washington is built on the Maryland side of the Potomac, which separates it from Alexandria, and a small stream, called Rock Creek, divides it from Georgetown.

The particular site of the Federal city was selected by President Washington; and it was laid out, and the streets, avenues, and the public squares, and the locations of the public buildings, were fixed and arranged under his direction. The capitol stands upon elevated ground in the eastern part of the city, and is surrounded by a highly cultivated park of about twenty acres in extent. The recent extension of the capitol is supposed to render a corresponding extension of the park necessary, and Congress has taken steps with the view of adding several acres to the grounds, by the purchase of adjacent squares. The executive mansion is located about one mile and a half west of the capitol; and Pennsylvania Avenue, the principal promenade and thoroughfare of the city, runs in a direct line from one to the other.

By an act approved February 27, 1801, Congress assumed exclusive jurisdiction over the District of Columbia, in accordance with the Constitution. That portion of the District which was ceded by Virginia, has since been receded to that State, so that the District now embraces only fifty square miles, all of which was originally a part of Maryland.

ORGANIZATION

OF

THE GENERAL GOVERNMENT.

STATE DEPARTMENT.

CREATED 27TH JULY, 1779.

SECRETARY OF STATE.

"There shall be an executive department, to be denominated the Department of Foreign Affairs; and there shall be a principal officer therein, to be called the Secretary for the Department of Foreign Affairs, who shall perform and execute such duties as shall, from time to time, be enjoined on or intrusted to him by the President of the United States, agreeably to the Constitution, relative to correspondences, commissions or instructions to or with public ministers or consuls from the United States, or to negotiations with public ministers from foreign States or princes, or to memorials or other applications from foreign public ministers or other foreigners, or to such other matters respecting foreign affairs, as the President of the United States shall assign to the said department; and furthermore, the said principal officer shall conduct the business of the said department in such manner as the President of the United States shall, from time to time, order or instruct." *Act of July* 27, 1779.

"The department of foreign affairs shall hereafter be denominated the Department of State, and the principal officer therein shall hereafter be called the Secretary of State." *Act of Sept.* 15, 1789.

ASSISTANT SECRETARY OF STATE.

"An officer shall be appointed in the department of State, to be called the assistant Secretary of State, . . . who shall perform all such duties in the office of the Secretary of State, belonging to that department, as shall be prescribed by the Secretary of State, or as may be required by law." *Act of March* 3, 1853.

The salary of the Secretary is $8,000,—Assistant Secretary, $3,000 per annum.

CLERKS.

The whole permanent clerical force allowed to the Department of State, consists of—

3 clerks of class	1,	salary	$1,200	per annum.
3 " " "	2,	"	1,400	" "
8 " " "	3,	"	1,600	" "
8 " " "	4,	"	1,800	" "
1 chief clerk,		"	2,200	" "

This department has the custody of the records, books, and papers of the department of foreign affairs under the confederation, and of the originals of all laws passed by Congress.

An annual appropriation of about eighty-five thousand dollars is required for the salaries and contingent expenses of the State Department.

TREASURY DEPARTMENT.

ESTABLISHED SEPT. 2, 1779.

"There shall be a Department of Treasury, in which shall be the following officers, namely, a Secretary of the Treasury, to be deemed head of the department, a comptroller, an auditor, a treasurer, a register, and an assistant to the Secretary of the Treasury, which assistant shall be appointed by the said secretary." *Act of Sept.* 2, 1789.

The office of assistant secretary was abolished, but subsequently rëestablished, to be appointed by the President and Senate.

ORGANIZATION OF THE DEPARTMENT.

There are now authorized by law and employed in the office of the secretary and the several bureaus and offices attached to the department in Washington, the following officers: —

	Secretary of the Treasury,	salary	$8,000	per annum.
	Assistant Secretary of the Treasury,	"	3,000	" "
2	Comptrollers,	"	3,000	each.
6	Auditors,	"	3,000	"
	Register of the Treasury,	"	3,000	
	Commissioner of Customs,	"	3,000	
	Treasurer of the United States,	"	3,000	
	Chief Clerk of the Department,	"	2,200	
13	Chief Clerks of Bureau,	"	2,000	each.
3	Disbursing Clerks,	"	2,000	"
12	Clerks (4th class),	"	1,800	"
104	Clerks (3d class),	"	1,600	"
155	Clerks (2d class),	"	1,400	"
61	Clerks (1st class),	"	1,200	"

The annual appropriation for the payment of the salaries of the officers and the contingent expenses of this department, amounts to something more than seven hundred thousand dollars.

DUTIES OF THE SECRETARY.

"To decide on the forms of keeping and stating accounts and making returns; and to grant, under the limitations herein established, or to be hereafter provided, all warrants for moneys to be issued from the treasury in pursuance of appropriations by law, ... and generally to perform all such services relative to the finances as he shall be directed to perform." 1 Stat. at Large, 65.

"The secretary of the treasury shall direct the superintendence of the collection of the duties on imports and tonnage, as he shall judge best." 1 Stat. 280.

"It shall be the duty of the secretary of the treasury to digest, prepare, and lay before Congress at the commencement of every session, a report on the subject of finance, containing estimates of the public revenue and public expenditures, and plans for improving or increasing the revenues from time to time, for the purpose of giving information to Congress in adopting modes of raising the money requisite to meet the public expenditures." 2 Stat. at Large, 79.

DUTIES OF ASSISTANT SECRETARY.

He "shall examine all letters, contracts, and warrants prepared for the signature of the secretary of the treasury and shall perform all other such duties in the office of the secretary of the treasury, now performed by some of the clerks, as may be devolved on him by the secretary of the treasury." 9 Stat. at Large, 396.

DUTIES OF COMPTROLLERS.

"It shall be the duty of the first comptroller to examine all accounts settled by the first and fifth auditors, and certify the balances arising thereon to the register; to countersign all warrants drawn by the secretary of the treasury, which shall be warranted by law; to report to the secretary, the official forms to be issued in the different offices for collecting the public revenue, and the manner and form of keeping and stating the accounts of the several persons employed therein; he shall also superintend the preservation of the public accounts subject to his revision, and provide for the regular payment of all moneys which may be collected." 3 Stat. at Large, 367.

"It shall be the duty of the first comptroller to superintend the recovery of all debts to the United States; to direct suits and legal proceedings and to take all such measures as may be authorized by the laws, to enforce prompt payments of all debts to the United States."

It is also his duty to report to Congress annually, the names of defaulters and cases requiring equitable relief.

"It shall be the duty of the second comptroller to examine all accounts settled by the second, third, and fourth auditors, and certify the balances arising thereon to the secretary of the department in which the expenditure has been incurred; to countersign all warrants drawn by the secretaries of the war and navy departments, which shall be warranted by law; to report to the said secretaries the official forms to be issued in the different offices for disbursing the public money in those departments, and the manner and form of keeping and stating the accounts of the persons employed therein; and it shall also be his duty to superintend the preservation of the public accounts subject to his revision." 3 Stat. at Large, 367.

COMMISSIONER OF CUSTOMS,

"Shall perform all the acts and exercise all the powers, now devolved by law on the first comptroller of the treasury relating to the receipt from customs and the accounts of collectors and other officers of the customs or connected therewith, to report to the secretary the official forms of all papers to be used in the different offices for collecting the public revenue." 9 Stat. at Large, 396.

TREASURER.

"It shall be the duty of the treasurer to receive and keep the moneys of the United States, and to disburse the same upon warrants drawn by the secretary of the treasury, countersigned by the comptroller, recorded by the register, and not otherwise." 1 Stat. at Large, 66.

AUDITORS.

"It shall be the duty of the auditor to receive all public accounts, and, after examination, to certify the balance and transmit the accounts with the vouchers and certificate, to the comptroller for his decision thereon; *provided,* that if any person whose account shall be so audited, be dissatisfied therewith, he may, within six months, appeal to the comptroller against such settlement." 1 Stat. 66.

Four additional auditors and one additional comptroller, were subsequently authorized, and it was made the "duty of the first auditor to receive all accounts accruing in the treasury department, and after examination to certify the balance and transmit the accounts, with the vouchers and certificate, to the first comptroller for his decision thereon.

"It shall be the duty of the second auditor to receive all accounts relative to the pay and clothing of the army, the subsistence of officers, bounties and premiums, military and hospital stores, and the contingent expenses of the war department.

"It shall be the duty of the third auditor to receive all accounts relative to the subsistence of the army, the quartermaster's department, and generally all accounts of the war department, other than those provided for.

"And it shall be the duty of the fourth auditor to receive all accounts arising in the navy department or relative thereto; and the second, third, and fourth auditors, aforesaid, shall examine the accounts respectively, and certify the balance, and transmit the accounts, with the vouchers and certificate, to the second comptroller for his decision thereon.

"And it shall be the duty of the fifth auditor to receive all accounts accruing in, or relative to, the department of State . . . . and those arising out of Indian affairs, and examine," &c. 3 Stat. 366.

The auditors are the final custodians of the settled accounts and vouchers, and are required to report annually to the secretary of the treasury.

"There shall be appointed by the President, with the consent of the Senate, an auditor of the treasury for the post-office department, whose duty it shall be to receive all accounts arising in said departments, or relative thereto, to audit and settle the same and certify their balances to the postmaster-general; *provided*, that if either the postmaster-general, or any person whose account shall be settled, be dissatisfied therewith, he may, within twelve months, appeal to the first comptroller of the treasury, whose decision shall be final and conclusive.

"The said auditor shall report to the postmaster-general, when required, the official forms of papers to be used by postmasters and other officers or agents of the department concerned in its receipts and payments, and the manner and form of keeping and stating its accounts. . . . . He shall close the accounts of the department quarterly, and transmit to the secretary of the treasury, quarterly statements of its receipts and expenditures." 5 Stat. at Large, 80.

THE REGISTER OF THE TREASURY.

"It shall be the duty of the register to keep all accounts of the receipts and expenditures of the public money, and of all debts due to or from the United States; . . . to record all warrants for the receipt or payment of moneys at the treasury, certify the same thereon, and to transmit to the secretary of the treasury copies of the certificates of balances of accounts adjusted as is herein directed." 1 Statutes at Large, 67.

THE SOLICITOR OF THE TREASURY.

"There shall be appointed by the President, &c., some suitable person, learned in the law, to be solicitor of the treasury, and that all and singular of the powers and duties which are by law vested in and required from the agent of the treasury of the United States, shall be transferred to, vested in, and required from the said solicitor of the treasury." [To direct and superintend all orders, suits, and proceedings in law or equity, for the recovery of money, chattels, lands, &c., in the name of the United States. Stat. 592.] 4 Statutes at Large, 414.

DEPARTMENT OF THE INTERIOR.

ESTABLISHED MARCH 3, 1849.

"There shall be created a new executive department, to be called the Department of the Interior; the head of which department shall be called the Secretary of the Interior, who shall be appointed by the President, by and with the advice and consent of the Senate, and who shall hold his office by the same tenure, and receive the same salary as the secretaries of the other executive departments, and who shall perform all the duties assigned to him by this act." 9 Stat. at Large, 395.

To the department of the interior is assigned the supervisory and appellate power over the following bureaus, to wit:—

The Patent office;
The General Land office;
The office of Indian Affairs;
The Pension office;
The office of Public Buildings;

and the supervisory power over the accounts of clerks, marshals, and other officers of the courts of the United States; over the lead and other mines of the United States; and over the inspector and wardens of the penitentiary of the District of Columbia.

ORGANIZATION OF THE DEPARTMENT.

Secretary of the Interior, salary	$8,000
Chief Clerk	2,200

	BUREAUS.	SALARIES.	
	Commissioner of General Land office	$3,000	
	Commissioner of Pensions	3,000	
	Commissioner of Indian Affairs	3,000	
	Commissioner of Patents	3,000	
	Commissioner of Public Buildings	2,000	
4	Chief Clerks of Bureaus	2,000	each.
3	Principal Clerks in General Land office	1,800	"
15	Clerks (class 4)	1,800	"
59	" (class 3)	1,600	"
88	" (class 2)	1,400	"
50	" (class 1)	1,200	"
12	Chief Examiners (Patent office)	2,500	"
12	Assistant " " "	1,800	"

The annual appropriations required for the payment of the salaries and contingent expenses of this department amount to about $660,000.

WAR DEPARTMENT.

CREATED AUGUST 7, 1779.

"There shall be an executive department to be denominated the Department of War; and there shall be a principal officer therein, to be called the Secretary for the Department of War, who shall perform and execute such duties as shall, from time to time, be enjoined on or intrusted to him by the President of the United States, agreeably to the Constitution, relative to military commissions or to the land-forces . . . warlike stores of the United States, or to such other matters respecting military . . . affairs, as the President of the United States shall assign to the said department . . . and furthermore the said principal officer shall conduct the business of the said department, in such manner as the President of the United States shall, from time to time, order or instruct." 1 Stat. at Large, 49.

"The secretary for the war department shall be and he is hereby authorized and directed to define and prescribe the species as well as the amount of supplies to be respectively purchased by the commissary-general's and the quartermaster-general's departments, and the respective duties and powers of the said departments respecting such purchases; and also to adopt and prescribe general regulations for the transportation, &c. And to fix and make reasonable allowances for the store-rent, storage, and salary of store-keepers necessary for the safe-keeping of all military stores and supplies." 2 Stat. at Large, 817.

ORGANIZATION OF THE DEPARTMENT.

Secretary of War, salary . . .	$8,000	per annum.
Chief Clerk	2,200	" "

BUREAU.

	Adjutant-General, Quartermaster-General, Commissary-General, Chief Engineer, Surgeon-General, Colonel of Ordnance, Colonel of Topographical Engineers,	all paid as officers of the army.
12	Clerks (class 4), salary . . .	$1,800 each per annum.
11	" (class 3), " . .	1,600 " " "
26	" (class 2), " . . .	1,400 " " "
15	" (class 1), " .	1,200 " " "

The annual appropriation for the support of the department (exclusive of the pay of the heads of the bureaus), is about $125,000.

NAVY DEPARTMENT.

ESTABLISHED APRIL 30, 1798.

"There shall be an executive department, under the denomination of the Department of the Navy, the chief officer of which shall be called the Secretary of the Navy, whose duty it shall be to execute such orders as he shall receive from the President of the United States, relative to the procurement of naval stores and materials, and the construction, armament, equipment and employment of vessels of war, as well as all other matters connected with the naval establishment of the United States." 1 Stat. at Large, 553.

"There shall be attached to the navy department the following bureaus, namely:

"I. A bureau of yards and docks.

"II. A bureau of construction, equipment, and repairs.

"III. A bureau of provisions and clothing.

"IV. A bureau of ordnance and hydrography.

"V. A bureau of medicine and surgery.

"The President of the United States by and with the advice and consent of the Senate, shall appoint from the captains in the naval service, a chief for each of the bureaus of navy-yards and docks, and of ordnance and hydrography, who shall each receive a salary of three thousand five hundred dollars per annum, in lieu of all other compensation whatever in the naval service. And shall in like manner appoint a chief of the bureau of construction, equipment and repairs, who shall be a skilful naval constructor; who shall receive for his services three thousand dollars per annum; and shall also appoint a chief of the bureau of provision and clothing — a purser of the navy of the United States of not less than ten years standing, . . . receiving for his services no compensation except his highest service pay as purser." 5 Stat. 579, and 9 Stat. 290.

"And shall in like manner appoint from the surgeons of the navy, a chief of the bureau of medicine and surgery, who shall receive for his services two thousand five hundred dollars per annum." 9 Stat. 290.

"When a captain of the navy shall be the chief of the bureau [of construction, &c.], he shall receive pay to which he would be entitled if upon other duty.

"The secretary of the navy shall assign and distribute among the said bureaus such of the duties of the navy department as he shall judge to be expedient and proper. And the duties of said bureaus shall be performed under the authority of the secretary of the navy; and their orders shall be considered as emanating from him, and shall have full force and effect as such." 9 Stat. at Large, 579.

The secretary of the navy is required to make an annual report of the expenditures and transactions of the department to Congress.

ORGANIZATION OF THE DEPARTMENT.

Secretary of the Navy, salary $8,000 per annum.

Chief Clerk, salary $2,200 per annum.

BUREAUS.

Chief of bureau of yards and docks, salary $3,500 per annum.
" " " " construction, &c. " 3,000 " "
" " " " provisions and clothing [pay as purser].
" " " " ordnance and hydrography, $3,500 per annum.
" " " " medicine and surgery, $2,500 per annum.

6 Clerks (class 4),	salary	$1,800	each	per	annum.
6 Clerks (class 3),	"	1,600	"	"	"
25 Clerks (class 2),	"	1,400	"	"	"
2 Clerks (class 1),	"	1,200	"	"	"

The annual appropriation for the support of the department is about $110,000.

POST-OFFICE DEPARTMENT.

ESTABLISHED SEPTEMBER, 1789.

"There shall be established at the seat of the government of the United States, a general post-office, under the direction of the postmaster-general. He shall establish post-offices and appoint postmasters at all such places as shall seem to him expedient, on the post-roads that are or may be established by law." 4 Stat. 102.

"There shall be appointed by the President of the United States, by and with the advice and consent of the Senate, a deputy-postmaster for each post-office, at which the commissions allowed to the postmaster amounted to $1,000 or upwards in the year ending 30th June, 1835, or which may in any subsequent year, terminating on the 30th day of June, amount to or exceed that sum; who shall hold his office for the term of four years, unless sooner removed by the President." 5 Stat. 84.

"He (the postmaster-general) shall give his assistants, the postmasters, and all other persons whom he shall employ or who may be employed in any of the departments of the general post-office, instructions relative to their duty. He shall provide for the carriage of the mails on all post-roads, that are or may be established by law, and as often as he, having regard to the productiveness thereof, and other circumstances, shall think proper. He may direct the route or road, where there are more than one, between places designated by law, for a post-road, which route shall be considered the post-road. He shall obtain from the postmasters, their accounts and vouchers for their receipts and expenditures, once in three months, or oftener, with the balance thereon arising, in favor of the general post-office. He shall pay all expenses which may arise in conducting the post-office, and in the conveyance of the mail, and all other necessary expenses arising on the collection of the revenue, and management of the general post-office. He shall prosecute offences against the post-office establishment. He shall once in three months, render to the secretary of the treasury, a quarterly account of all the receipts and expenditures in the said department, to be adjusted and settled as other public accounts. He shall also superintend the business of the department in all the duties that are or may be assigned to it. *Provided,* that in case of the death, resignation, or removal from office of the postmaster-general, all his duties shall be performed by his senior assistant (the first assistant postmaster-general), until a successor shall be appointed, and arrive at the general post-office, to perform the business." 4 Stat. 102.

ORGANIZATION OF THE DEPARTMENT.

Postmaster-General,	salary	$8,000
Chief Clerk,	"	2,200

BUREAUS.

First Assistant Postmaster-General, (At the head of the Appointment office).	salary	$3,000
Second Assistant Postmaster-General, (At the head of the Contract office).	"	$3,000
Third Assistant Postmaster-General, (At the head of the Finance office).	"	$3,000

6 Clerks	(class 4),	salaries each	$1,800	per annum.
29 Clerks	(class 3),	" "	1,600	" "
33 Clerks	(class 2),	" "	1,400	" "
14 Clerks	(class 1),	" "	1,200	" "

The annual appropriations required for the payment of salaries and contingent expenses of this department, amount to about one hundred and seventy thousand dollars.

ATTORNEY-GENERAL.

"There shall also be appointed, a meet person learned in the law, to act as attorney-general for the United States, who shall be sworn or affirmed to a faithful execution of his office; whose duty it shall be to prosecute and conduct all suits in the Supreme Court in which the United States shall be concerned, and to give his advice and opinion upon questions of law, when required by the President of the United States, or when requested by the heads of any of the departments, touching any matters that may concern their departments." Act of 1789. 1 Stat. at Large, 93.

By a clause in the general appropriation bill passed March 3, 1859, the attorney-general is allowed to appoint an assistant attorney-general, at a salary of $3,000 per annum; two clerks at $1,600 each, and one clerk at $1,400 per annum.

The annual appropriations for the payment of the salaries and contingent expenses of the attorney-general's office, is about $17,500.

ELECTORAL VOTES FOR PRESIDENT AND VICE-PRESIDENT OF THE UNITED STATES OF AMERICA.

ELECTION OF 1789.	G. Washington, of Virginia.	John Adams, of Massachusetts.	Sam'l Huntingdon, of Conn.	John Jay, of N. York.	John Hancock, of Mass.	R. H. Harrison, of Maryland.	George Clinton, of New York.	John Rutledge, of S. Carolina.
New Hampshire	5	5	..	..	..	..	..	..
Massachusetts	10	10	..	..	..	..	..	..
Connecticut	7	5	2	..	..	..	..	..
New Jersey	6	1	..	5	..	..	..	..
Pennsylvania	10	8	..	..	2	..	..	..
Delaware	3	..	..	3	..	..	..	..
Maryland	6	..	..	..	..	6	..	..
Virginia	10	5	..	1	1	..	3	..
South Carolina	7	..	..	..	1	..	..	6
Georgia	5	..	..	..	..	..	..	..
	69	34	2	9	4	6	3	6

John Milton, of Ga. received 2, and J. Armstrong, of Ga., and B. Lincoln, of Mass. 1 each.

ELECTION OF 1793.	G. Washington, of Virginia.	John Adams, of Massachusetts.	George Clinton, of New York.	Thos. Jefferson, of Virginia.	Aaron Burr, of New York.
New Hampshire	6	6	..	..	..
Massachusetts	16	16	..	..	..
Rhode Island	4	4	..	..	..
Connecticut	9	9	..	..	..
Vermont	3	3	..	..	..
New York	12	..	12	..	..
New Jersey	7	7	..	..	..
Pennsylvania	15	14	1	..	..
Delaware	3	3	..	..	..
Maryland	8	8	..	..	..
Virginia	21	..	21	..	..
Kentucky	4	..	..	4	..
North Carolina	12	..	12	..	1
South Carolina	8	7	..	..	..
Georgia	4	..	4	..	..

Election of 1797.	John Adams, of Mass.	Thos. Jefferson, of Va.	Thos. Pinckney, of S. C.	Aaron Burr, of N. York.	Sam'l Adams, of Mass.	O. Ellsworth, of Conn.	John Jay, of N. York.	Geo. Clinton, of N. York.
Tennessee	..	3	..	3	..	..	..	..
Kentucky	..	4	..	4	..	..	..	..
Georgia	..	4	..	..	..	..	..	4
South Carolina . .	..	8	8	..	..	..	..	..
North Carolina . .	1	11	1	6	..	..	..	..
Virginia	1	20	1	1	15	..	..	3
Maryland	7	4	4	3	..	..	..	..
Delaware	3	..	3	..	..	..	..	..
Pennsylvania . . .	1	14	2	13	..	..	..	..
New Jersey . . .	7	..	7	..	..	..	..	..
New York	12	..	12	..	..	..	..	..
Connecticut . . .	9	..	4	..	..	..	5	..
Rhode Island . . .	4	..	..	..	..	4	..	..
Massachusetts . .	16	..	13	..	..	1	..	..
Vermont	4	..	4	..	..	..	..	..
New Hampshire . .	6	..	..	..	..	6	..	..
	71	68	59	30	15	11	5	7

S. Johnston, of N. C. received 3; J. Iredell, of N. C. 3; G. Washington, of Va. 2; C. C. Pinckney, of S. C. 1; and John Henry, of Md. 2.

Election of 1801.	Thos. Jefferson, of Va.	Aaron Burr, of N. Y.	John Adams, of Mass.	C. C. Pinckney, of S. C.	John Jay, of N. York.
New Hampshire	..	..	6	6	..
Massachusetts	..	..	16	16	..
Rhode Island	..	..	4	3	1
Connecticut	..	..	9	9	..
Vermont	..	..	4	4	..
New York	12	12	..	..	..
New Jersey	..	..	7	7	..
Pennsylvania	8	8	7	7	..
Delaware	..	..	3	3	..
Maryland	5	5	5	5	..
Virginia	21	21	..	..	..
Kentucky	4	4	..	..	..
North Carolina	8	8	4	4	..
Tennessee	3	3	..	..	..
South Carolina	8	8	..	..	..
Georgia	4	4	..	..	..
	73	73	65	64	1

The vote for Thomas Jefferson and Aaron Burr being equal, the House of Representatives proceeded on Wednesday, February 11, 1801, to the choice of *a*

President of the United States. On the first ballot eight States voted for Thomas Jefferson, of Virginia, six States voted for Aaron Burr, of New York, and the votes of two States were divided. The balloting continued until Tuesday, 17th Feb. 1801, when on the thirty-sixth ballot the votes of ten States were given for Thomas Jefferson, of Virginia, the votes of four States for Aaron Burr, of New York, and the votes of two States in blank, and Thomas Jefferson, of Virginia, was elected.

Aaron Burr, as Vice-President, took the oath of office, and entered upon his duties on 4th of March, 1801.

Election of 1805.	PRESIDENT.		VICE-PRESIDENT.	
	Thomas Jefferson, of Virginia.	Charles Cotesworth Pinckney, of South Carolina.	George Clinton, of New York.	Rufus King, of New York.
New Hampshire	7	..	7	..
Massachusetts	19	..	19	..
Rhode Island	4	..	4	..
Connecticut	..	9	..	9
Vermont	6	..	6	..
New York	19	..	19	..
New Jersey	8	..	8	..
Pennsylvania	20	..	20	..
Delaware	..	3	..	3
Maryland	9	2	9	2
Virginia	24	..	24	..
North Carolina	14	..	14	..
South Carolina	10	..	10	..
Georgia	6	..	6	..
Tennessee	5	..	5	..
Kentucky	8	..	8	..
Ohio	3	..	3	..
	162	14	162	14

Election of 1809.	President.			Vice-President.				
	James Madison, of Virginia.	George Clinton, of New York.	C. C. Pinckney, of South Carolina.	George Clinton, of New York.	James Madison, of Virginia.	James Monroe, of Virginia.	John Langdon, of New Hampshire.	Rufus King, of New York.
New Hampshire . .	..	..	7	..	..	..	..	7
Massachusetts . . .	..	..	19	..	..	..	..	19
Rhode Island . . .	..	..	4	..	..	..	..	4
Connecticut . . .	..	..	9	..	..	..	..	9
Vermont	6	..	..	..	..	3	6	..
New York	13	6	..	13	3	..	..	..
New Jersey . . .	8	..	..	8	..	..	..	..
Pennsylvania . . .	20	..	..	20	..	..	..	..
Delaware	..	..	3	..	..	..	..	3
Maryland	9	..	2	9	..	..	..	2
Virginia	24	..	..	24	..	..	..	..
North Carolina . .	11	..	3	11	..	..	..	3
South Carolina . .	10	..	..	10	..	..	..	..
Georgia	6	..	..	6	..	..	..	..
Kentucky	7	..	..	7	..	..	..	..
Tennessee	5	..	..	5	..	..	..	..
Ohio	3	..	..	..	..	..	3	..
	122	6	47	113	3	3	9	47

Election of 1813.	President.		V. President.	
	James Madison, of Virginia.	De Witt Clinton, of New York.	Elbridge Gerry, of Massachusetts.	Jared Ingersoll, of Pennsylvania.
New Hampshire	..	8	1	7
Massachusetts	..	22	2	20
Rhode Island	..	4	..	4
Connecticut	..	9	..	9
Vermont	8	..	8	..
New York	..	29	..	29
New Jersey	..	8	..	8
Pennsylvania	25	..	25	..
Delaware	..	4	..	4
Maryland	6	5	6	5
Virginia	25	..	25	..
North Carolina	15	..	15	..
South Carolina	11	..	11	..
Georgia	8	..	8	..
Kentucky	12	..	12	..
Tennessee	8	..	8	..
Ohio	7	..	7	..
Louisiana	3	..	3	..
	128	89	131	86

Election of 1817.	President.		Vice-President.				
	Jas. Monroe, of Virginia.	Rufus King, of New York.	Daniel D. Tompkins, of N. Y.	John E. Howard, of Maryland.	James Ross, of Pennsylvania.	John Marshall, of Virginia.	Rob't G. Harper, of Maryland.
New Hampshire	8	..	8	..	..	..	..
Massachusetts	..	22	..	22	..	..	..
Rhode Island	4	..	4	..	..	..	..
Connecticut	..	9	..	..	5	4	..
Vermont	8	..	8	..	..	..	..
New York	29	..	29	..	..	..	..
New Jersey	8	..	8	..	..	..	..
Pennsylvania	25	..	25	..	..	..	..
Delaware	..	3	..	..	..	..	3
Maryland	8	..	8	..	..	..	..
Virginia	25	..	25	..	..	..	..
North Carolina	15	..	15	..	..	..	..
South Carolina	11	..	11	..	..	..	..
Georgia	8	..	8	..	..	..	..
Kentucky	12	..	12	..	..	..	..
Tennessee	8	..	8	..	..	..	..
Ohio	8	..	8	..	..	..	..
Louisiana	3	..	3	..	..	..	..
Indiana	3	..	3	..	..	..	..
	183	34	183	22	5	4	3

ELECTION OF 1821.	PRESIDENT.		VICE-PRESIDENT.				
	James Monroe, of Virginia.	John Q. Adams, of Massachusetts.	Daniel D. Tompkins, of N. York.	Richard Stockton, of New Jersey.	Robert G. Harper, of Maryland.	Richard Rush, of Pennsylvania.	Daniel Rodney, of Delaware.
New Hampshire	7	1	7	..	..	1	..
Massachusetts	15	..	7	8	..	..	..
Rhode Island	4	..	4	..	..	..	..
Connecticut	9	..	9	..	..	..	..
Vermont	8	..	8	..	..	..	..
New York	29	..	29	..	..	..	..
New Jersey	8	..	8	..	..	..	..
Pennsylvania	24	..	24	..	..	..	..
Delaware	4	..	..	..	..	..	4
Maryland	11	..	10	..	1	..	..
Virginia	25	..	25	..	..	..	..
North Carolina	15	..	15	..	..	..	..
South Carolina	11	..	11	..	..	..	..
Georgia	8	..	8	..	..	..	..
Kentucky	12	..	12	..	..	..	..
Tennessee	7	..	7	..	..	..	..
Ohio	8	..	8	..	..	..	..
Louisiana	3	..	3	..	..	..	..
Indiana	3	..	3	..	..	..	..
Mississippi	2	..	2	..	..	..	..
Illinois	3	..	3	..	..	..	..
Alabama	3	..	3	..	..	..	..
Maine	9	..	9	..	..	..	..
Missouri	3	..	3	..	..	..	..
	231	1	218	8	1	1	4

Election of 1825.	President.				Vice-President.				
	Andrew Jackson, of Tennessee.	John Q. Adams, of Massachusetts.	William H. Crawford, of Georgia.	Henry Clay, of Kentucky.	John C. Calhoun, of South Carolina.	Nathan Sanford, of New York.	Nathaniel Macon, of North Carolina.	Andrew Jackson, of Tennessee.	Martin Van Buren, of New York.
New Hampshire	..	[illegible]	..	..	7	..	..	1	..
Massachusetts	..	15	..	..	15	..	..	..	..
Rhode Island	..	4	..	..	3	..	..	..	..
Connecticut	..	8	..	..	..	..	..	8	..
Vermont . .	..	7	..	..	7	..	..	..	..
New York .	1	26	5	4	29	7	..	..	..
New Jersey .	8	..	..	..	8	..	..	..	..
Pennsylvania	28	..	..	..	28	..	..	.	..
Delaware . .	..	1	2	..	1	..	..	..	..
Maryland . .	7	3	1	..	10	..	..	1	..
Virginia . .	..	..	24	..	..	.	24	..	..
North Carolina	15	..	..	..	15	..	..	..	..
South Carolina	11	..	..	..	11	..	..	..	.
Georgia . .	..	..	9	..	..	..	..	..	9
Kentucky .	..	..	..	14	7	7	..	..	..
Tennessee .	11	..	..	..	11	..	..	..	..
Ohio . . .	..	..	..	16	..	16	..	..	..
Louisiana .	3	2	..	..	5	..	..	..	..
Indiana . .	5	..	..	..	5	..	..	..	..
Mississippi .	3	..	..	..	3	..	..	..	..
Illinois . . .	2	1	..	..	3	..	..	..	..
Alabama . .	5	..	..	..	5	..	..	..	..
Maine . . .	..	9	..	..	9	..	..	..	..
Missouri . .	..	..	..	3	..	..	..	3	..
	99	84	41	37	182	30	24	13	9

For Vice-president, Henry Clay, of Kentucky, received two.

Neither of the persons voted for as President having received a majority of the votes, it devolved upon the House of Representatives to choose a President from the three highest on the list of those voted for by the electors for President, which three were, Andrew Jackson, John Quincy Adams, and William H. Crawford. The votes of thirteen States were given for John Quincy Adams; the votes of seven States for Andrew Jackson, and the votes of four States for William H. Crawford. John Quincy Adams, having received a majority of the votes of all the States of this Union, was duly elected President of the United States for four years, to commence on the 4th of March, 1825.

Election of 1829.	President.		Vice-President.		
	Andrew Jackson, of Tennessee.	John Q. Adams, of Massachusetts.	John C. Calhoun, of S. Carolina.	Richard Rush, of Pennsylvania.	William Smith, of South Carolina.
Maine	1	8	1	8	..
New Hampshire	..	8	..	8	..
Massachusetts	..	15	..	15	..
Rhode Island	..	4	..	4	..
Connecticut	..	8	..	8	..
Vermont	..	7	..	7	..
New York	20	16	20	16	..
New Jersey	..	8	..	8	..
Pennsylvania	28	..	28	..	..
Delaware	..	3	..	3	..
Maryland	5	6	5	6	..
Virginia	24	..	24	..	..
North Carolina	15	..	15	..	..
South Carolina	11	..	11	..	..
Georgia	9	..	2	..	7
Kentucky	14	..	14	..	..
Tennessee	11	..	11	..	..
Ohio	16	..	16	..	..
Louisiana	5	..	5	..	..
Mississippi	3	..	3	..	..
Indiana	5	..	5	..	..
Illinois	3	..	3	..	..
Alabama	5	..	5	..	..
Missouri	3	..	3	..	..
	178	83	171	83	7

Election of 1832.	President.				Vice-President.				
	Andrew Jackson, of Tennessee.	Henry Clay, of Kentucky.	John Floyd, of Virginia.	William Wirt, of Maryland.	M. Van Buren, of New York.	John Sergeant, of Pennsylvania.	William Wilkins, of Pennsylvania.	Henry Lee, of Massachusetts.	Amos Ellmaker, of Pennsylvania.
Maine . . .	10	..	..	..	10	..	..	..	..
N. Hampshire	7	..	..	..	7	..	..	..	..
Massachusetts	..	14	..	..	..	14	..	..	..
Rhode Island	..	4	..	..	..	4	..	..	..
Connecticut	..	8	..	..	..	8	..	..	..
Vermont . .	..	..	..	7	..	..	..	..	7
New York .	42	..	..	..	42	..	..	..	..
New Jersey .	8	..	..	..	8	..	..	..	..
Pennsylvania	30	..	..	..	..	..	30	..	..
Delaware .	..	3	..	..	..	3	..	..	..
Maryland .	3	5	..	..	3	5	..	..	..
Virginia . .	23	..	..	..	23	..	..	..	..
North Carolina	15	..	..	..	15	..	..	..	..
South Carolina	..	..	11	..	..	..	..	11	..
Georgia . .	11	..	..	..	11	..	..	..	..
Kentucky .	..	15	..	..	..	15	..	..	..
Tennessee .	15	..	..	..	15	..	..	..	..
Ohio . . .	21	..	..	..	21	..	..	..	..
Louisiana .	5	..	..	..	5	..	..	..	..
Mississippi .	4	..	..	..	4	..	..	..	..
Indiana . .	9	..	..	..	9	..	..	..	..
Illinois . .	5	..	..	..	5	..	..	..	..
Alabama . .	7	..	..	..	7	..	..	..	..
Missouri . .	4	..	..	..	4	..	..	..	..
	219	49	11	7	189	49	30	11	7

Election of 1836.	President.					Vice-President.			
	M. Van Buren, of New York.	Wm. H. Harrison, of Ohio.	Hugh L. White, of Tenn.	Daniel Webster, of Mass.	W. P. Mangum, of N. Carolina.	R. M. Johnson, of Kentucky.	Francis Granger, of New York.	John Tyler, of Virginia.	William Smith, of Alabama.
Maine . . .	10	..	..	..	..	10	..	..	..
N. Hampshire	7	..	..	..	..	7	..	..	..
Massachusetts	..	..	..	14	..	..	14	..	..
Rhode Island	4	..	..	..	..	4	..	..	..
Connecticut	8	..	..	..	..	8	..	..	..
Vermont . .	..	7	..	..	..	..	7	..	..
New York .	42	..	..	..	..	42	..	..	..
New Jersey	..	8	..	..	..	..	8	..	..
Pennsylvania	30	..	..	..	..	30	..	..	..
Delaware .	..	3	..	..	..	..	3	..	..
Maryland .	..	10	..	..	..	..	..	10	..
Virginia . .	23	..	..	..	..	..	..	..	23
North Carolina	15	..	..	..	..	15	..	..	..
South Carolina	..	..	..	..	11	..	..	11	..
Georgia . .	..	..	11	..	..	..	..	11	..
Kentucky .	..	15	..	..	..	..	15	..	..
Tennessee .	..	..	15	..	..	..	..	15	..
Ohio . . .	..	21	..	..	..	..	21	..	..
Louisiana, .	5	..	..	..	..	5	..	..	..
Mississippi .	4	..	..	..	..	4	..	..	..
Indiana . .	..	9	..	..	..	..	9	..	..
Illinois . .	5	..	..	..	..	5	..	..	..
Alabama .	7	..	..	..	..	7	..	..	..
Missouri .	4	..	..	..	..	4	..	..	..
Arkansas .	3	..	..	..	..	3	..	..	..
Michigan .	3	..	..	..	..	3	..	..	..
	170	73	26	14	11	147*	77	47	23

*Elected by the Senate.

States.	Election of 1840.*					Election of 1844.			
	President.		Vice-President.			President.		V. President.	
	Wm. H. Harrison, of Ohio.	M. Van Buren, of New York.	John Tyler, of Virginia.	R. M. Johnson, of Kentucky.	L. W. Tazewell, of Virginia.	James K. Polk, of Tennessee.	Henry Clay, of Kentucky.	George M. Dallas, of Pennsylvania.	T. Frelinghuysen, of New York.
Maine . . .	10	..	10	..	..	9	..	9	..
N. Hampshire	..	7	..	7	..	6	..	6	..
Massachusetts	14	.	14	..	..	..	12	..	12
Rhode Island	4	..	4	..	..	..	4	..	4
Connecticut	8	..	8	..	..	..	6	..	6
Vermont . .	7	..	7	..	..	..	6	..	6
New York .	42	..	42	..	..	36	..	36	..
New Jersey	8	..	8	..	..	..	7	..	7
Pennsylvania	30	..	30	..	..	26	..	26	..
Delaware .	3	..	3	..	..	..	3	..	3
Maryland .	10	..	10	..	..	..	8	..	8
Virginia . .	..	23	..	22	..	17	..	17	..
North Carolina	15	..	15	..	..	..	11	..	11
South Carolina	..	11	..	..	11	9	..	9	..
Georgia . .	11	..	11	..	..	10	..	10	..
Kentucky .	15	..	15	..	..	..	12	..	12
Tennessee .	15	..	15	..	..	..	13	..	13
Ohio . . .	21	..	21	..	..	..	23	..	23
Louisiana .	5	..	5	..	..	6	..	6	..
Mississippi .	4	..	4	..	..	6	..	6	..
Indiana . .	9	..	9	..	..	12	..	12	..
Illinois . .	..	5	..	5	..	9	..	9	..
Alabama . .	..	7	..	7	..	9	..	9	..
Missouri . .	..	4	..	4	..	7	..	7	..
Arkansas .	..	3	..	3	..	3	..	3	..
Michigan .	3	..	3	..	..	5	..	5	..
	234	60	234	48	11	170	105	170	105

* James K. Polk received one electoral vote.

Election of 1848.	President.		V. President.	
	Z. Taylor, of Louisiana.	Lewis Cass, of Michigan.	M. Fillmore, of New York.	W. O. Butler, of Kentucky.
Maine	..	9	..	9
New Hampshire	..	6	..	6
Massachusetts	12	..	12	..
Rhode Island	4	..	4	..
Connecticut	6	..	6	..
Vermont	6	..	6	..
New York	36	..	36	..
New Jersey	7	..	7	..
Pennsylvania	26	..	26	..
Delaware	3	..	3	..
Maryland	8	..	8	..
Virginia	..	17	..	17
North Carolina	11	..	11	..
South Carolina	..	9	..	9
Georgia	10	..	10	..
Kentucky	12	..	12	..
Tennessee	13	..	13	..
Ohio	..	23	..	23
Louisiana	6	..	6	..
Mississippi	..	6	..	6
Indiana	..	12	..	12
Illinois	..	9	..	9
Alabama	..	9	..	9
Missouri	..	7	..	7
Arkansas	..	3	..	3
Michigan	..	5	..	5
Florida	3	..	3	..
Texas	..	4	..	4
Iowa	..	4	..	4
Wisconsin	..	4	..	4
	163	127	163	127

States.	Election of 1852.				Election of 1856.					
	President.		V. President.		President.			Vice-President.		
	Franklin Pierce.	Winfield Scott.	William R. King.	Wm. A. Graham.	James Buchanan.	John C. Fremont.	Millard Fillmore.	J. C. Breckinridge.	William L Dayton.	And. J. Donelson.
Maine	8	..	8	..	..	8	..	..	8	..
N. H.	5	..	5	..	..	5	..	..	5	..
Mass.	..	13	..	13	..	13	..	..	13	..
R. Island	4	..	4	..	..	4	..	..	4	..
Conn.	6	..	6	..	..	6	..	..	6	..
Vt. .	..	5	..	5	..	5	..	..	5	..
N. Y.	35	..	35	..	..	35	..	..	35	..
N. J.	7	..	7	..	7	..	..	7	..	..
Penn.	27	..	27	..	27	..	..	27	..	..
Del. .	3	..	3	..	3	..	..	3	..	..
Md. .	8	..	8	..	..	..	8	..	..	8
Va. .	15	..	15	..	15	..	..	15	..	..
N. C.	10	..	10	..	10	..	..	10	..	..
S. C.	8	..	8	..	8	..	..	8	..	..
Georgia	10	..	10	..	10	..	..	10	..	..
Ky. .	..	12	..	12	12	..	..	12	..	..
Tenn.	..	12	..	12	12	..	..	12	..	..
Ohio.	23	..	23	..	..	23	..	..	23	..
La. .	6	..	6	..	6	..	..	6	..	..
Miss.	7	..	7	..	7	..	..	7	..	..
Indiana	13	..	13	..	13	..	..	13	..	..
Illinois	11	..	11	..	11	..	..	11	..	..
Ala. .	9	..	9	..	9	..	..	9	..	..
Mo. .	9	..	9	..	9	..	..	9	..	..
Ark.	4	..	4	..	4	..	..	4	..	..
Mich.	6	..	6	..	..	6	..	..	6	..
Florida	3	..	3	..	3	..	..	3	..	..
Texas	4	..	4	..	4	..	..	4	..	..
Iowa	4	..	4	..	..	4	..	..	4	..
Wis. .	4	..	4	..	..	4	..	..	4	..
Cal. .	4	..	4	..	4	..	..	4	..	..
	254	42	254	42	174	113	8	174	113	8

EXECUTIVE ADMINISTRATIONS.

WASHINGTON'S CABINET.

1789 TO 1797.

Secretaries of State.

Thomas Jefferson, of Virginia, Sept. 26, 1789.
Edmund Randolph, of Virginia, Jan. 2, 1794.
Timothy Pickering, of Pa., Dec. 10, 1795.

Secretaries of the Treasury.

Alexander Hamilton, of New York, Sept. 11, 1789.
Oliver Wolcott, Jr., of Connecticut, Feb. 3, 1795.

Secretaries of War.

Henry Knox, of Massachusetts, Sept. 12, 1789.
Timothy Pickering, of Pennsylvania, Jan. 2, 1795.
James McHenry, of Maryland, Jan. 27, 1796.

Secretaries of the Navy.

None appointed in Washington's administration.

Postmasters-General.

Samuel Osgood, of Massachusetts, Sept. 26, 1789.
Timothy Pickering, of Pennsylvania, Aug. 12, 1791.
Joseph Habersham, of Georgia, Feb. 25, 1795.

Attorneys-General.

Edmund Randolph, of Virginia, Sept. 26, 1789.
William Bradford, of Pennsylvania, Jan. 28, 1794.
Charles Lee, of Virginia, Dec. 10, 1795.

Average annual expenditure, exclusive of public debt, $1,986,588

JOHN ADAMS'S CABINET.

1797 TO 1801.

Secretaries of State.

Timothy Pickering, of Pennsylvania (held over).
John Marshall, of Virginia, May 13, 1800.

Secretaries of the Treasury.

Oliver Wolcott, of Connecticut (held over).
Samuel Dexter, of Massachusetts, Dec. 31, 1800.

Secretaries of War.

James McHenry, of Maryland (held over).
John Marshall, of Virginia, May 7, 1800.
Samuel Dexter, of Massachusetts, May 13, 1800.
Roger Griswold, of Connecticut, Feb. 3, 1801.

Secretaries of the Navy.

George Cabot, of Massachusetts, May 3, 1798.
Benjamin Stoddert, of Maryland, May 21, 1798.

Postmaster-General.

Joseph Habersham, of Georgia (held over).

Attorney-General.

Charles Lee, of Virginia (held over).

Average annual expenditure, exclusive of public debt, $5,287,088.

THOMAS JEFFERSON'S CABINET.

1801 TO 1809.

Secretary of State.

James Madison, of Virginia, March 5, 1801.

Secretary of the Treasury.

Albert Gallatin, of Pennsylvania, May 14, 1801.

Secretary of War.

Henry Dearborn, of Massachusetts, March 5, 1801.

Secretaries of the Navy.

Benjamin Stoddert, of Maryland (held over).
Robert Smith, of Maryland, July 15, 1801.
Jacob Crowninshield, of Massachusetts, March 2, 1805.

Postmasters-General.

Joseph Habersham, of Georgia (held over).
Gideon Granger, of Connecticut, Nov. 28, 1801.

Attorneys-General.

Levi Lincoln, of Massachusetts, March 5, 1801.
Robert Smith, of Maryland, March 2, 1805.
John Breckinridge, of Kentucky, Dec. 23, 1805.
Cæsar A. Rodney, of Pennsylvania, Jan. 20, 1807.

Average annual expenditure, exclusive of public debt, $5,142,598.

JAMES MADISON'S CABINET.

1809 TO 1817.

Secretaries of State.

Robert Smith, of Maryland, March 6, 1809.
James Monroe, of Virginia, April 2, 1811.

Secretaries of the Treasury.

Albert Gallatin, of Pennsylvania (held over).
George W. Campbell, of Tennessee, Feb. 9, 1814.
Alexander James Dallas, of Pennsylvania, Oct. 6, 1816.
William H. Crawford, of Georgia, Oct. 22, 1816.

Secretaries of War.

William Eustis, of Massachusetts, March 7, 1809.
John Armstrong, of Pennsylvania, Jan. 13, 1813.
James Monroe, of Virginia, Sept. 27, 1814.
William H. Crawford, of Georgia, March 3, 1815.

Secretaries of the Navy.

Paul Hamilton, of South Carolina, March 7, 1809.
William Jones, of Pennsylvania, Jan. 12, 1813.
Benj. W. Crowninshield, of Massachusetts, Dec. 17, 1814.

Postmasters-General.

Gideon Granger, of Connecticut (held over).
Return Jonathan Meigs, jr., of Ohio, March 19, 1814.

Attorneys-General.

Cæsar A. Rodney, of Pennsylvania (held over).
William Pinkney, of Maryland, Dec. 11, 1811.
Richard Rush, of Pennsylvania, Feb. 10, 1814.

Average annual expenditure, exclusive of public debt, $18,085,617.

JAMES MONROE'S CABINET.

1817 TO 1825.

Secretary of State.

John Quincy Adams, of Massachusetts, March 5, 1817.

Secretary of the Treasury.

William H. Crawford, of Georgia, March 5, 1817.

Secretary of War.

John Caldwell Calhoun, of South Carolina, Oct. 8, 1817.
[Mr. George Graham was appointed acting Sec'y of War in the recess of the Senate.]

Secretaries of the Navy.

Benj. W. Crowninshield, of Massachusetts (held over).
Smith Thompson, of New York, Nov. 9, 1818.
John Rodgers, of New York, Sept. 1, 1823.
Samuel L. Southard, of New Jersey, Dec. 9, 1823.

Postmasters-General.

Return J. Meigs, jr., of Ohio (held over).
John McLean, of Ohio, Dec. 9, 1823.

Attorneys-General.

Richard Rush, of Pennsylvania (held over).
William Wirt, of Virginia, Nov. 13, 1817.

Average annual expenditure, exclusive of public debt, $13,045,431.

JOHN QUINCY ADAMS'S CABINET.

1825 to 1829.

Secretary of State.

Henry Clay, of Kentucky, March 7, 1825.

Secretary of the Treasury.

Richard Rush, of Pennsylvania, March 7, 1825.

Secretaries of War.

James Barbour, of Virginia, March 7, 1825.
Peter B. Porter, of New York, May 26, 1828.

Secretary of the Navy.

Samuel L. Southard, of New Jersey (held over).

Postmaster-General.

John McLean, of Ohio (held over).

Attorney-General.

William Wirt, of Virginia (held over).

Average annual expenditure, exclusive of public debt, $12,625,478.

ANDREW JACKSON'S CABINET.

1829 to 1837.

Secretaries of State.

Martin Van Buren, of New York, March 6, 1829.
Edward Livingston, of Louisiana, May 24, 1831.
Louis McLane, of Delaware, May 29, 1833.
John Forsyth, of Georgia, June 27, 1834.

Secretaries of the Treasury.

Samuel D. Ingham, of Pennsylvania, March 6, 1829.
Louis McLane, of Delaware, Aug. 8, 1831.
William J. Duane, of Pennsylvania, May 29, 1833.
Roger B. Taney, of Maryland, Sept. 23, 1833.
Levi Woodbury, of New Hampshire, June 27, 1834.

Secretaries of War.

John H. Eaton, of Tennessee, March 9, 1829.
Lewis Cass, of Ohio, Aug. 1, 1831.

Secretaries of the Navy.

John Branch, of North Carolina, March 9, 1829.
Levi Woodbury, of New Hampshire, May 23, 1831.
Mahlon Dickerson, of New Jersey, June 30, 1834.

Postmasters-General.

William T. Barry, of Kentucky, March 9, 1829.
Amos Kendall, of Kentucky, May 1, 1835.

Attorneys-General.

Jno. M. Berrien, of Georgia, March 9, 1829.
Roger Brooke Taney, of Maryland, July 20, 1831.
Benjamin F. Butler, of New York, November 15, 1833.

Average annual expenditure, exclusive of public debt, $18,068,301

MARTIN VAN BUREN'S CABINET.

1837 to 1841.

Secretary of State.

John Forsyth, of Georgia (held over).

Secretary of the Treasury.

Levi Woodbury, of New Hampshire (held over).

Secretary of War.

Joel R. Poinsett, of South Carolina, March 7, 1837.

Secretaries of the Navy.

Mahlon Dickerson, of New Jersey (held over).
James Kirke Paulding, of New York, June 20, 1838.

Postmasters-General.

Amos Kendall, of Kentucky (held over).
John M. Niles, of Connecticut, May 25, 1840.

Attorneys-General.

Benjamin F. Butler, of New York (held over).
Felix Grundy, of Tennessee, July 7, 1838.
Henry D. Gilpin, of Pennsylvania, Jan. 10, 1840.

Average annual expenditure, exclusive of public debt, $28,047,173.

WILLIAM HENRY HARRISON'S CABINET.

Secretary of State.

Daniel Webster, of Massachusetts, March 5, 1841.

Secretary of the Treasury.

Thomas Ewing, of Ohio, March 5, 1841.

Secretary of War.

John Bell, of Tennessee, March 5, 1841.

Secretary of the Navy.

George E. Badger, of North Carolina, March 5, 1841.

Postmaster-General.

Francis Granger, of New York, March 6, 1841.

Attorney-General.

John J. Crittenden, of Kentucky, March 5, 1841.

JOHN TYLER'S CABINET.

Secretaries of State.

Daniel Webster, of Massachusetts (held over).
Abel P. Upshur, of Virginia, July 24, 1843.
John C. Calhoun, of South Carolina, March 6, 1844.

Secretaries of the Treasury.

Thomas Ewing, of Ohio (held over).
Walter Forward, of Pennsylvania, Sept. 13, 1841.
John C. Spencer, of New York, March 3, 1843.
George M. Bibb, of Kentucky, June 15, 1844.

Secretaries of War.

John Bell, of Tennessee (held over).
John C. Spencer, of New York, Oct. 12, 1841.
James Madison Porter, of Pennsylvania, March 8, 1843.
William Wilkins, of Pennsylvania, Feb. 15, 1844.

Secretaries of the Navy.

George E. Badger, of North Carolina (held over).
Abel P. Upshur, of Virginia, Sept. 13, 1841.
David Henshaw, of Massachusetts, July 24, 1843.
Thomas W. Gilmer, of Virginia, Feb. 15, 1844.
John Y. Mason, of Virginia, March 14, 1844.

Postmasters-General.

Francis Granger, of New York (held over).
Charles A. Wickliffe, of Kentucky, Sept. 13, 1841.

Attorneys-General.

John J. Crittenden, of Kentucky (held over).
Hugh S. Legaré, of South Carolina, Sept. 13, 1841.
John Nelson, of Maryland, July 1, 1843.

Average annual expenditure, exclusive of public debt, $23,541,238.

JAMES KNOX POLK'S CABINET.

1845 TO 1849.

Secretary of State.

James Buchanan, of Pennsylvania, March 5, 1845.

Secretary of the Treasury.

Robert J. Walker, of Mississippi, March 5, 1845.

Secretary of War.

William L. Marcy, of New York, March 5, 1845.

Secretaries of the Navy.

George Bancroft, of Massachusetts, March 10, 1845.
John Y. Mason, of Virginia, September 9, 1846.

Postmaster-General.

Cave Johnson, of Tennessee, March 5, 1845.

Attorneys-General.

John Y. Mason, of Virginia, March 5, 1845.
Nathan Clifford, of Maine, October 17, 1846.
Isaac Toucey, of Connecticut, 1848.

Average annual expenditure, exclusive of public debt, $36,681,101.

ZACHARY TAYLOR'S CABINET.

1849 TO 1850.

Secretary of State.

John M. Clayton, of Delaware, March 7, 1849.

Secretary of the Treasury.

William M. Meredith, of Pennsylvania, March 7, 1849.

Secretary of War.

George W. Crawford, of Georgia, March 7, 1849.

Secretary of the Navy.

William B. Preston, of Virginia, March 7, 1849.

Secretary of the Interior.

Thomas Ewing, of Ohio, March 7, 1849.

Postmaster-General.

Jacob Collamer, of Vermont, March 7, 1849.

Attorney-General.

Reverdy Johnson, of Maryland, March 7, 1849.

Annual expenditure, exclusive of public debt, $31,074,347.

MILLARD FILLMORE'S CABINET.

1850 TO 1853.

Secretaries of State.

Daniel Webster, of Massachusetts, July 20, 1850.
Edward Everett, of Massachusetts, November, 1852.

Secretary of the Treasury.

Thomas Corwin, of Ohio, July 20, 1850.

Secretary of War.

Charles M. Conrad, of Louisiana, August 15, 1850.

Secretaries of the Navy.

William A. Graham, of North Carolina, July 20, 1850
John P. Kennedy, of Maryland, 1852.

Secretaries of the Interior.

Tho. M. T. McKennan, of Pennsylvania, August 15, 1850
Alexander H. H. Stuart, of Virginia, September 12, 1850.

Postmasters-General.

Nathan K. Hall, of New York, July 20, 1850.
Samuel D. Hubbard, of Connecticut, 1852.

Attorney-General.

John J. Crittenden, of Kentucky, July 20, 1850.

Average annual expenditure, exclusive of public debt, $44, 805,721.

FRANKLIN PIERCE'S CABINET.

Secretary of State.

William L. Marcy, of New York, March 7, 1853.

Secretary of the Treasury.

James Guthrie, of Kentucky, March 7, 1853.

Secretary of War.

Jefferson Davis, of Mississippi, March 7, 1853.

Secretary of the Navy.

James C. Dobbin, of North Carolina, March 7, 1853.

Secretaries of the Interior.

Robert McLelland, of Michigan, March 7, 1853.

Postmaster-General.

James Campbell, of Pennsylvania, March 7, 1853.

Attorney-General.

Caleb Cushing, of Massachusetts, March 7, 1853.

Average annual expenditures, exclusive of public debt, $55,872,028.

JAMES BUCHANAN'S CABINET.

Secretary of State.

Lewis Cass, of Michigan, March, 1857.

Secretary of the Treasury.

Howell Cobb, of Georgia, March, 1857.

Secretary of War.

John B. Floyd, of Virginia, March, 1857.

Secretary of the Navy.

Isaac Toucey, of Connecticut, March, 1857.

Secretary of the Interior.

Jacob Thompson, of Mississippi, March, 1857.

Postmaster-General.

Aaron V. Brown, of Tennessee, March, 1857.
Joseph Holt of Kentucky, 1859.

Attorney-General.

Jeremiah S. Black, of Pennsylvania, 1857.

LISTS OF OFFICERS OF THE GOVERNMENT FROM 1789 TO 1860.

SUPREME COURT OF THE UNITED STATES.

Chief Justices.

John Jay, of New York,	appointed	26th Sept., 1789.
William Cushing, of Mass.,	"	27th Jan., 1796.
Oliver Ellsworth, of Ct.,	"	4th March, 1796.
John Marshall, of Va.,	"	31st Jan., 1801.
Roger B. Taney,	"	15th March, 1836.

Associate Justices.

John Rutledge, of S. C.,	appointed	26th	Sept., 1789.
William Cushing, of Mass.,	"	27th	" "
Robert H. Harrison, of Md.,	"	28th	" "
James Wilson, of Pa.,	"	29th	" "
John Blair, of Va.,	"	30th	" "

James Iredell, of N. C., Feb. 10, 1790, in place of R. H. Harrison, resigned.

Thomas Johnson, of Md., Nov. 7, 1791, in place of John Rutledge, resigned.

William Patterson, of N. Y., March 4, 1793, in place of T. Johnson, resigned.

Sam'l Chase, of Md., Jan. 27, 1796, in place of John Blair, resigned.

Bushrod Washington, of Va., Dec. 20, 1798, in place of James Wilson, deceased.

Alfred Moore, of N. C., Dec. 10, 1799, in place of James Iredell, deceased.

William Johnson, of S. C., March 26, 1800, in place of Alfred Moore, resigned.

Thomas Todd, of Ky., March 3, 1807.

Brockholst Livingston, of N. Y., Nov. 10, 1806, in place of W. Patterson, deceased.

Levi Lincoln, of Mass., Jan. 3, 1811, declined.

John Quincy Adams, Feb. 22, 1811, declined.

Joseph Story, of Mass., Nov. 18, 1811, in place of William Cushing, deceased.

Gabriel Duval, of Md., Nov. 18, 1811, in place of Sam'l Chase, deceased.

Smith Thompson, of N. Y., Sept. 1, 1823, in place of B. Livingston, deceased.

Robert Trimble, of Ky., May 9, 1826, in place of Thomas Todd, deceased.

John McLean, of Ohio, March 7, 1829, in place of R. Trimble, deceased.

Henry Baldwin, of Pa., Jan. 6, 1830, in place of B. Washington, deceased.

James M. Wayne, of Ga., Jan. 9, 1835, in place of W. Johnson, deceased.

Philip P. Barbour, of Va., March 15, 1836, in place of G. Duval, resigned.

William Smith, of Ala., March 8, 1837, declined.

John Catron, of Tenn., March 8, 1837.

John McKinley, of Ala., April 22, 1837.

Peter V. Daniel, of Va., March 3, 1841, in place of P. P. Barbour, deceased.

Samuel Nelson, of N. Y., Feb. 14, 1845, in place of Smith Thompson, deceased.

Levi Woodbury, of N. H., Sept. 30, 1845, in place of Joseph Story, deceased.

Robert C. Grier, of Pa., Aug. 4, 1846, in place of H. Baldwin, deceased.

Benjamin R. Curtis, of Mass., 1852, in place of Levi Woodbury, deceased.

John A. Campbell, of Ala., March, 1853, in place of John McKin ley, deceased.

Nathan Clifford, of Me. ——, 1859, in place of B. R. Curtis, re signed.

VICE-PRESIDENTS OF THE UNITED STATES.

John Adams,	elected	1789
Thomas Jefferson,	"	1797
Aaron Burr,	"	1801
George Clinton,	"	1805
Elbridge Gerry,	"	1813
Daniel D. Tompkins,	"	1817
John C. Calhoun,	"	1825
Martin Van Buren,	"	1833
Richard M. Johnson,	"	1837
John Tyler,	"	1841
George M. Dallas,	"	1845
Millard Fillmore,	"	1849
William Rufus King,	"	1853
John Cabell Breckinridge,	"	1857

PRESIDENTS PRO TEMPORE OF THE SENATE.

1789 TO 1860.

John Langdon,	New Hampshire.
Richard Henry Lee,	Virginia.
John Langdon,	New Hampshire.
Ralph Izard,	South Carolina.
Henry Tazewell,	Virginia.
Samuel Livermore,	New Hampshire.
William Bingham,	Pennsylvania.
William Bradford,	Rhode Island.
Jacob Read,	South Carolina.
Theodore Sedgwick,	Massachusetts.

John Lawrence,	New York.
James Ross,	Pennsylvania.
Samuel Livermore,	New Hampshire.
Uriah Tracy,	Connecticut.
John Eager Howard,	Maryland.
James Hillhouse,	Connecticut.
Abraham Baldwin,	Georgia.
Stephen R. Bradley,	Vermont.
John Brown,	Kentucky.
Jesse Franklin,	North Carolina.
Joseph Anderson,	Tennessee.
Samuel Smith,	Maryland.
Stephen R. Bradley,	Vermont.
John Milledge,	Georgia.
Andrew Gregg,	Pennsylvania.
John Gaillard,	South Carolina.
John Pope,	Kentucky.
William H. Crawford,	Georgia.
Joseph B. Varnum,	Massachusetts.
John Gaillard,	South Carolina.
James Barbour,	Virginia.
John Gaillard,	South Carolina.
Nathaniel Macon,	North Carolina.
Samuel Smith,	Maryland.
Littleton W. Tazewell,	Virginia.
Hugh L. White,	Tennessee.
George Poindexter,	Mississippi.
John Tyler,	Virginia.
William R. King,	Alabama.
Samuel L. Southard,	New Jersey.
Willie P. Mangum,	North Carolina.
David R. Atchison,	Missouri.
William R. King,	Alabama.
David R. Atchison,	Missouri.
Jesse D. Bright,	Indiana.
James M. Mason,	Virginia.
Benjamin Fitzpatrick,	Alabama.

SPEAKERS OF THE HOUSE OF REPRESENTATIVES.

F. A. Muhlenberg, of Pa.,	from March 4, 1789, to	March 3, 1791
	and from Dec. 2, 1793, to	" 3, 1795
Jonathan Trumbull, of Ct.,	from Oct. 24, 1791, to	" 2, 1793
Jonathan Dayton, of N. J.,	" Dec. 7, 1795, to	" 3, 1799
Theodore Sedgwick, of Mass.,	" " 2, 1799, to	" 3, 1801
Nathaniel Macon, of N. C.,	" " 7, 1801, to	" 3, 1807
J. B. Varnum, of Mass.,	" Oct. 26, 1807, to	" 3, 1811
Henry Clay, of Ky.,	" Nov. 4, 1811, to	Aug. 2, 1812
	and " Dec. 4, 1815, to	May 15, 1820
	and " " 1, 1823, to	March 3, 1825
Langdon Cheves, of S. C.,	" " 6, 1813, to	" 3, 1815
John W. Taylor, of N. Y.,	" Nov. 12, 1820, to	" 3, 1821
	and " Dec. 4, 1825, to	" 3, 1827
Philip P. Barbour, of Va.,	" " 3, 1821, to	" 3, 1823
Andrew Stevenson, of Va.,	" " 3, 1827, to	June 20, 1834
John Bell, of Tenn.,	" " 1, 1834, to	March 3, 1835
James K. Polk, of Tenn.,	" " 7, 1835, to	" 3, 1839
Robert M. T. Hunter, of Va.,	" " 7, 1839, to	" 3, 1841
John White, of Ky.,	" May 31, 1841, to	" 3, 1843
John W. Jones, of Va.,	" Dec. 4, 1843, to	" 3, 1845
John W. Davis, of Indiana,	" " 3, 1845, to	" 3, 1847
Robert C. Winthrop, of Mass.,	" " 3, 1847, to	" 3, 1849
Howell Cobb, of Ga.,	" " 3, 1849, to	" 3, 1851
Linn Boyd, of Ky.,	" " 3, 1851, to	" 3, 1855
Nathaniel P. Banks, of Mass.,	" " 3, 1855, to	" 3, 1857
James L. Orr, of S. C.,	" " 3, 1857, to	" 3, 1859
William Pennington, of N. J.,	" Jan. 1860, to	" 3, 1861

MEMBERS OF CONVENTIONS AND CONGRESSES,

PRIOR TO THE ADOPTION OF THE CONSTITUTION.

Convention of Commissioners, assembled at Boston, 1643, to form Articles of Confederation for the United Colonies of New England.

From the Colony of New Plymouth.

Edward Winslow, William Collier.

From the Colony of Massachusetts Bay.

John Winthrop,
Thomas Dudley,
Simon Bradstreet,
William Hawthorne,
——— Gibbons,
——— Tyng.

From the Colony of Connecticut.

John Haynes, Edward Hopkins.

From the Colony of New Haven.

Theophilus Eaton, Thomas Greyson.

CONGRESS CONVENED AT ALBANY IN 1754.

New York.

James Delancey,
Joseph Murray,
William Johnson,
John Chambers,
William Smith.

New Hampshire.

Theodore Atkinson,
Richard Wibird,
Mesheck Ware,
Henry Sherburne.

Connecticut.

William Pitkin,
Roger Wolcott,
Elisha Williams.

Massachusetts.

Thomas Hutchinson, Oliver Partridge,
Samuel Wells, John Worthington.
John Chandler,

Rhode Island.

Stephen Hopkins, Martin Howard.

Pennsylvania.

John Penn, Richard Peters,
Benjamin Franklin, Isaac Norris.

Maryland.

Benjamin Tasker, Abraham Barnes.

CONGRESS OF 1765.

Massachusetts.

James Otis, Timothy Ruggles.
Oliver Partridge,

Rhode Island.

Metcalf Bowler, Henry Ward.

Connecticut.

Eliphalet Dyer, William S. Johnson.
David Rowland,

New York.

Robert R. Livingston, William Bayard,
John Cruger, Leonard Lispenard.
Philip Livingston,

New Jersey.

Robert Ogden, Joseph Borden.
Hendrick Fisher,

Pennsylvania.

John Dickinson,	George Bryan.
John Morton,	

Delaware.

Jacob Kollock,	Cæsar Rodney.
Thomas McKean,	

Maryland.

William Murdock,	Thomas Ringgold.
Edward Tilghman,	

South Carolina.

Thomas Lynch,	John Rutledge.
Christopher Gadsden,	

Nine colonies represented by twenty-eight delegates, assembled in the city of New York, on Monday, October 7, 1765, and TIMOTHY RUGGLES, of Massachusetts, was elected President.

Being duly organized, they commenced their business by the adoption of the following resolution: —

Resolved, That the committee of each colony shall have one voice only, in determining any questions that shall arise in the Congress.

THE CONTINENTAL CONGRESS.

1774 to 1788.

PRESIDENTS.

Peyton Randolph,	Virginia,	1774
Henry Middleton,	South Carolina,	1774
Peyton Randolph,	Virginia,	1775
John Hancock,	Massachusetts,	1775–6
Henry Laurens,	South Carolina,	1777
John Jay,	New York,	1778
Samuel Huntington,	Connecticut,	1779–80
Thomas McKean,	Delaware,	1781

John Hanson,	Maryland,	1781
Elias Boudinot,	New Jersey,	1782
Thomas Mifflin,	Pennsylvania,	1783
Richard Henry Lee,	Virginia,	1784–5
Nathaniel Gorham,	Massachusetts,	1786
Arthur St. Clair,	Pennsylvania,	1787
Cyrus Griffin,	Virginia,	1788

MEMBERS.

New Hampshire.

Bartlett, Josiah
Blanchard, Jonathan
Folsom, Nathaniel
Foster, Abiel
Frost, George
Gilman, John Taylor
Gilman, Nicholas
Langdon, John
Langdon, Woodbury
Livermore, Samuel
Long, Pierce
Peabody, Samuel
Sullivan, John
Thornton, Matthew
Wentworth, John, Jr.
Whipple, William
White, Phillips
Wingate, Paine.

Massachusetts.

Adams, John
Adams, Samuel
Cushing, Thomas
Dana, Francis
Dane, Nathan
Gerry, Elbridge
Gorham, Nathaniel
Hancock, John
Higginson, Stephen
Holton, Samuel
Jackson, Jonathan
King, Rufus
Lovell, James
Lowell, John
Osgood, Samuel
Otis, Samuel A.
Paine, Robert T.
Partridge, George
Sedgwick, Theodore
Sullivan, James
Thatcher, George
Ward, Artemas.

Rhode Island.

Arnold, Jonathan
Arnold, Peleg
Collins, John
Cornell, Ezekiel
Ellery, William
Hazard, Jonathan

Hopkins, Stephen
Howell, David
Manning, ——
Marchant, Henry
Miller, Nathan
Mowry, ——
Varnum, James M.
Ward, Samuel.

Connecticut.

Adams, Andrew
Cook, Joseph P.
Deane, Silas
Dyer, Eliphalet
Edwards, Pierpont
Ellsworth, Oliver
Hillhouse, William
Hosmer, Titus
Huntington, Benjamin
Huntington, Samuel
Johnson, William S.
Law, Richard
Mitchell, Stephen M.
Root, Jesse
Sherman, Roger
Spencer, Joseph
Strong, Jedediah
Sturges, Jonathan
Treadwell, John
Trumbull, Joseph
Wadsworth, James
Wadsworth, Jeremiah
Williams, William
Wolcott, Oliver.

New York.

Alsop, John
Benson, Egbert
Boerum, Simon
Clinton, George
DeWitt, Charles
Duane, James
Duer, William
Floyd, William
Gansevoort, Leonard
Hamilton, Alexander
Haring, John
Jay, John
Lansing, John
Lawrence, John
Lewis, Francis
Livingston, Philip
Livingston, Robert R.
Livingston, Walter
Low, Isaac
L'Hommedieu, Ezra
Morris, Gouverneur
Morris, Lewis
M'Dougall, Alexander
Paine, Ephraim
Platt, Zephaniah
Schuyler, Philip
Scott, John Morris
Smith, Melancthon
Wisner, Henry
Yates, Abraham, Jr.
Yates, Peter W.

New Jersey.

Beatty, John
Boudinot, Elias
Burnett, W.
Cadwallader, Lambert
Clark, Abraham
Condict, Silas
Cooper, John
Crane, Stephen
Dayton, Elias
De Hart, John
Dock, Samuel
Elmer, Jonathan
Fell, John
Frelinghuysen, Frederick
Henderson, Thomas
Hopkinson, Francis
Hornblower, Josiah
Houston, Wm. C.
Kinsey, James
Livingston, William
Neilson, John
Scheurman, J.
Scudder, Nathaniel
Sergeant, Jonathan D.
Smith, Richard
Stewart, ——
Stockton, Richard
Symmes, John C.
Witherspoon, John.

Pennsylvania.

Allen, Andrew
Armstrong, John
Attlee, Samuel
Bayard, John
Biddle, Edward
Bingham, William
Clarkson, Matthew
Clingan, William
Clymer, George
Dickinson, John
Fitzsimmons, Thomas
Franklin, Benjamin
Galloway, Joseph
Gardner, Joseph
Hand, ——
Henry, William
Humphreys, Charles
Ingersoll, Jared
Irwine, ——
Jackson, David
Matlack, Timothy
McClure, James
Meredith, ——
Mifflin, Thomas
Morris, Charles
Morris, Robert
Montgomery, John
Morton, John
Muhlenburg, Frederick A.
Peters, Richard
Pettit, Charles
Read, ——
Reed, Joseph
Rhodes, Samuel
Roberdeau, Daniel
Ross, George

Rush, Benjamin
Searle, James
Shippen, William
Smith, James
Smith, Jonathan B.
Smith, Thomas
St. Clair, Arthur
Taylor, George
Willing, Thomas
Wilson, James
Wynkoop, Henry.

Delaware.

Bedford, Gunning
Bedford, Gunning, Jr.
Dickinson, John
Dickinson, Philemon
Evans, John
Kearney, Dyre
McComb, Eleazer
Mitchell, Nathaniel
McKean, Thomas
Patton, John
Perry, William
Read, George
Rodney, Cæsar
Rodney, Thomas
Sykes, James
Tilton, James
Van Dyke, Nicholas
Vining, John
Wharton, Samuel.

Maryland.

Alexander, Robert
Carmichael, William
Carroll, Charles
Carroll, Daniel
Chase, Jeremiah T.
Chase, Samuel
Contee, Benjamin
Forbes, James
Forest, Uriah
Goldsborough, Robert
Hall, John
Hanson, John
Harrison, William
Hemsley, William
Henry, John
Hindman, William
Howard, John E.
Jenifer, D. of St. Thomas
Johnson, Thomas
Lee, Thomas Sim
Lloyd, Edward
Martin, Luther
McHenry, James
Paca, William
Plater, George
Potts, Richard
Ramsay, Nathaniel
Ridgely, Richard
Rogers, John
Ross, David
Rumsey, Benjamin
Scott, Gustavus
Seney, Joshua
Smith, William
Stone, Thomas
Tilghman, Mathew
Wright, Turbett.

Virginia.

Adams, Thomas
Banister, John
Bland, Richard
Bland, Theodorick
Braxton, Carter
Brown, John
Carrington, Edward
Fitzhugh, ——
Fleming, William
Grayson, William
Griffin, Cyrus
Hardy, Samuel
Harrison, Benjamin
Harvie, John
Henry, James
Henry, Patrick
Jefferson, Thomas
Jones, Joseph
Lee, Arthur
Lee, Francis Lightfoot
Lee, Henry
Lee, Richard Henry
Madison, James Jr.
Mercer, James
Mercer, John F.
Monroe, James
Nelson, Thomas
Page, Mann
Pendleton, Edmund
Randolph, Edmund
Randolph, Peyton
Smith, Merewether
Washington, George
Wythe, George.

North Carolina.

Ashe, John B.
Bloodworth, Timothy
Blount, William
Burke, Thomas
Burton, Robert
Caswell, Richard
Cumming, William
Harnett, Cornelius
Hawkins, Benjamin
Hewes, Joseph
Hill, Whitmill
Hooper, William
Johnston, Samuel
Jones, Allen
Jones, Willie
Nash, Abner
Penn, John
Sitgreaves, John
Sharpe, William
Spaight, Richard D.
Swan, John
Williams, John
Williamson, Hugh
White, Alexander.

South Carolina.

Bee, Thomas
Beresford, Richard
Bull, John
Butler, Pierce

Drayton, Wm. Henry
Eveleigh, Nicholas
Gadsden, Christopher
Gervais, John L.
Heyward, Thomas, Jr.
Huger, Daniel
Hutson, Richard
Izard, Ralph
Kean, John
Kinloch, Francis
Laurens, Henry
Lynch, Thomas
Lynch, Thomas, Jr.
Matthews, John
Middleton, Arthur
Middleton, Henry
Motte, Isaac
Parker, John
Pinckney, Charles
Ramsay, David
Read, Jacob
Rutledge, Edward
Rutledge, John
Trapier, Paul
Tucker, Thomas T.

Georgia.

Baldwin, Abraham
Brownson, Nathan
Bullock, Archibald
Clay, Joseph
Few, William
Gibbons, William
Gwinnett, Button
Habersham, John
Hall, Lyman
Houston, John
Houston, William
Howley, Richard
Jones, Noble Wimberley
Langworthy, Edward
Pierce, W.
Telfair, Edward
Walton, George
Wood, Joseph
Zubly, John J.

THE CONSTITUTIONAL CONVENTION OF 1787.

New Hampshire.

Nicholas Gilman
John Langdon
*John Pickering
*Benjamin West.

Massachusetts.

*Francis Dana
Elbridge Gerry
Nathaniel Gorham
Rufus King
Caleb Strong.

Connecticut.

Oliver Ellsworth
William Samuel Johnson
Roger Sherman.

New York.

Alexander Hamilton,
John Lansing, Jr.
Robert Yates.

New Jersey.

David Brearly
*Abraham Clark
Jonathan Dayton
William Churchill Houston
William Livingston
*John Neilson
William Paterson.

Pennsylvania.

George Clymer
Thomas Fitzsimons
Benjamin Franklin
Jared Ingersoll
Thomas Mifflin
Gouverneur Morris
Robert Morris
James Wilson.

Delaware.

Richard Bassett
Gunning Bedford
Jacob Broom
John Dickinson
George Read.

Maryland.

Daniel Carroll
Daniel of St. Thomas Jenifer
Luther Martin
James McHenry
John Francis Mercer.

Virginia.

John Blair
*Patrick Henry (declined)
James Madison, Jr.
George Mason
James McClung
Edmund Randolph
George Washington
George Wythe.

North Carolina.

William Blount
*Richard Caswell (declined)
William Richardson Davie
*Willie Jones (declined)
Alexander Martin
Richard Dobbs Spaight
Hugh Williamson.

South Carolina.

Pierce Butler
Charles Pinckney
Charles Cotesworth Pinckney
John Rutledge.

Georgia.

Abraham Baldwin
William Few
William Houston
*Nathaniel Pendleton
William Pierce
*George Walton.

Those gentlemen marked with an * did not attend the Convention during its sitting.

SIGNERS OF THE DECLARATION OF INDEPENDENCE.

JOHN HANCOCK, PRESIDENT OF THE CONGRESS.

From *New Hampshire.*

Josiah Bartlett,	age at signing, 46 years.	Died,	1795
Matthew Thornton,	" 62 "	"	1803
William Whipple,	" 46 "	"	1785

Massachusetts.

John Adams,	age at signing, 40 years.	Died,	1826
Samuel Adams,	" 53 "	"	1803
Elbridge Gerry,	" 32 "	"	1814
John Hancock,	" 39 "	"	1793
Robert Treat Paine,	" 45 "	"	1804

Connecticut.

Samuel Huntington,	age at signing,	44 years.	Died,	1796
Roger Sherman,	"	55 "	"	1783
William Williams,	"	45 "	"	1811
Oliver Wolcott,	"	50 "	"	1797

Rhode Island.

William Ellery,	age at signing,	48 years.	Died,	1820
Stephen Hopkins,	"	71 "	"	1785

New York.

William Floyd,	age at signing,	41 years.	Died,	1821
Francis Lewis,	"	63 "	"	1803
Philip Livingston,	"	60 "	"	1778
Lewis Morris,	"	50 "	"	1798

New Jersey.

John Witherspoon,	age at signing,	54 years.	Died,	1794
Abraham Clark,	"	50 "	"	1794
John Hart,	"	63 "	"	1780
Francis Hopkinson,	"	39 "	"	1790
Richard Stockton,	"	46 "	"	1781

Pennsylvania.

George Clymer,	age at signing,	37 years.	Died,	1813
Benjamin Franklin,	"	70 "	"	1790
Robert Morris,	"	43 "	"	1806
John Morton,	"	52 "	"	1777
George Ross,	"	46 "	"	1779
Benjamin Rush,	"	31 "	"	1813
James Smith,	"	— "	"	1806
George Taylor,	"	60 "	"	1781
James Wilson,	"	34 "	"	1798

Delaware.

Thomas McKean,	age at signing, 42 years.	Died, 1817
George Read,	" 42 "	" 1798
Cæsar Rodney,	" 46 "	" 1783

Maryland.

Charles Carroll,	age at signing, 38 years.	Died, 1832
Samuel Chase,	" 35 "	" 1811
William Paca,	" 40 "	" 1799
Thomas Stone,	" 34 "	" 1787

Virginia.

Carter Braxton,	age at signing, 40 years.	Died, 1797
Benjamin Harrison,	" — "	" 1791
Thomas Jefferson,	" 33 "	" 1826
Francis Lightfoot Lee,	" 42 "	" 1797
Richard Henry Lee,	" 44 "	" 1794
Thomas Nelson, Jr.,	" 37 "	" 1789
George Wythe,	" 50 "	" 1806

North Carolina.

Joseph Hews,	age at signing, 46 years.	Died, 1779
William Hooper,	" 34 "	" 1790
John Penn,	" 35 "	" 1809

South Carolina.

Thomas Heyward, Jr.,	age at signing, 30 years.	Died, 1804
Thomas Lynch, Jr.,	" 26 "	" 1779
Arthur Middleton,	" 34 "	" 1787
Edward Rutledge,	" 26 "	" 1800

Georgia.

Button Gwinnet,	age at signing, 44 years.	Died, 1777
Lyman Hall,	" 45 "	" 1790
George Walton,	" 36 "	" 1804

UNITED STATES GOVERNMENT.

THE EXECUTIVE.

JAMES BUCHANAN, of Penn., *President of the United States,*	salary,	$25,000
JOHN C. BRECKINRIDGE, of Kentucky, *Vice-President,*	"	6,000

THE CABINET.

LEWIS CASS, of Michigan, *Secretary of State,*	salary,	$8,000
HOWELL COBB, of Georgia, *Secretary of the Treasury*	"	8,000
JACOB THOMPSON, of Mississippi, *Secretary of the Interior*	"	8,000
ISAAC TOUCEY, of Connecticut, *Secretary of the Navy,*	"	8,000
JOHN B. FLOYD, of Virginia, *Secretary of War,*	"	8,000
JEREMIAH S. BLACK, of Pennsylvania, *Attorney-General,*	"	8,000
JACOB HOLT, of Kentucky, *Postmaster-General,*	"	8,000

THE JUDICIARY.

SUPREME COURT OF THE UNITED STATES.

ROGER B. TANEY, of Maryland, *Chief Justice,* salary, $8,000.

JOHN M'LEAN, of Ohio,	*Associate*	*Justice.*	JOHN A. CAMPBELL, of Ala.,	*Ass.*	*Justice*
JAMES M. WAYNE, of Ga.,	"	"	SAMUEL NELSON, of N. Y.,	"	"
JOHN CATRON, of Tenn.,	"	"	ROBERT C. GRIER, of Penn.,	"	"
	"	"	NATHAN CLIFFORD, of Me.,	"	"

Salary of Associate Justices, $6,000. Court meets first Monday in December, at Washington.

MINISTERS TO FOREIGN COUNTRIES.

ENVOYS EXTRAORDINARY AND MINISTERS PLENIPOTENTIARY.

Country.	Capital.	Ministers.	Salary.
Brazil,	Rio Janeiro,	Richard K. Meade, Va.,	$12,000
Chili,	Santiago,	John Bigler, Cal.,	10,000
China,	Canton,	William B. Reed, Pa.,	12,000
France,	Paris,	Charles J. Faulkner, Va.,	17,500
Great Britain,	London,	George M. Dallas, Pa.,	17,500

Country	Capital.	Ministers.	Salary
Mexico,	Mexico,	Robert M. McLane, Md.,	$12,000
Peru,	Lima,	John R. Clay, Pa.,	10,000
Prussia,	Berlin,	Joseph A. Wright, Ind.,	12,000
Russia,	St. Petersburg,	Francis W. Pickens, S. C.,	12,000
Spain,	Madrid,	William Preston, Ky.,	12,000
	MINISTERS	RESIDENT.	
Argentine Confederation,	Parana,	B. C. Yancey, Ga.,	7,500
Austria,	Vienna,	J. Glancy Jones, Pa.,	9,000
Belgium,	Brussels,	E. Y. Fair, Ala.,	7,500
Bolivia,	La Pas,	John C. Smith, Ct.,	7,500
Denmark,	Copenhagen,	J. M. Buchanan, Md.,	7,500
Ecuador,	Quito,	C. R. Buckalew, Pa.,	7,500
Guatemala,	Guatemala,	B. L. Clarke, Ky.,	7,500
Naples,	Naples,	Joseph R. Chandler, Pa.,	7,500
Netherlands,	Hague,	Henry C. Murphy, N. Y.,	7,500
New Granada,	Bogota,	Alexander Dimitry, La.,	7,500
Nicaragua,	Nicaragua,	M. B. Lamar, Texas,	7,500
Portugal,	Lisbon,	G. W. Morgan, Ohio,	7,500
Rome,	Rome,	J. P. Stockton, N. J.,	7,500
Sardinia,	Turin,	John M. Daniel, Va.,	7,500
Sweden and Norway,	Stockholm,	Benjamin F. Angel, N. Y.,	7,500
Switzerland,	Berne,	Theodore S. Fay, Mass.,	7,500
Turkey,	Constantinople,	James Williams, Tenn.,	7,500
Venezuela,	Caraccas,	E. A. Turpin, N. Y.,	7,500
	COMMISSIONER.		
Sandwich Islands,	Honolulu,	J. W. Borden, Indiana,	7,500

THIRTY-SIXTH CONGRESS.

SENATE—66 MEMBERS.

JOHN C. BRECKINRIDGE, of Kentucky, *President, ex-officio.*

EXPIRES.	ALABAMA.	
1861	Benjamin Fitzpatrick,	Wetumpka.
1865	Clement C. Clay, jr.,	Huntsville.
	ARKANSAS.	
1861	Robert W. Johnson,	Pine Bluff.
1865	William K. Sebastian,	Helena.
	CALIFORNIA.	
1861	William M. Gwin,	San Franc'o.
1863	Milton S. Latham,	

EXPIRES.	CONNECTICUT.	
1867	Lafayette S. Foster,	Norwich.
1863	James Dixon,	Hartford.
	DELAWARE.	
1863	James A. Bayard,	Wilmingt'n.
1865	Willard Saulsbury,	Georget'wn
	FLORIDA.	
1861	David L. Yulee,	Homapassa.
1863	Stephen R. Mallory,	Pensacola.

EXPIRES.	GEORGIA.	
1861	Alfred Iverson,	Columbus.
1865	Robert Toombs,	Washington.
	ILLINOIS.	
1861	Lyman Trumbull,	Alton.
1865	Stephen A. Douglas,	Chicago.
	INDIANA,	
1861	Graham N. Fitch,	Logansport.
1863	Jesse D. Bright,	Jeffer'ville.
	IOWA.	
1867	James Harlan,	Mt. Pleasant.
1865	James W. Grimes,	Burlington.
	KENTUCKY.	
1861	John J. Crittenden,	Frankfort.
1865	Lazarus W. Powell,	Henderson.
	LOUISIANA.	
1861	John Slidell,	N. Orleans.
1865	Judah P. Benjamin,	N. Orleans.
	MAINE.	
1863	Hannibal Hamlin,	Hampden.
1865	William P. Fessenden,	Portland.
	MASSACHUSETTS.	
1863	Charles Sumner,	Boston.
1865	Henry Wilson,	Natick.
	MARYLAND.	
1867	James A. Pearce,	Chestert'wn.
1863	Anthony Kennedy,	Baltimore.
	MICHIGAN.	
1863	Zachariah Chandler,	Detroit.
1865	Kingsley S. Bingham,	Kensington.
	MINNESOTA.	
1863	Henry M. Rice,	St. Paul.
1865	Morton S. Wilkinson,	Blue Earth Co.
	MISSISSIPPI.	
1863	Jefferson Davis,	Hurricane,
1865	Albert G. Brown,	Terry, Hinds Co.
	MISSOURI.	
1861	James S. Green,	Canton.
1863	Trusten Polk,	St. Louis.
	NEW HAMPSHIRE.	
1867	Daniel Clark,	Manchester.
1863	John P. Hale,	Dover.

EXPIRES.	NEW YORK.	
1861	William H. Seward,	Auburn.
1863	Preston King,	Ogdensburg.
	NEW JERSEY.	
1863	John R. Thompson,	Princeton.
1865	John C. Ten Eyck,	Burlington.
	NORTH CAROLINA.	
1861	Thomas L. Clingman,	Asheville.
1865	Thomas Bragg,	Raleigh.
	OHIO.	
1861	George E. Pugh,	Cincinnati.
1863	Benjamin F. Wade,	Jefferson.
	OREGON.	
1861	Joseph Lane,	Winchester.
1865	[Vacancy.]	
	PENNSYLVANIA.	
1861	William Bigler,	Clearfield.
1863	Simon Cameron,	Harrisburg.
	RHODE ISLAND.	
1863	James F. Simmons,	Providence.
1865	Henry B. Anthony,	Providence.
	SOUTH CAROLINA.	
1861	James H. Hammond,	Beech Isl'd.
1865	James Chesnut, jr.,	Camden.
	TENNESSEE.	
1863	Andrew Johnson,	Greenville.
1865	A. O. P. Nicholson,	Columbia.
	TEXAS.	
1863	Louis T. Wigfall,	Marshall.
1865	John Hemphill,	Austin.
	VERMONT.	
1861	Jacob Collamer,	Woodstock.
1863	Solomon Foot,	Rutland.
	VIRGINIA.	
1863	James M. Mason,	Winchester.
1865	Robert M. T. Hunter,	Loyds.
	WISCONSIN.	
1861	Charles Durkee,	Kenosha.
1863	James R. Doolittle,	Racine.

HOUSE OF REPRESENTATIVES — 237 MEMBERS.

WILLIAM PENNINGTON, of New Jersey, *Speaker.*
JOHN W. FORNEY, of Pennsylvania, *Clerk.*

ALABAMA.

James A. Stallworth, Evergreen.
James L. Pugh, Eufaula.
David Clopton, Crawford.
Sydenham Moore, Greensboro'.
George S. Houston, Athens.
Williamson R. W. Cobb, Bellefonte.
Jabez L. M. Curry, Talladega.

ARKANSAS.

Thomas C. Hindman, Helena.
Albert Rust, Little Rock.

CALIFORNIA.

Charles L. Scott, Sonora.
John C. Burch, Weaverville.

CONNECTICUT.

Dwight Loomis, Rockville.
John Woodruff, New Haven.
Alfred A. Burnham, Windham.
Orris S. Ferry, Norwalk.

DELAWARE.

William G. Whiteley, Newcastle.

FLORIDA.

George S. Hawkins, Pensacola.

GEORGIA.

Peter E. Love, Thomsville.
Martin J. Crawford, Columbus.
Thomas Hardeman, jr., Macon.
Lucius J. Gartrell, Atalanta.
John W. Underwood, Rome.
James Jackson, Athens.
Joshua Hill, Madison.
John J. Jones, Lester's Dis't.

ILLINOIS.

Elihu B. Washburne, Galena.
John F. Farnsworth, St. Charles.
Owen Lovejoy, Princeton.
William Kellogg, Canton.
Isaac N. Morris, Quincy.
John A. McClernand,
James C. Robinson, Marshall.
Philip B. Fouke, Belleville.
John A. Logan, Benton.

INDIANA.

William J. Niblack, Vincennes.
William H. English, Vienna.
William M. Dunn, Madison.
William S. Holman, Aurora.
David Kilgore, Muncietown.
Albert G. Porter, Indianapolis.
John G. Davis, Rockville.
James Wilson, Crawfordsville.
Schuyler Colfax, South Bend.
Charles Case, Fort Wayne.
John U. Pettit, Wabash.

IOWA.

Samuel R. Curtis, Keokuk.
William Vandever, Dubuque.

KENTUCKY.

Henry C. Burnett, Cadiz.
Samuel O. Peyton, Hartford.
Francis M. Bristow, Elkton.
William C. Anderson, Danville.
John Y. Brown, Elizabethtown.
Green Adams, Barboursville.
Robert Mallory, La Grange.
William E. Sims, Paris.
Laban T. Moore, Louisa.
John W. Stevenson, Covington.

LOUISIANA.

Edward Bouligny, New Orleans.
Miles Taylor, Donaldsonville.
Thomas G. Davidson, East Feliciana.
John M. Landrum, Shreveport.

MAINE.

Daniel E. Somes, Biddeford.
John J. Perry, Oxford.
Ezra B. French, Damariscotta.
Freeman H. Morse, Bath.
Israel Washburn, jr., Orono.
Stephen C. Foster, Pembroke.

MARYLAND.

James A. Stewart, Cambridge.
Edwin H. Webster, Belair.
J. Morrison Harris, Baltimore.
Henry Winter Davis, Baltimore.
Jacob M. Kunkel, Frederick.
George W. Hughes, West River.

MASSACHUSETTS.

Thomas D. Eliot, New Bedford.
James Buffinton, Fall River.

Charles F. Adams,	Quincy.
Alexander H. Rice,	Boston.
Anson Burlingame,	Cambridge.
John B. Alley,	Lynn.
Daniel W. Gooch,	Melrose.
Charles R. Train,	Framingham.
Eli Thayer,	Worcester.
Charles Delano,	Northampton.
Henry L. Dawes,	Adams.

MICHIGAN.

George B. Cooper,	Jackson.
William A. Howard,	Detroit.
Henry Waldron,	Hillsdale.
Francis W. Kellogg,	Kelloggville.
De Witt C. Leach,	Lansing.

MINNESOTA.

Cyrus Aldrich,	Chatfield.
William Windom,	Winona.

MISSISSIPPI.

Lucius Q. C. Lamar,	Abbeville.
Reuben Davis,	Aberdeen.
William Barksdale,	Columbus.
Otho R. Singleton,	Canton.
John J. McRae,	State Line.

MISSOURI.

J. Richard Barrett, Francis P. Blair,	St. Louis.
Thomas L. Anderson,	Palmyra.
John B. Clark,	Fayette.
James Craig,	St. Joseph.
Samuel H. Woodson,	Independence.
John S. Phelps,	Springfield.
John W. Noell,	Perryville.

NEW HAMPSHIRE.

Gilman Marston,	Exeter.
Mason W. Tappan,	Bradford.
Thomas M. Edwards,	Keene.

NEW JERSEY.

John T. Nixon,	Bridgeton.
John L. N. Stratton,	Mount Holly.
Garnett B. Adrain,	N. Brunswick.
Jetur R. Riggs,	Paterson.
William Pennington,	Newark.

NEW YORK.

Luther C. Carter,	Flushing.
James Humphrey,	Brooklyn.
Daniel E. Sickles,	New York.
Thomas J. Barr,	New York.
William B. Maclay,	New York.
John Cochrane,	New York.
George Briggs,	New York.
Horace F. Clark,	New York.
John B. Haskin,	Fordham.
Charles H. Van Wyck,	Bloomingburg.
William S. Kenyon,	Kingston.
Charles L. Beale,	Kinderhook.
Abraham B. Olin,	Troy.
John H. Reynolds,	Albany.
James B. McKean,	Saratoga Spr.
George W. Palmer,	Plattsburg.
Francis E. Spinner,	Mohawk.
Clark B. Cochrane,	Schenectady.
James H. Graham,	Delhi.
Roscoe Conkling,	Utica.
R. Holland Duell,	Cortlandville.
M. Lindley Lee,	Fulton.
Charles B. Hoard,	Watertown.
Charles B. Sedgwick,	Syracuse.
Martin Butterfield,	Palmyra.
Emory B. Pottle,	Naples.
Alfred Wells,	Ithaca.
William Irvine,	Corning.
Alfred Ely,	Rochester.
Augustus Frank,	Warsaw.
Silas M. Burroughs,	Medina.
Elbridge G. Spaulding,	Buffalo.
Reuben E. Fenton,	Frewsburg.

NORTH CAROLINA.

William N. H. Smith,	Murfreesboro'.
Thomas Ruffin,	Goldsboro'.
Warren Winslow,	Fayetteville.
Lawrence O'B. Branch,	Raleigh.
John A. Gilmer,	Greensboro'.
James M. Leach,	Lexington.
Burton Craige,	Salisbury.
Zebulon B. Vance,	Ashville.

OHIO.

George H. Pendleton,	Cincinnati.
John A. Gurley,	Cincinnati.
Chas. L. Vallandigham,	Dayton.
William Allen,	Greenville.
James M. Ashley,	Toledo.
William Howard,	Batavia.
Thomas Corwin,	Lebanon.
Benjamin Stanton,	Bellefontain.
John Carey,	Carey.
Carey A. Trimble,	Chillicothe.
Charles D. Martin,	Lancaster.
Samuel S. Cox,	Columbus.
John Sherman,	Mansfield.
Harrison G. Blake,	Medina.
William Helmick,	New Philad'ia.
Cydnor B. Tompkins,	McConnells'lle.
Thomas C. Theaker,	Bridgeport.
Sidney Edgerton,	Akron.
Edward Wade,	Cleveland.
John Hutchins,	Warren.
John A. Bingham,	Cadiz.

OREGON.

Lansing Stout,	Portland.

PENNSYLVANIA.

Thomas B. Florence,	Philadelphia.
Edward Joy Morris,	Philadelphia.
John P. Verree,	Philadelphia.
William Millward,	Philadelphia.
John Wood,	Conshohocken.
John Hickman,	Westchester.
Henry C. Longenecker,	Allentown.
John Schwartz,	Reading.
Thaddeus Stevens,	Lancaster.
John W. Killinger,	Lebanon.
James H. Campbell,	Pottsville.
George W. Scranton,	Scranton.
William H. Dimmick,	Honesdale.
Galusha A. Grow,	Glenwood.
James T. Hale,	Bellefonte.
Benjamin F. Junkin,	Bloomfield.
Edward McPherson,	Gettysburg.
Samuel S. Blair,	Hollidaysburg.
John Covode,	Lockport St'n.
William Montgomery,	Washington.
James K. Moorhead,	Pittsburg.
Robert McKnight,	Allegheny City.
William Stewart,	Mercer.
Chapin Hall,	Warren.
Elijah Babbit,	Erie.

RHODE ISLAND.

Christopher Robinson,	Cumberland.
William D. Brayton,	Warwick.

SOUTH CAROLINA.

John McQueen,	Society Hill.
William Porcher Miles,	Charleston.
Lawrence M. Keitt,	Orangeburg.
Milledge L. Bonham,	Edgefield.
John D. Ashmore,	Anderson.
William W. Boyce,	Winsboro'.

TENNESSEE.

Thomas A. R. Nelson,	Jonesboro'.
Horace Maynard,	Knoxville.
Reese B. Brabson,	Chattanooga.
William B. Stokes,	Smithville.
Robert Hatton,	Lebanon.
James H. Thomas,	Columbia.
John V. Wright,	Purdy.
James M. Quarles,	Clarksville.
Emerson Etheridge,	Dresden.
William T. Avery,	Memphis.

TEXAS.

John H. Reagan,	Palestine.
Andrew J. Hamilton,	Austin.

VERMONT.

Ezekiel P. Walton,	Montpelier.
Justin S. Morrill,	Strafford.
Homer E. Royce,	East Berkshire.

VIRGINIA.

Muscoe R. H. Garnett,	Loretto.
John S. Millson,	Norfolk.
Daniel C. Dejarnette,	Bowl'g Greene.
Roger A. Pryor,	Petersburg.
Thomas S. Bocock,	Appomattox, C. H.
Shelton F. Leake,	Charlottesville.
William Smith,	Warrenton.
Alexander R. Boteler,	Shepherdstown.
John T. Harris,	Harrisonburg.
Sherrard Clemens,	Wheeling.
Elbert G. Jenkins,	Green Bottom.
Henry A. Edmundson,	Salem.
Elbert S. Martin,	Lee, C. H.

WISCONSIN.

John F. Potter,	East Troy.
C. C. Washburn,	La Crosse.
Charles H. Larrabee,	Horicon.

Delegates from Territories.

KANSAS.

Marcus J. Parrot,	Leavenworth City.

NEBRASKA.

Experience Eastabrook,	Omaha City.

Contested by Samuel G. Daily.

NEW MEXICO.

Miguel A. Otero,	Albuquerque.

UTAH.

William H. Hooper,	Salt Lake City.

WASHINGTON.

Isaac I. Stephens,	Olympia.

INDEX TO THE CONSTITUTION.